STAND OF THE THUNDERBIRDS

STAND OF THE THUNDERBIRDS

180th Infantry Regiment and the Battle of Frémifontaine

MICHAEL REYKA, PHD

CASEMATE
Pennsylvania & Yorkshire

Published in the United States of America and Great Britain in 2025 by
CASEMATE PUBLISHERS
1950 Lawrence Road, Havertown, PA 19083, USA
and
47 Church Street, Barnsley, S70 2AS, UK

Hardcover Edition: ISBN 978-1-63624-582-9
Digital Edition: ISBN 978-1-63624-583-6

A CIP record for this book is available from the British Library

Printed and bound in the United Kingdom by CPI Group (UK) Ltd, Croydon, CR0 4YY
Typeset in India by DiTech Publishing Services

For a complete list of Casemate titles, please contact:

CASEMATE PUBLISHERS (US)
Telephone (610) 853-9131
Fax (610) 853-9146
Email: casemate@casematepublishers.com
www.casematepublishers.com

CASEMATE PUBLISHERS (UK)
Telephone (0)1226 734350
Email: casemate@casemateuk.com
www.casemateuk.com

Cover images: (Front) Thunderbirds patch. (Michael Reyka); Tank Destroyer passing through Bourg while carrying 2nd Battalion soldiers. (Courtesy of NARA, 180th Infantry Regiment photo collection); (back) Steve C. Reyka's Boot Camp portrait. (Courtesy of Michael Reyka); 45th Division infantrymen as they don a new type of winter combat jacket on October 31, 1944 (U.S. Signal Corps, 111-SC 195862/NARA).

The Publisher's authorised representative in the EU for product safety is Authorised Rep Compliance Ltd., Ground Floor, 71 Lower Baggot Street, Dublin D02 P593, Ireland.
www.arccompliance.com

This book is dedicated to my father, Steve C. Reyka, who served as an H Company heavy machine gunner with the 45th Infantry Division, 2nd Battalion, 180th Infantry Regiment, in Italy and France during World War II. In the dense forest surrounding the village of Frémifontaine, France, during the first week of October 1944, the 2nd Battalion was on the brink of total annihilation when enemy troops and tanks surrounded all three of its rifle companies along with their H Company heavy weapons attachments. Faced with the probability of impending death or capture, the battalion confronted and defended against this formidable attack through determination, courage, strength, and tenacity—words that have come to be associated with the 45th Infantry Division and its motto, *Semper Anticus* (Always Forward).

This book is also dedicated to my children and grandchildren. May this story offer strength and courage throughout their lives. No matter how powerful, no matter how overwhelming and no matter how unexpected the challenge and the associated fear, stress, and cost, always keep fighting with every ounce of strength you possess within. In doing so, you will realize you are capable of accomplishing much more than you ever imagined. *Semper Anticus*!

Contents

Acknowledgements

Much gratitude is expressed to Jean-Marie Siret for his interest in my quest, as well as his insight and assistance in arranging this personal journey into a brief, but significant, segment of my father's life as a 45th Division "Thunderbird." Jean-Marie's willingness to serve as our guide, introduce us to French villagers who shared with me their personal stories, and conduct reconnaissance of the villages we visited throughout our journey created the framework for this exploration into the history associated with the 180th Regiment and my father's secret struggle. His knowledge of the French countryside, the remote villages, the culture, and the history allowed us to reach our objectives. His commitment to the 45th Infantry Division, and his appreciation for my deeply personal need to understand my father's secrets, was an essential element of this once-in-a-lifetime adventure. The villagers I met as we followed the footsteps of the 180th troops across the countryside added depth to the journey; I am grateful for their openness and transparency. Their names are included in the chapters that follow. All welcomed the opportunity to share their personal stories with me. A few smiled and quietly gazed in anticipation of what I would find along my journey. The war was a significant and traumatic part of their lives and each had spent decades processing the experience.

I must also express appreciation to Larry Gregorio, my colleague and friend of 35 years. Having served as a professor of French literature and language for more than three and a half decades, his skillful use of the French language, and his affinity for French culture, provided a seamless communication process. The relationship he formed with Jean-Marie assisted in the clarification of villagers' statements and the complex historical descriptions shared throughout our journey.

I am especially grateful for my daughter's companionship on this journey. Tara's inquisitive nature and intuitive need to understand led her forward throughout this exploration into her grandfather's life. Having had the opportunity to share this journey with her was especially meaningful to me.

Finally, a note of appreciation to my friend and trusted colleague David Gonzalez, MD. His expertise as a psychiatrist provided insight into the concept of fishing as a therapeutic activity and the connection to behavioral health. In response, I have developed an understanding of how my father's lifelong love of fishing and his simple relationship with the activity served to ease his secret struggle.

Prologue

As we drove into Frémifontaine that evening, we passed a group of hunters. They were gathering from the fields and the woods in preparation to close the day's hunt. Several looked inquisitively through the window of the car to catch a glimpse of the "visiting Americans" as Jean-Marie pointed out the location of an event still known to the local hunters. During the course of a patrol in early October 1944, an American jeep hit a mine and exploded along a road crossing the Sep, a wooded area on the high ground near the village.[1] According to clues picked up on the ground at the point of the explosion, the jeep had been equipped with a radio and villagers marveled at the device. In a crater created by the explosion, part of the engine still exists and reinforces the name given to the area by local hunters—"the place of the jeep."[2]

We drove along the winding Frémifontaine road up to the location of the monument; as our car approached the intersection at the top of the hill in front of the monument, I noticed approximately forty villagers had gathered for the ceremony, as well as the mayor, the regional chief of police, the color guard, and the local fire department dressed in formal ceremonial blue uniforms and brightly polished chrome helmets.

The Frémifontaine mayor, Etienne Pourcher, introduced himself and we quietly joined the group of villagers along the side of the road to the right of the monument. Jean-Marie, smiling and looking quite pleased and excited, stood in the middle of the intersection and spoke in French to the rather large group. When Jean-Marie shared that joining the group this evening was the son of an American soldier who had fought at Frémifontaine during the battle to liberate the village, a collective gasp could be heard among the crowd. People looked at each other and then looked around to find the American visitors. Jean-Marie's big smile and direct eye contact with me acknowledged to the crowd my presence and they began to applaud as they looked in our direction. He had patiently waited to share this secret with the villagers at that precise moment. Still smiling, Jean-Marie called to a young girl in the crowd and introduced her as Mademoiselle Leonie as she quietly walked to his side. She held a piece of paper in her hands and shyly began reading aloud to the group. Jean-Marie still seemed excited and proud as he listened to her read from the paper. I wondered if he was proud of her willingness to speak publicly at the event as I attempted to understand what was responsible for the excitement shown on his face. As the young girl spoke in French, I heard her say "Steve Reyka" and realized the purpose of this ceremony. Jean-Marie had arranged a memorial for my father.

> Steve Reyka of the heavy arms company of the Second Battalion of the 180th Regiment of American Infantry, and a native of Cleveland, Ohio, underwent here while he was with his unit on the 6th and 7th of October 1944, the powerful German counterattack that was aimed at taking back the villages of Grandvillers and Frémifontaine. He participated in the intense combat that the American troops fought in during the days that followed in order to take back the lost ground. On the 10th of October, stricken by Pneumonia, he was evacuated to the American military hospital in Xertigny. After having recovered and having gone back into service, he was wounded in the neck under conditions that have not been completely determined because of a fire in the American archives in St. Louis, Missouri. He survived the conflict and left those dear to him in 1984 when he passed away. Today, 66 years afterwards, to the exact day, Michael Reyka, a hospital administrator from Gettysburg and preparing a doctorate degree, completes here before this monument a pilgrimage that he has undertaken, in the company of his daughter and a friend, for several days in France in the footsteps of his father. The latter, never having spoken to his son Michael of his experience during the course of WWII. After consulting numerous documents and archives, Michael has been able to recount these experiences and retrace his father's path.[3]

Following the reading, the mayor motioned for me to join him. With the regional chief of police and the young girl who had read my father's memorial, we walked across the intersection and up the narrow gravel path to the 45th Division monument where I had stood earlier that morning under the brief glow of the sun's rays. The mayor carried a flowered wreath, which we placed at the foot of the granite structure.

I stood in silence in front of the 45th Division emblem and thought of my father's experiences in this small village nearly seventy years earlier. The French National Anthem was played. After a moment of silence, the United States National Anthem was played. As the music played, I closed my eyes for a few moments, in deep reflection and emotion, and opened them to see the firemen in full ceremonial uniforms, standing at attention behind the monument, smiling at me with the same enthusiasm I had seen on Jean-Marie's face. They too seemed to understand what this moment, and this journey, meant to me.

As the sun slowly set, seemingly melting into the dense woods, and as the darkness of the forest slowly surrounded the 45th Division monument, we returned to our sedan and followed Jean-Marie, the mayor, and the villagers down the winding street to the Frémifontaine town hall for a welcome reception. Wine and light hors d'oeuvres had been prepared for the event.

Several villagers shared stories of the war and their personal experiences during the battle to liberate their small town. René Phulpin recounted the story of his younger brother, Daniel, burning his hand on their basement stove as they took shelter from the artillery bombardment. Daniel was taken to the American aid station—the station that cared for my father following the intense fighting. René thanked me, in honor of my father and the rest of the 180th Regiment, for liberating his village. He held direct eye contact and conveyed sincerity in his tone and his words as he said in French, "If your father had not liberated us, we would be a German province now."[4] Each villager who spoke with us still seemed sincerely appreciative of what the American troops had sacrificed here at Frémifontaine, and angry at the thought of the German invasion and occupation—nearly seventy years after the event. There remained a sense of joy and solidarity among the group.

After an hour, we said goodbye to Jean-Marie, who had been our invaluable guide throughout our trip, and returned to our car. It was dark when we left the small village of Frémifontaine and the sky was filled with bright stars. The journey was over and our mission complete. I had walked in my father's footsteps and stood on the same ground where he had experienced the fight of his life. He carried that fight in his subconscious mind throughout the course of his life. Despite the obstacles, he and his 180th Regiment comrades embodied the motto of the 45th Infantry Division—*Semper Anticus* (Always Forward)! He made it home, but something had been lost. Part of him was left behind in the dark forest surrounding this small rural village and he was never again the person who wrote an emotional letter home following his 19th birthday. I never knew that man, but at least I had finally gained a better understanding of him, and I am grateful for the opportunity to have gained a glimpse into the events that most certainly contributed to his perplexing silence, subtle sadness, and somewhat distant relationships.

Introduction

My father had a "bad experience in the war" as my cousin Helen was once told by her mother, but it was not defined by one experience. It was the combination of his battle experiences with H Company of the 180th Infantry Regiment and a final horrific conflict near Frémifontaine, France.

It began with living outside in the cold, rain, and snow for more than three months at Anzio in ice-cold, water-filled, foxholes while German SS troops attempted to completely destroy the 45th Division and its supporting units. It included the amphibious beach assault on Southern France in the summer heat of 1944, the relentless pursuit of the Germans northward toward their homeland, along with the liberation of innumerable French villages and towns along the way. And it culminated with the horrible hand-to-hand combat in the French forests during early October 1944—when the Germans decided to stop running and turn to defend their homeland with the last of their strength—that inflicted the deepest psychological and emotional wounds. Something happened in the dark forests at the foothills of the Vosges Mountains that stood out from my father's overall experiences—something occurred that left a profound scar on his life, much more significant than the physical scar on his neck.

Stories of his youth, told by aunts and cousins over the years, as well as old photographs, are consistent with the image of a gentle and loving personality conveyed through letters that he wrote to his family. He participated in the Civilian Conservation Corps (CCC) in his late teens in the winter of 1940, and was stationed at a CCC camp in Burns, Oregon. On small pieces of lined paper, he wrote a letter home to his sister, Mary, on January 26, 1941.

Dear Mary,

How are you and the rest of the family getting along? I am not feeling so hot because I have a sore throat. But otherwise I'm OK. I'm still having a swell time out here. I received your letter yesterday and was happy to hear from you. Boy I sure miss you and Ma and Pa a lot. I'll be home about the middle of June. That isn't so long from now. I'm glad to hear that the boss is going to send you to school and give you a job in the office. I'm awfully glad to hear that Ma and Pa are getting along swell and it makes me feel so happy. I'm sorry to hear that George went to the Army. I hope he will write to me from Mississippi. Tell Eli and Sophie that I said hello. I'm sorry that I'm not home to taste any of that pig that you bought, boy I bet it's good. I'm sorry and kind of feel bad that I wasn't home for Holy Night supper. I'm glad to hear that Ann is feeling fine. Mary, I don't have a steady girl out here but I'm sending you some pictures of a few of the girls that I know. Please do me a favor and tell Ann to send me all of her negatives that she has at home and I will have two sets of pictures made out here and I'll send one set home and I would like to have the other set. Mary, you asked me if I needed anything and that you would send them to me. Well, I need some cigarettes and stamps badly if you can please send them soon. And ask Pa to send me a couple of bucks if he can because I'm broke. But if he can't it's alright. Well, I guess I will close now. So long.

Love to all, Steve
P.S. Our camp mail address is changed to
Steve Reyka
P.O. Box 791, Burns, Oregon

My father wrote this letter shortly after his 19th birthday and three years before he landed on the beaches of Anzio. He was a quiet and gentle man, but I never knew him to be open and transparent with his emotions toward me, my siblings, or toward my mother. The love and tenderness conveyed in that letter to his sister went into hiding, or was somehow left in the dark pine forest of Frémifontaine, and a subtle, silent, sadness filled the void.

Hidden in small box of photographs and documents that had long since been forgotten until this research into my father's experience as a Thunderbird, I found a postcard that he sent home to his mother, Helen, for Mother's Day 1944. The small postcard with scalloped edges is made of white linen fabric over heavy paper. Purple embroidered flowers with green leaves and pink embroidered letters convey the message, "To my dear mother from your loving son." The hand-written message on the back reads, "Dear Mom, Hope that you like this little card. I'm feeling fine and hope that all at home are just as well. I love and miss you very much. I think of you every minute of the day. I'll close with all my love. Your son, Steve." He was engaged in heavy fighting along the Anzio beachhead on Mother's Day 1944 as the 45th Division continued to stand its ground against the relentless German assault. The intense and costly breakout that occurred in the last days of May brought the prolonged stalemate to an end through sheer Allied force and determination as the exhausted troops advanced to Rome in the early days of June. Whether he bought the postcard in Rome after Mother's Day or at a rest area behind the front lines earlier in the month will remain a mystery. However, the love and tender expression of emotion are consistent with the tone of the letter he sent home from CCC camp prior to the war.

My father's violent engagements with German troops ceased when he left the field of battle on October 10, 1944, near Frémifontaine after falling ill with pneumonia, pleurisy (inflammation of the tissues that line the lungs and chest cavity, which restricts the ability to expand the lungs), and an upper respiratory infection. When his medical conditions

Mother's Day card sent home from Europe in 1944. (Courtesy of Michael Reyka)

had resolved, he began to share with the hospital medical and nursing personnel the stories of his experiences in battle, particularly those in the foothills of the Vosges Mountains. Subsequently, he did not return to the front lines. The medical board felt it was inappropriate to send him back into battle at that particular time and recommended he return to duty as Class "B" with reassignment to a non-combat unit. When reading the original medical documents, I had the sense the medical staff were saying, "Well done, soldier, you've seen and done enough, we're not sending you back there." Following 55 days in the hospital recovering from pneumonia, sinus infections, and dental concerns, he was eventually transferred to active duty with a military police unit in Paris for the remainder of the war.

The experiences in the forests around Frémifontaine haunted him for the remainder of his life. According to official medical records written during his hospital stay, "… He got along rather well in Southern France until he reached the woods near Epinal [*sic*]—was trapped five times and 'froze' on one occasion but was able to carry on in a few minutes." The woods mentioned in the report were actually 15 miles further east near the village of Frémifontaine—he likely hadn't known the name of the small village when he was speaking with the medical staff. This intense battle at Frémifontaine was the final episode in his combat experience. It was the silent breaking point. He left the field of battle near this small village after spending 175 consecutive days on the front line.

Nightmares repeatedly haunted him long after the war. I can recall hearing them on at least two occasions during my childhood. One caused me to leave my bed and walk into my parents' room in the middle of the night to see if he was alright. As I stood in the doorway, my mother calmly said, "It's okay. He just had a bad dream. You can go back to bed." I have come to believe he carried all of those horrible memories with him throughout the course of his life. He never dealt with them—he simply tucked them away, visible to others only through occasional nightmares that were brushed off as "bad dreams." We had no reason to think otherwise.

World War II was perhaps the pivotal moment of my father's life, as it was for so many of his generation. His experience in the dense forests between Épinal and Frémifontaine at the foothills of the Vosges

Mountains in eastern France was far more intense than can be imagined by anyone who was not present. In addition to the soldiers who fought in hand-to-hand combat, the citizens of Frémifontaine were profoundly affected by the violence they witnessed. Many were children and young adults at the time of the battle, but the memories remain focal points in their lives.

My search for the story of my father's war began with two seemingly insignificant memories from my childhood: my father pointing to a photograph of a Browning water-cooled .30-caliber machine gun in a World War II weapons book borrowed from my elementary school library, and one brief reference to a large scar along the side of his neck, indicating it was received during the war. Beyond those two statements, he never referenced the war or his involvement in the conflict. During my early research, I mentioned the neck scar to every 180th Regiment veteran with whom I interacted—it had been the primary focus of my investigation. Similar to so many other veterans, my father's records had been lost in the extensive 1973 St. Louis National Archives fire. His medical records from the Veterans Affairs offered limited insight into the wound. However, I eventually realized the scar did not hold the answers to my questions. It was not the story that needed to be told.

The traditional history books and published biographies failed to provide insight and answers to personal questions involving my father's hidden experiences during World War II. It became clear I needed a different approach far less traditional and more expansive in both scope and depth for any hope of success. Resources available locally and regionally had been exhausted and my next logical move therefore involved visiting the French countryside where the events occurred in the autumn of 1944.

Initial interest in the concept resulted in a simple internet search of the 180th Regiment's operations in that region. I located Jean-Marie Siret's site, dedicated to the 45th Infantry Division, after only a few hours. From previous research, I knew an intense battle between the 180th Regiment's three battalions and a large number of German troops occurred in a small village near the foothills of the Vosges Mountains. As I exchanged initial email conversations with Jean-Marie, I eventually realized he lives in the small village where such a battle occurred—Frémifontaine—and he had become a local resource for that specific military conflict. Through Jean-Marie's personal research, he had excavated and retrieved hundreds of artifacts from the field of battle surrounding the village. In addition, he facilitated the dedication of a monument to commemorate the 45th Division's sacrifices in liberating the village from its German occupiers. Although I didn't realize it at the time of my initial discussions with Jean-Marie, the village of Frémifontaine was the site of my father's most harrowing military experiences.

After exchanging brief emails for several weeks, Jean-Marie offered to be my guide should I decide to visit Frémifontaine. It seems unbelievable this initial inquiry would so easily place me in contact with Jean-Marie—an expert in this important battle and who, on a daily basis, walks the very ground where it occurred. Shortly after his invitation to serve as my guide, and without much organized thought, I asked my daughter if she had any interest in visiting France to retrace her grandfather's footsteps.

Once rational thought began to find its way into the situation, I realized that neither Tara nor I spoke French. Frémifontaine is a small village located in the rural districts of eastern France—not a traditional tourist area where residents would be expected to speak conversation-level English. I immediately contacted my colleague and friend of 25 years, Larry Gregorio, to ask several questions related to French culture and to ask for his advice regarding resources. Larry had previously assisted me in the translation of Jean-Marie's email messages, since Jean-Marie spoke limited English and felt more comfortable writing in French. Larry was a PhD-prepared professor of French literature and language at Gettysburg College—a career spanning more than thirty years. At some point during the discussion, I casually stated, "It would certainly be helpful if we had someone like you with us on this journey." Larry responded, "Well, I'm on sabbatical next semester. I don't have any plans." I recall feeling perplexed and uncertain as to my next words. After a few moments, I cautiously asked, "If I cover your plane fare and lodging, would you join us as our personal interpreter?" Larry thought for a moment and replied, "I've never been to that area of France. Sure, I'll go."

We had an objective; we had a personal guide waiting for us in France and we had an expert interpreter. Now, we needed a detailed plan, but I didn't know where to begin the journey. We continued to communicate with Jean-Marie in the weeks that followed.

October was eventually selected for several reasons, including Larry's availability, my work schedule, Tara's college course schedule, and the time required to complete travel arrangements. By coincidence, it was also the month the fighting in and around Frémifontaine actually occurred in 1944.

In preparation for the trip, Tara and I visited the Barnes & Noble bookstore in Camp Hill, Pennsylvania, on one non-specific evening in late August in an effort to purchase books and maps of the general Bourg region. Admittedly clueless in this regard, we approached two women at the information desk in the center of the store and asked for assistance. The young store employee with whom we spoke turned to a petite older women standing next to her and told us she would assist in finding the specific materials. Appearing to be in her mid-seventies, the woman had distinguished gray hair pulled up neatly in a tight bun. She had a hint of Audrey Hepburn's poise. We followed her quietly to the rack of folded maps and began to scan the titles. We explained our interest in Bourg, France, but clarified we were not certain as to its specific location. She casually responded, "I know that area, I grew up in the region." Tara and I looked at each other as the woman searched through the maps. This couldn't be possible. I asked the woman to repeat her statement and she replied, "I spent many of my childhood years there, only thirty miles from Bourg." Tara smiled. It seemed as though this trip was destined to occur. Eventually, when all of the reservations were made and the tickets obtained, we realized our arrangements would place us in Frémifontaine on the same date my father left the field of battle in 1944—a remarkable coincidence.

CHAPTER I

Always Forward—180th Infantry Regiment and the 45th Division

The 45th Division was known for its tough soldiers, not because they were fearless, but because they experienced fear like every other soldier in combat and yet kept fighting. The original men of the 45th were primarily Oklahoma farmhands, cowboys, oilfield workers, and Native Americans. They were tough men that worked sun up until sun down. My father joined them as a replacement; a city boy from Cleveland.

He received his basic training from the 78th "Lightning" Division at Camp Butler in North Carolina. Under the command of Major General Edwin Parker, the newly formed division was tasked with producing combat-ready reinforcements and, by late 1943, had earned a reputation for effectiveness in its objective. Following combat training, my father and his comrades made their way to Hampton Roads, Virginia, where they boarded ships on January 23, 1944, and sailed for Oran, Algeria. Oran was a staging area that allowed few comforts for the troops. Arriving reinforcements were assigned to tents with straw mattresses resting on the dirt floors while waiting for the next convoy that transported them to Naples and then onto Anzio. The convoy of 35 ships started moving on February 18 with its escorts "scurrying up and down the flanks of the convoy like sheep dogs keeping the flock together."[1] Troops gained sight of the erupting Mount Vesuvius volcano in the distance as the convoy sailed north along the Italian coastline on February 24.

My father joined the 45th Infantry on February 28, 1944, as a replacement at the Anzio beachhead. Fresh out of training, his arrival on the beachhead was met with heavy shelling of the Anzio harbor, forcing his ship to anchor a few miles offshore and shuttle him close enough to wade through the surf with his infantry gear and rifle. He proceeded directly to the newly constructed 45th Infantry reserve location in the Padiglione Woods approximately a mile south of the 45th's line, where he spent several days receiving instructions and training. He then moved on foot during the night of March 1 and joined H Company and 2nd Battalion already positioned on the north side of the "Bowling Alley," the name soldiers assigned to the long, flat, straight main road between Padiglione and Carroceto, north of Anzio.

As a 21-year-old replacement, my father was thrust into the final phases of a battle between a sizeable army of Hitler's elite forces and the advancing Allied forces, each side attempting to annihilate each other. It was estimated that, between February 29 and March 4, the Germans lost 30 percent of their tanks and more than 3,500 soldiers either killed, wounded, or captured.[2] The 180th sustained significant losses during the week immediately prior to my father's arrival when the Germans launched a massive attack in an effort to drive the "Thunderbirds" back into the sea. Enemy forces had attacked both shoulders of the line and then pounded the center with tanks and swarms of infantry that advanced down the "Bowling Alley" main road. "Every available man, cooks and drivers, mechanics and storemen, clerks, even men from the Docks Operating Companies, were brought up from the rear to stem the tide."[3] Second Battalion sustained the brunt of the attack in response to its position on the battlefield:

> In those five days, some 400 men of the 45th Division had been killed, 2,000 were wounded, and a thousand were listed as missing in action. Many of the missing were now prisoners, but others had simply been obliterated by the nearly constant artillery and mortar bombardments or buried forever under the mud of Anzio. Another 2,500 Thunderbirds had been evacuated for non-battle causes—immersion foot, exhaustion, and exposure.[4]

Casualties among 180th troops escalated to the point that B Company's commanding officer refused to accept any replacements unless they were battle trained. "The new soldier was either killed, wounded, or went out of his mind under the conditions that existed."[5] Second Battalion's losses necessitated my father's assignment to H Company to ensure the continued deployment of the defensive firepower of the Browning water-cooled heavy machine gun. By the time he landed on the beaches of southern France, he had acquired significant combat experience and was well prepared for the relentless fighting and continued advance northward toward Germany.

The 180th Infantry Regiment was a component of the 45th Infantry Division during World War II and, specifically, the European Theater of Operations (ETO). General William W. Eagles was the commanding officer of the 45th and Colonel Robert L. Dulaney served as the commanding officer of the 180th Infantry Regiment. Known as the "Thunderbirds," the 45th Infantry Division and its elements entered the ETO with its southern France amphibious landing on August 15, 1944, and continued through the Rhineland and central Europe campaigns until the end of the war. Overall casualties sustained by the 45th Division throughout the ETO totaled 26,449.[6]

Each of the 45th's three infantry regiments (180th, 157th, 179th) consisted of three battalions (1st, 2nd, and 3rd) and within each battalion were unique staff positions referred to as "S" officers. Each of these officers had very specific roles within the unit: S-1 officers were responsible for personnel and administrative issues; S-2s managed intelligence and security; S-3s had oversight of operations and mission planning; and S-4s were responsible for supplies and logistics. Because S-2s had a very significant role during active combat operations, the S-2 journals are referenced in numerous locations throughout this book. S-2s must know and understand the battalion's area of operations, including enemy strength and locations, the terrain, civilian population, local infrastructure, and weather conditions.[7] The most important task of S-2s in combat is to gather and communicate enough information in a timely manner so commanders can make critical battlefield decisions. S-2 officers have the most direct influence on the tactics chosen during battle. It is believed that "If the S-2 succeeds, the battalion is almost always successful; if the S-2 fails, the battalion is almost certainly doomed to defeat and the unnecessary loss of American lives."[8] The S-2 journals provide detailed descriptions of specific events and actions along with their locations, dates and times, including detailed radio communications from the front lines.

The battalions were further divided into companies. Second Battalion consisted of E, F, G, and H Companies. The rifle companies formed E, F, and G, while H Company served as the heavy weapons unit in support of the rifle companies, providing heavy machine guns and mortars. Company H never fought together as an independent company. Rather, it was broken up and distributed throughout the battalion to fight along with rifle-company squads and platoons as needed.[9] For this reason, it has been difficult, if not impossible, for anyone to tell the unit-specific story of a heavy weapons company. Therefore, this unique journey to understand my father's combat experiences will need to involve all four battalion companies with a relentless effort to determine which company he had been fighting with during specific battles. If successful in this effort, I would be able to know exactly what he experienced in the dark forests of eastern France and gain greater insight into understanding the man.

Many of the 45th veterans with whom I had spoken with over the years said they were scared to death, and yet they continued to fight no matter what the Germans threw at them. One veteran shared, "It's hard to explain. At that time, we moved so fast—you were tired. You almost prayed that you'd be killed, captured, or wounded. You were so tired you could hardly move. It's hard to explain. You're scared."[10] My father was likely no different. He was not fearless. Only an insane person could be fearless under such conditions. Time after time these men faced the unknown; he witnessed death and destruction very close to him, and he faced and escaped his own probable death, yet he and his comrades kept going back to the front lines. Even after being surrounded by the Germans on five different occasions in the woods near Frémifontaine, France, in the autumn of 1944, he was able to continue fighting and carry on with his duties. A member of the German 6th SS Mountain Division wrote, "The 45th Infantry Division 'Thunderbirds' was an outfit with many battle-hardened soldiers, veterans of considerable mountain fighting … it had far more experience in actual mountain warfare than did we."[11] General Jacob L. Devers, in his letter of appreciation to the men of the 45th Division, wrote:

> The officers and men of the 45th Infantry Division have reached heights of bravery and self-sacrifice which all Americans may well set before themselves

> as future standards of conduct. Seldom has a group of men been called upon to endure such hardships, and never has man responded more gallantly than did the infantrymen in the 45th … Since the 45th served under my command in Italy, France and Germany, I have seen for myself the courage, determination and fidelity which have become a part of your tradition. I shall never fear for the safety of our country as long as the ideals of the 45th Infantry Division remain steadfast in our heritage.[12]

Early research brought me face-to-face with some of the H Company veterans who had served alongside my father. Their stories and specific memories of life as front-line combat soldiers with H Company were helpful in understanding the basic conditions he experienced as a heavy-machine-gun team member. Byrd Austin served as the H Company commander's jeep driver during the entire time my father was assigned to 2nd Battalion. His memory was foggy, but he acknowledged that my father's name sounded familiar to him. Given Byrd's position, it is likely the two of them interacted to some degree on more than one occasion. After all, the unit was small—the entire company could have fit into a school bus.[13] In addition, Byrd was known to be a bit of a "character." Cecil Bell, a friend of Byrd and fellow 2nd Battalion soldier, shared:

> Whenever we got paid, that's when the poker games would start. One time there was four or five guys playing poker, just sittin' on a blanket, low ball with the Joker wild, and Byrd walked up with a hand grenade; he had taken the powder out of it, and he said, "I don't know how to work this thing." He pulled the pin and dropped it on the blanket. You talk about people scattering.[14]

Clinton Charles served as the H Company clerk through Italy, France, and Germany. Only one person was assigned to this unique and important role within H Company responsible for the many administrative responsibilities including distribution of payroll within the unit. Clinton was the only person who assisted the captain with the process of personally handing each soldier his pay. No matter how impersonal or fleeting the contact, I'm certain Clinton interacted with my father each payday throughout the entire time they were assigned to H Company.[15]

Joseph Margotta was a sergeant with H Company's 1st Platoon of heavy machine guns. He told me a heavy-machine-gun team had between six and eight men. It included a gunner who carried the machine gun, referred to as the #1 man, a tripod carrier, known as the #2 man, and between four and six ammunition runners. There were two people at the gun when it was firing: the gunner who was aiming and pulling the trigger, and the #2 man who was feeding the belts into the gun. The Browning 1917A1 heavy machine gun was water cooled and recoil operated. Its .30-caliber ammunition came in 250-round belts made of fabric. With a well-trained crew, the gun could fire 450 to 600 rounds per minute; its water jacket kept the barrel from burning out in combat. The gun, with tripod and water, weighed 93 pounds. Sergeant Margotta led several machine-gun squads and had been assigned to H Company throughout the same period of time as my father. He was captured in the woods near Frémifontaine after having been surrounded and engaged in fierce fighting in early October 1944.[16] At the time of my discussion with Joseph in Sleepy Hollow, New York, I had not yet realized the significance of this battle as it related to my father. Unfortunately, when I began to sense a possible connection, I learned through a disconnected phone number and the presence of a medical death certificate that Joseph had passed away.

Joseph Margotta may have been the key to understanding, but he was gone. I needed another path forward. This inquiry into my father's silence was moving from archive-specific research and casual conversations with World War II veterans to an expedition-style journey across France in a manner that embraces the 45th Division motto, *Semper Anticus* (Always Forward).

While conducting research at the National Archives and Records Administration in College Park, Maryland, I came across a photograph in a 180th Regiment folder that showed a group of soldiers riding on the back of a tank destroyer (TD) through Bourg, France, on September 4, 1944. In the middle of the group, appearing to tip his helmet toward the camera, is a soldier with a striking resemblance to my father. The facial features, cheekbones, body shape and the posture are hauntingly reminiscent. He often sat in a relaxed manner with his head slightly tilted to one side similar to the soldier in the photo. Through my research, I knew that 2nd Battalion was in Bourg on September 4 and I suspected my father had been in H Company's 1st Platoon with Sergeant Margotta

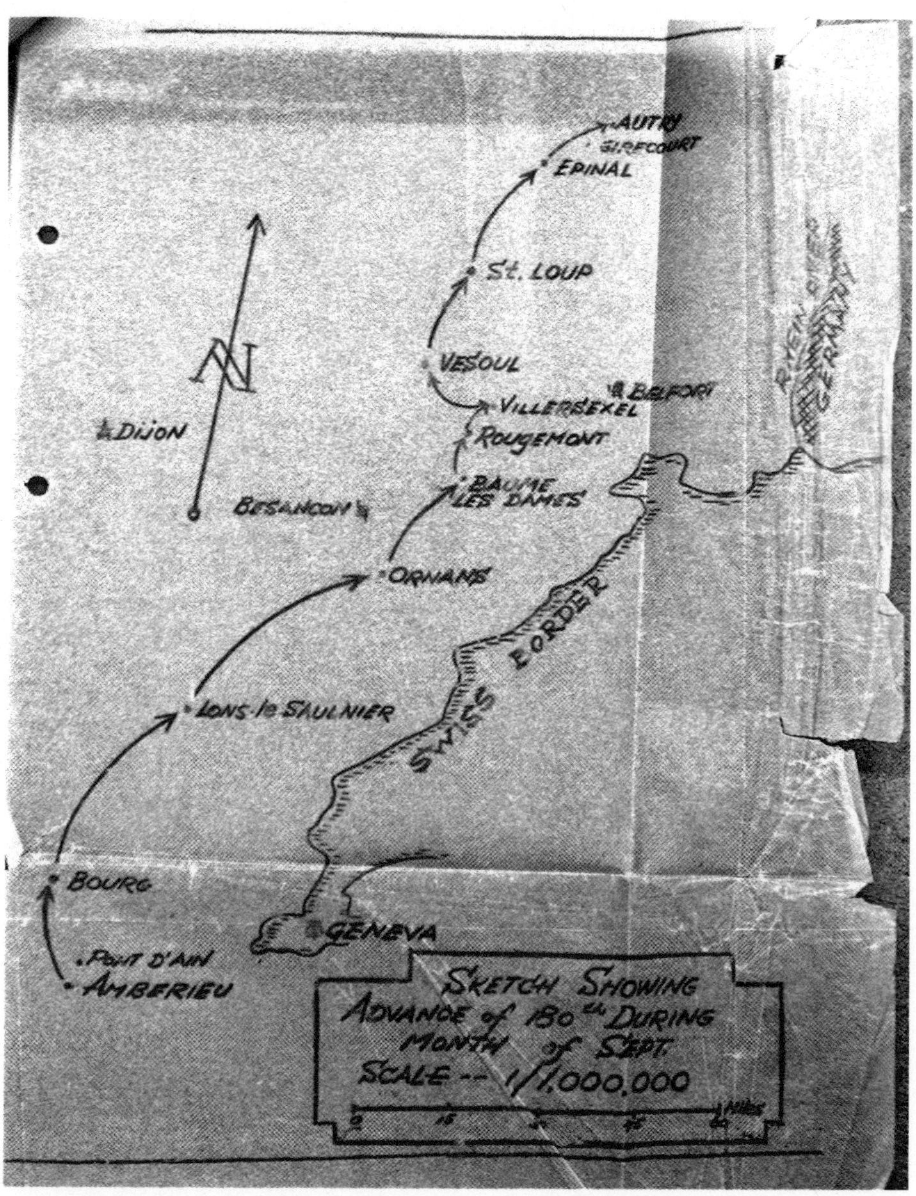

Sketch showing advance of the 180th Infantry during the month of September 1944. Sketch located in Headquarters 45th Infantry Division Transmittal of Organizational History, Operations Report of the 180th Infantry Regiment, September 1–30, 1944. (Document courtesy of the 45th Infantry Division Museum Archives. Photo by Michael Reyka on location at museum archives in Oklahoma City, Oklahoma)

because he also told me my father's name was familiar to him. If it were possible for me to identify someone else on the TD, I might be able to confirm this assumption. I compared the photo with H Company photographs taken on May 29, 1945, at the Dachau Concentration Camp and searched for the soldier without a helmet sitting next to my father. In the 1st Platoon photograph, only two men had a similar hairline, and only one of the two had the same check bones, ears, jaw line, facial expression, and unusually long legs as the soldier in the TD photo. The resemblance was startling. The soldier was Arthur Heeringa, 1st Platoon, H Company, and he had been assigned to a heavy-machine-gun team. His name is listed along with my father's name in an H Company roster included in the 180th Infantry Regiment General Order (GO) #34, dated July 11, 1944, that awards both men the Combat Infantry Badge "for exemplary conduct in action against the enemy."

Convinced my father was indeed the soldier on the TD, Bourg seemed to be the perfect location to begin my expedition-style journey into my father's secret past that he protected so diligently, in the same location and in front of the same house where the Army photographer captured the photo in 1944.

CHAPTER 2

Bourg—The Beginning

The plane landed in Paris before dawn. My daughter, Tara, as well as long-time colleague and friend, Larry, accompanied me on the transatlantic flight that initiated this expedition-style journey. Tara, a graduate student completing her final semester in pursuit of a master's degree in public health, agreed to join the expedition with a plan that included visiting internet cafes along the way to transmit course papers to various professors within the timeframes established in the syllabuses. Larry, a tenured professor of French literature and language and expert in French dialog, with no trace of Western accent, was our interpreter. Once away from the aircraft gates, Charles-de-Gaulle Airport appeared relatively silent in those early hours as we navigated our way through the seemingly endless corridors and layers of alternating escalators that led to the subterranean train station beneath Terminal 2. Our lingering drowsiness convinced Larry to approach two police officers in an effort to clarify the correct location of the train that would shuttle us 15 miles northwest to the city. The ride from the Charles-de-Gaulle Airport to Paris seemed to drag on as we fought the desire to sleep, not helped by the optical boredom associated with the inside of a train car. Nevertheless, anticipation continued to push us forward as the train stopped and our tired legs carried us up the subway staircase tunnel, eventually emerging into the heart of Paris. A light rain had fallen overnight and the wet sidewalks and dripping cafe awnings added to the ambiance of the still-dark city streets. Waiters prepared outdoor tables for the morning customers as cafes opened. The gray, damp, morning should have seemed depressing and disappointing, but in Paris it felt mystical and nostalgic—the culmination of numerous old movies and writings that I experienced throughout my life.

The walk, which was more of a hazy or somewhat dazed stroll resulting from the jet lag, escorted our tired bodies several blocks before selecting an open cafe along the sidewalk and sitting at a small round table closest to the street. An attentive waiter, dressed in dark slacks and a crisp white shirt, briskly moved toward our table as he slung a pressed towel over his arm. "Bonjour, bonjour. Bienvenue." Larry's conversation was brief, but whatever he said to the confident and lively waiter caused him to return with coffee and fresh pastries. The fresh croissant crumbled as my fork pressed through the warm delicate pastry. Coffee was served in small white-porcelain cups with matching saucers. Glancing around at the people reading newspapers folded strategically in front of them, this moment seemed routine for them—nothing special.

Hailing a taxi and traveling to the student district near Notre-Dame Cathedral and The Louvre was relatively easy given Larry's familiarity with the local processes and the culture. The dialog between him and the taxi driver drifted off as it reached the back seat through the sounds of rain drops and car horns. Larry eventually pointed as the driver slowed and pulled to the curb, allowing us to step out into the brightening surroundings and continue wandering along the riverside streets of the fabled city as the morning progressed. Arched bridges crossed the Seine River in systematic spacing, each reflecting a style and character uniquely different from the others. The sky above Paris remained overcast and several ominous clouds gathered over the city, silhouetting historic structures. Notre-Dame appeared to be the unsuspecting victim of one such cloud as a local painter patiently transferred the moment onto his canvas. A wide footbridge with decorative iron railings displayed hundreds of padlocks of all shapes and sizes randomly placed on both sides of the bridge. Local students and young lovers had created a tradition of inscribing their initials or names on the locks before attaching them to the iron grids along the railings and then throwing the keys over the side to rest forever on the riverbed.

Fatigue and exhaustion had begun to catch up as we greeted the desk clerk at our hotel, The Grand Hôtel des Balcons on Rue Casimir Delavigne, where the opportunity for a few hours of sleep in comfortable beds finally presented itself. At dinner, the conversation centered on the details of our journey that would begin the following morning in the town of Bourg, located several hours south of Paris. Jean-Marie, our guide whom we would soon meet, had identified the house depicted in the photograph that appeared to show my father and his fellow 180th Infantry Regiment soldiers riding on the back of a tank destroyer through Bourg in early September 1944.

★★★

Accompanied by Tara and Larry, I planned to retrace my father's steps through the French countryside during the autumn months of 1944, crossing rivers and passing through villages he and the rest of the 180th Infantry Regiment had successfully crossed and liberated nearly seven decades earlier. Although so many years had passed since the regiment's soldiers had walked this ground, many of the landmarks, houses, and buildings remain relatively unchanged. The road signs have been replaced and the road surfaces improved over the decades, but the rural landscape has been relatively untouched by the course of time. We intended to follow the advance of my father's infantry battalion as the soldiers fought their way northeast into the Vosges Mountains and into a fierce and devastating battle involving the small village of Frémifontaine. Many of his deepest secrets were formed in this village—secrets that haunted him, awakened him from sleep, and that he silently took to his grave. It remained my hope those secrets would be exposed through this expedition across the French countryside as we retraced the 180th Infantry Regiment's path.

The image of a 45th Division soldier described in historical documents that I reviewed did not align with my memories of this man. I felt compelled to travel halfway around the world to a country where I could not speak the native language, where I had never considered visiting prior to this research, and yet where I believed important insight and deeply personal answers awaited me. The inquiry had not ended with the completion of my journal that helped to uncover and expose my father's military assignments—that was merely the first phase that established the framework for expanded and more meaningful inquiry. There was something still to discover in France about the man I knew as my father. Something profound and unimaginable happened to him as an infantry soldier that buried itself deep within his psyche, resulting in a lifetime of behaviors commonly associated with post-traumatic stress disorder (PTSD). Initially referred to as battle fatigue or shell shock, PTSD can look different from person to person, depending upon how the individual processes the traumatic event. My father's suspected PTSD manifested itself in silence, emotional distance, recurring nightmares, and a subtle sadness that seemed to loom just beneath his conscious thoughts and within his relationships. These symptoms appeared to increase as he aged, especially the sadness and introspective nature of his personality. My research convinced me he experienced something profoundly terrifying in October 1944 while fighting with his unit. I needed to know what changed this strong young man, what impacted how he viewed himself and his environment, and understand the events that impacted and altered the course of his life. He most certainly struggled with PTSD-related symptoms throughout his 42 years of life following the war. He brought the battle home with him. If there was something for me to learn about my father in eastern France, I would either discover it during this journey or I would accept the realization it could never be known to me or anyone else. Quite possibly, there is also something to learn about my own life in the form of lessons and insight into dealing with adversity, fear, and emotional trauma.

★★★

I had learned a great deal about my father's military experience throughout the five years prior to this journey, despite his lifelong silence regarding his experiences and his premature death in the autumn of 1984. Yet, throughout my life, the quiet nature and the subtle sadness in his personality eluded me. He frequently seemed introspective and reflective of things that were invisible to me. This was a common trait that could be seen to varying degrees regardless of the environment or the situation or the people around him—at least from my perspective. There were certainly moments of laughter and smiles and happiness—he wasn't angry or openly depressed. There was simply a subtle sadness lingering just below the surface. It was something only I could sense for some unknown reason.

My father loved the outdoors and he frequently fished. He never used expensive fishing tackle; what he owned was limited to a few rods, a tackle box, and a pair of river waders. He kept things simple. He didn't brag about his catches, nor did he boast about his sportsman-related skills. It seemed that fishing wasn't a competition, neither was it an elaborate process. The many childhood memories of fishing with my father involve what I interpreted as quiet peacefulness along river banks. He never said much. He just fished. As a child, I wasn't interested in quiet peacefulness; I was bored, frequently reeling in my fishing line over and over again to see if some sneaky little fish had stolen the worm from my hook (I was convinced it had because my bobber stopped bobbing—every few minutes). My patient father would eventually say, "Just leave it out there for a while so the fish can find it" and then he returned to his peaceful place, recognizable to me only through his face and his eyes staring into the distance across the water to something elusive.

During the early years of my youth, he fished lakes. A photo album filled with black-and-white postcard-size images of large fish strung across thin ropes between the posts of old wooden boat docks rested on the lower shelf of the built-in oak bookcases on either side of the living room fireplace in my childhood home. I had never seen so many large fish. I recall wondering how he could have possibly caught all of them, since there were no people in the photographs. At my young age I hadn't quite grasped the concept he had been on a Canadian fishing trip with a group we later referred to as his "poker buddies." The group initially formed in the Army Reserves during the late 1940s and early 1950s where he served as a master sergeant. Dave, Dan, George, and several others whose names have slipped my memory over the years formed the core of the group that sustained the decades that followed. They travelled to Kings Bad River Outpost on Caugee's Bay near Ontario for their fishing expeditions. I have no memories of those fishing trips as they started prior to my birth and apparently ended when I was a toddler. Nevertheless, I can still see the images in my mind even though I haven't held that photo album in my hands for more than fifty years.

During my preteen years, my father periodically fished a small lake in northern Tennessee, near the small town of Crossville located along Route 40 between Nashville and Knoxville. The small Cleveland-based manufacturing company where he worked for multiple decades produced custom advertising items related to many of the major tire companies such as Goodyear, Firestone, BF Goodrich, and Dunlop. During that era, small tire franchises existed across the United States and these local businesses ordered custom-printed ice scrapers, key chains, pens, and ashtrays which they gave away with gratitude to loyal customers. The most unique item was a three-inch glass ashtray dropped into the center of a miniature replica of a rubber car or truck tire (these continue to show up in antique stores across the country). The tire designs changed every few years, based upon new models released by the tire manufacturers. They looked and felt like real tires—just a great deal smaller. Intended as functional ash trays, they also made favorite toys for the family springer spaniel after the glass insert was removed. The Crossville Rubber Company produced the tires using molds provided by my father's company. Once or twice a year, he traveled to Crossville for a few days of business and a few days of fishing. Ed Kmet was his counterpart at the Crossville Rubber Company. The two men became close friends.

Ed had a small aluminum fishing boat on Lake Holiday and they spent many morning hours catching Smallmouth Bass and Bluegill. When the business trip occurred during the summer months, we occasionally made it a family vacation for the week. Those trips to Crossville are the summer vacations I remember most. My father's dialect would change at the first gas station we visited after crossing the Tennessee state line. His traditional greeting of "hello" became "howdy." Rather than an attempt at humor, he was seemingly trying to fit into his environment. Even as a child I was certain the Ohio license plate as well as the manufactured accent undermined his attempt to masquerade as a local. One of the rustic cabins at the Cumberland Mountain State Park, located just a few miles from Ed's house on Mimosa Lane, served as our home for the week.

Our days were spent exploring the park and our evenings were either spent at Ed's house visiting with his family and cooking fried fish or BBQ chicken on the patio grill or meeting them for dinner at the state park restaurant. Built in collaboration with the Civil Works Administration and the Civilian Conservation Corps (CCC) during the late 1930s, the park was one of the many New Deal initiatives that helped to bring the United States out of the Great Depression. Under the direction of the National Park Service, the CCC built the Byrd Creek Dam, creating the 50-acre Byrd Lake in the center of the park. My brothers and I fished the banks behind the cabins and along the boathouse, but my father's focus was the much larger Lake Holiday, which he always referred to as "City Lake." He loved spending time on that rural Crossville lake. On one occasion during my early teenage years, I overheard him tell a small group of extended family that it was his favorite place in the entire world.

We never joined him on the lake. He and Ed usually fished by themselves. I always assumed it was related to the fact that the boat was a small aluminum vessel with limited seating. But I later developed a different perspective. During my early research into his World War II experiences, I talked with Ed about some of the events I discovered. Ed listened patiently through the telephone and then eventually said, "Michael, some things are just best left unsaid."

Ed had been in the military as well during World War II. He had been in the Navy, but suggested he too had many memories he had not shared and would prefer to forget. At that moment, I realized his fishing trips on City Lake were in some way associated with a common history between two servicemen. They both were drawn to the peace, tranquility, and comradery of fishing. There were traditions and simple unspoken processes associated with their fishing trips. Any uncertainty typically involved the number of fish they would catch and the weather conditions they would endure. In a sense, they were in control of their surroundings and their experiences. They were free from pressures, stressors, and threats. They were safe.

Fishing is often an effective way in which to divert attention from frustrations, concerns, and psychological pressures. People who struggle with chronic anxiety or depression have been known to benefit from the reprieve offered by fishing with groups of friends or even fishing alone.

Friends provide comradely support and encouragement around a common and non-threatening activity, while the peace and solitude of connecting with nature can reduce stress and offer the opportunity for moments of psychological balance against life's demands and pressures. Fishing isn't necessarily an activity associated with isolation or silence. Rather, being outdoors shifts one's focus from artificial irritants such as phones, car horns, machines, and the chatter or cackle of crowds to the calming and rational sounds of nature—the wind rolling through the trees along the riverbank, the water current splashing against rocks, and the musical frequencies produced by varieties of birds encompassing the space all around. There is order and balance, consistency, and even predictability. For some, fishing functions as a form of meditation, a chance to get away from whatever may be weighing upon the mind and subsequently the body. Extensive research indicates a direct link between prolonged stress and physical illness, including high blood pressure, stroke, heart attack, cancer, and other diseases (my father experienced most of these medical conditions). Quite simply, fishing provides the opportunity to embrace and enjoy some peace and quiet at both a conscious and subconscious level. For veterans struggling with PTSD, fishing can be a method for calming the battles that perpetuate, and sometimes rage, within their minds.

★★★

As a heavy-machine-gun operator with H Company of the 2nd Battalion during World War II, my father had been assigned to support E, F, and G Rifle Companies on the front lines of battle throughout France. He survived the war, although this outcome appears to defy statistical explanation. Heavy machine gunners didn't last long during combat once they gave away their position by firing the weapon; their life expectancy was measured in minutes. He was no doubt exhausted and challenged by exposure to the elements but continued to fight across France through what likely amounted to the basic determination to survive. This was not the man I knew throughout my childhood. My memories did not include personality traits associated with determination, confidence, resourcefulness, tenacity, or courage (however you define that word). I found it difficult to even envision my quiet and unassuming father in this situation. The historical puzzle pieces didn't fit together. I was overwhelmingly perplexed, and even slightly skeptical, regarding his involvement in this historic battle across the landscape of Europe. Nevertheless, military records and dates, including the H Company morning reports, indicate he was present from the amphibious landing of the 45th Division on the beaches of southern France in August 1944, through countless small villages and larger French cities and eventually engaged in brutal hand-to-hand combat in and around the village of Frémifontaine.

Operation *Dragoon* was the name eventually given to the campaign in southern France. The amphibious operation plans called for Major General Lucian Truscott's US VI Corps headquarters and the 3rd, 36th and 45th Infantry Divisions to lead the assault at three beaches codenamed Alpha, Delta and Camel, followed by several French divisions. At 8:00 a.m. on the morning of August 15, the 180th and 157th Regiments of the 45th Division climbed down the nets into landing craft and stormed the center of the beachhead along Delta beach east of St. Maxime. The 179th Regiment landed later in the day and served as reserve.[1] More than 94,000 men and approximately 11,000 vehicles landed on the beaches of southern France on the first day of Operation *Dragoon* despite enemy attempts to halt the

A landing craft, carrying troops and vehicles, approaches the 45th Division beaches north of St. Maxime on D-Day of the invasion of southern France. Seventh Army, August 15, 1944. (U.S. Signal Corps photo, 111-SC 192902/NARA)

operation at sea. Throughout the day on the 15th and into the night, the *Luftwaffe* repeatedly bombed the Allied fleet off the coast of southern France. Allied P-38 Lightning fighter planes responded but ships were nevertheless sunk. German *Schnellboots* (fast boats) harassed the convoy of ships throughout the night under the cover of darkness.[2]

German ground defenses varied along the beaches, but initial resistance overall was lighter than anticipated. The 180th Regiment's 1st Battalion on the right-hand side of the landing zone met significant enemy resistance on its northward path along the coastal road toward St. Aygulf, advancing only two miles during the first day. The 3rd Battalion on the left advanced to the high ground and the 2nd Battalion in the middle successfully advanced four miles into the hills near Maures.[3] The lengthy and costly battles at Anzio, as a direct result of remaining stationary on the beachhead while German units strengthened their forces, were fresh in the minds of Operation *Dragoon* commanders. In response, General Truscott recommended US forces advance west and move immediately away from the beaches before the Germans could respond. General Alexander Patch, commander of the Seventh Army, agreed and ordered the 45th and 3rd Divisions to advance westward toward Toulon and Marseille. German troops were under Hitler's order to defend these coastal towns to the last man.[4] Enemy resistance increased as the regiment's initial attack forces moved inland along the coastal road on August 16. German machine guns and mortars inflicted many casualties until Allied tanks were called in to silence the well-entrenched enemy weapons. The effort proved challenging as the first tank to engage German positions was knocked out by the direct hit of an antitank gun and two additional tanks were destroyed by German mines when attempting to flank the enemy positions. Second Battalion advanced into Vidauban during the morning hours after encountering heavy resistance from enemy machine gun and antitank guns as well as a column of German vehicles and artillery.[5] The 45th Division and its regiments continued northward following the road to Aspres, Grenoble, Voiron, and Meximieux as it fought at a relentless pace toward Bourg. A German Panzer Division battle group attempted to slow the advancing 45th Division by unleashing an attack to the rear of the 45th's main force and into the streets of Meximieux where it engaged two companies of the 179th Regiment held in reserve. Losses were heavy on both sides.[6]

Within the first 17 days following the southern France landing, the 45th Division fought its way northward to Bourg at a relentless pace as the enemy retreated toward Germany, resisting the American advance with fierce firefights and deadly roadblocks along the way. By the end of August, the 180th Regiment had completed its objective ahead of schedule, advancing a distance of approximately 400 miles. Second Battalion assembled south of Montferrat on August 29 and the following day marched to Montelieu.[7] Enemy resistance continued as the regiment fought its way into Pont d'Ain, south of Bourg. Shortly before 1:00 a.m. on September 1, 3rd Battalion reported to the regimental S-3, "the Germans are on the north bank of the river and are setting Pont d'Ain afire," and by 8:00 p.m. the regimental S-3 received a report that Pont d'Ain had been destroyed. Enemy troops retreated to the north and south after building a five-foot high timber roadblock north of the crossroad and destroying the bridge 1,000 yards beyond that. Seven German tanks were reported leaving town and moving to the high ground.[8]

Soldiers of the 45th Infantry Division advance northward to the front lines north of St. Maxime, southern France on August 16, 1944. (U.S. Signal Corps, 111-SC 271433/NARA)

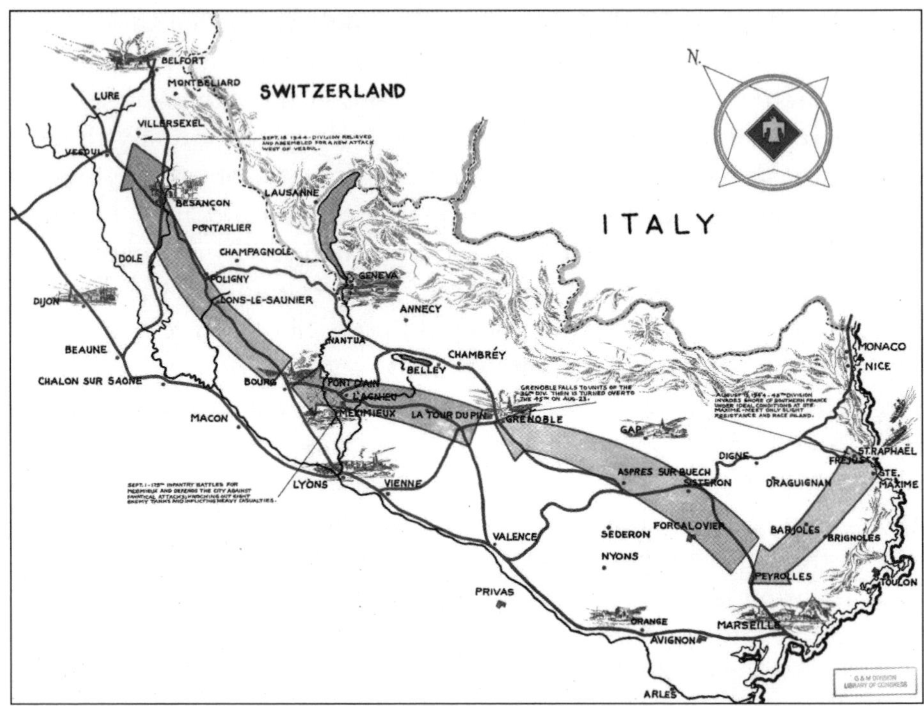

The 45th Division's advance toward Bourg. (U.S. Army, 45th Infantry Division)

During the early morning hours of September 4, 1944, the 2nd Battalion of the 180th Regiment, attacked in a westerly direction toward Bourg, advancing to the highway known as Route Nationale. A large number of enemy troops were concentrated and waiting in the woods south of Bourg[9] as the regiment approached.

I was soon to arrive in the same French town, many decades after he and the 180th had liberated it in 1944. What would I find? What would the structures and the landscape reveal in comparison to the historical narratives and photographs as well as the images they have created in my mind? I was about to learn the answers to these and other questions through immersion in the landscape and the culture. The anticipation generated an image as I quietly stepped back in time to events long past. Although people were present all around me, I felt as though I was the only one who could see beyond the present and into the hazy mist of a previous time.

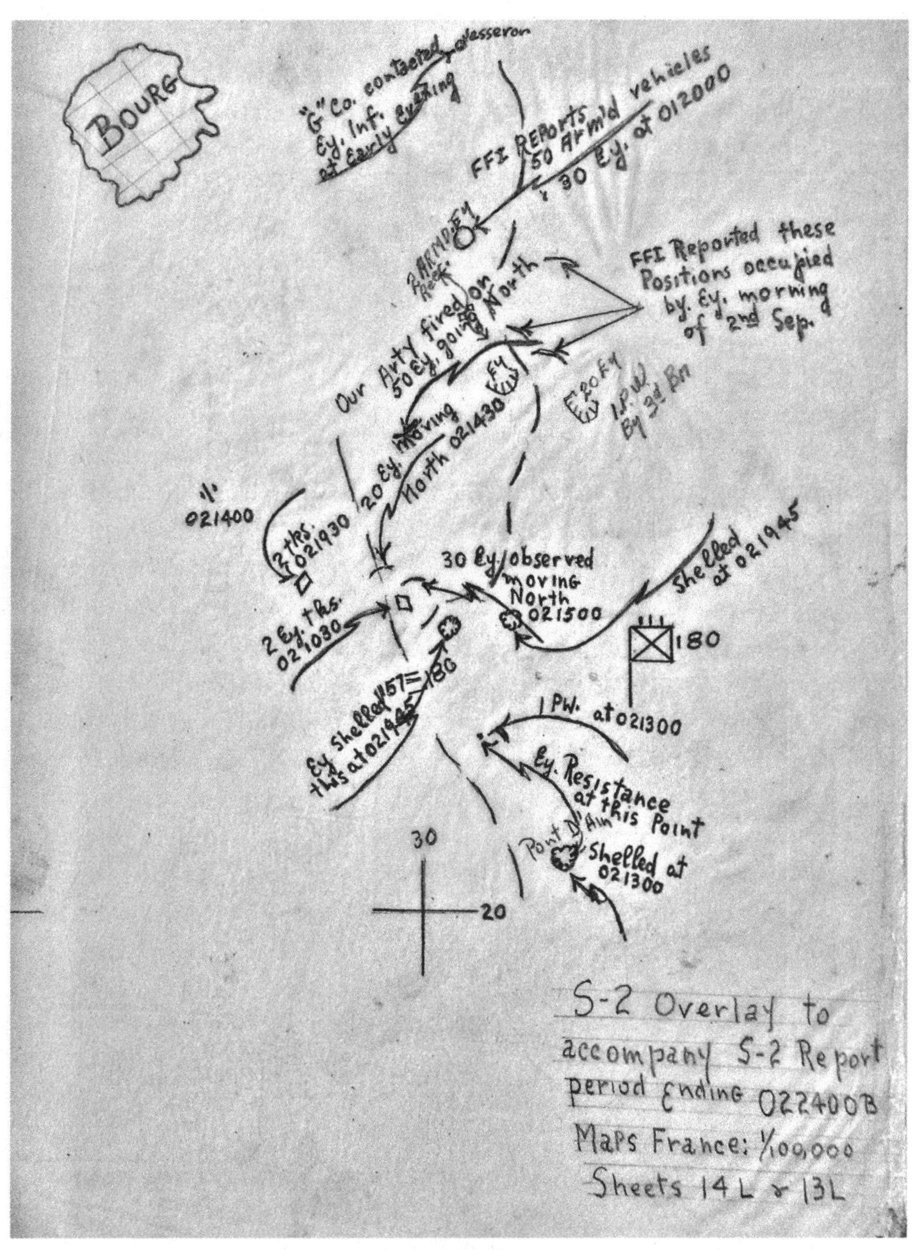

Sketched map overlay showing enemy resistance and fighting near Bourg on September 2, 1944. Sketch located in Headquarters 180th Infantry S-2 Journal, September 1944. (Document courtesy of the 45th Infantry Division Museum Archives. Photo by Michael Reyka on location at museum archives in Oklahoma City, Oklahoma)

Our royal-blue rented BMW turned left onto Boulevard de Brou, the main road leading into Bourg from the south, after passing through the northern more-recently developed areas of Bourg, and advanced toward the old center of the town. The various cars parked along the roadside left several options for our rental car as it came to rest across from rows of streetside shops. The weathered concrete sidewalk led us southward, searching the distant structures on the opposite side of the street in hope of gaining a glimpse of the house shown in the photograph I had found in the National Archives—the photo that appears to show my father riding on the back of a tank destroyer. We walked a significant distance before finally recognizing the house at the southern edge of town. A small tree grew along the curb and partially obstructed my view. Nevertheless, the structure was unmistakable. While standing in the same location as the original photographer, I imagined the sights and the sounds around him at the time; the sound of the tank engines, the dirt and dust from the tank tracks, the tired faces of the soldiers, as well as the old Frenchman and the young child standing along the curb waving to them as the warm autumn sun shone down. The cast-iron sign seen along the road in the original photograph, signifying the southernmost city limits of Bourg, had long since been removed and the road had been paved at some point within the near seven decades since the tanks and trucks had rolled through town. Where the child had stood waving to the soldiers, my daughter, Tara, stood in the same location, staring into the street at the precise spot where the tank destroyer had passed in September 1944. It was a moment that seemed to defy time as I compared the two images. Tara had never met her grandfather—he died a year prior to her birth. Yet, in this small town in France, she took the first steps into a powerful segment of his life—a brief but profound experience that changed the man in ways I had yet to determine.

The original stucco surface of the house had accumulated significant dirt, but the windows and first-floor shutters matched the photograph. The wide vertical trim on the right front corner of the house had been removed at some point in time. The outline of the original material, however, was clearly visible against the stucco surface, suggesting the revision had been fairly recent or the owner had simply failed to paint the area following the removal.

It was noon. I felt the warm sunlight on my face and recognized the shadows in front of me were only slightly different than those in the original photograph. Given the slight variation in both shadow angle and length across the road surface, I estimated the tank had likely passed the house around 10:00 a.m. We walked northward along the sidewalk, focusing on each house, each structure, and each large tree, imagining my father experiencing the same sights as he rode on the back of the tank destroyer. A large, white-stone church with a mosaic-tiled roof, standing along the east side of the road opposite the house, clearly existed in 1944.

According to the 180th Regiment S-2 Journal transcripts of the original radio reports, the northern main road into Bourg was reported to be bustling with enemy tanks, trucks, and troops ahead of the advancing Americans. Several bridges had been destroyed by enemy forces in an attempt to slow the advancing American troops. The German troops were retreating north, attempting to stay ahead of the advancing Thunderbirds, but 45th Division commanders knew they could turn and fight at any time. The Germans had occupied this ground for several years before the Americans arrived and were well equipped with weapons, vehicles, and infantry. Some began to question whether the Germans were retreating or simply moving to an established fortified area where they would have an advantage—the forested terrain in the foothills of the Vosges Mountains.

The 180th Regiment soldiers were no doubt distracted from the danger by the response of French residents; perhaps their concerns were lightened, if only for a short time:

> The people of Bourg gave the 45th Division one of its most gala welcomes. The liberated populace went wild as the division's armor and doughboys made their way through the crowded streets. The hardened and battle-worn men of the 45th received their first joyous tribute from the French with customary good nature. Civilians and excited French resistance fighters alike hailed the Americans as liberators.[10]

The progress of our journey led away from Bourg and northward through the small villages of Saint-Étienne-Dubois, through Villemottier, through Cologny, and across the River Loue to the ancient French city of Besançon, which the 3rd Infantry Division liberated in September 1944 while fighting along the 45th Division's left flank. During the liberation,

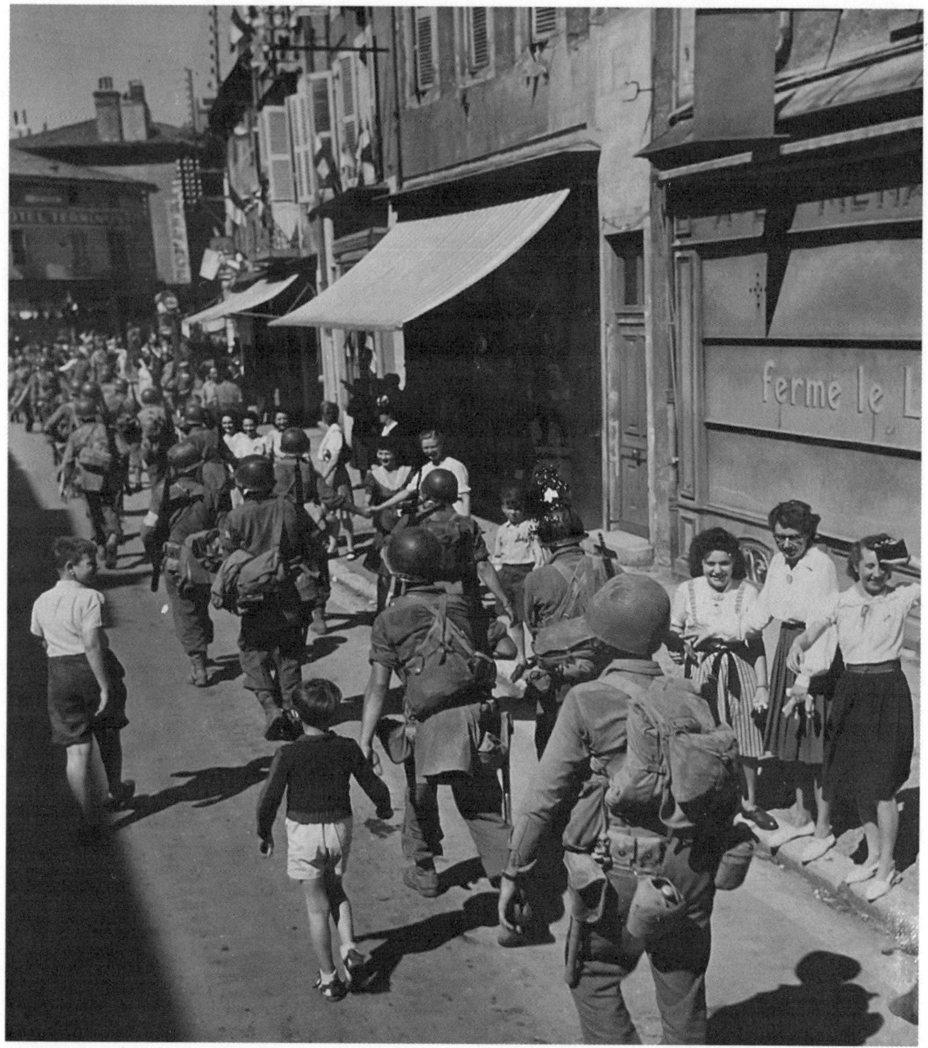

Soldiers of the 45th Division are greeted and cheered by the citizens of Bourg on September 4, 1944. (U.S. Signal Corps, 111-SC, 194990/NARA)

the 3rd Division's 1st Battalion of the 7th Infantry Regiment entered the city from the north, the 2nd Battalion entered from the west, and one of its infantry companies crossed the river before making contact with the 1st Battalion of the 30th Regiment while the 30th Regiment's 3rd Battalion attacked the high ground outside of the city.[11] By September 8, the 3rd Infantry Division had captured 450 prisoners and had killed a German major general in the liberation of Besançon[12] after heavy fighting through the city streets.

The sun had already set as we entered and prepared to spend the night in this historic city. Colorful floodlights illuminated the old stone buildings while cafes drew small crowds of people to their outdoor tables, even on a brisk autumn evening. A small, round rod-iron table with red-and-white checkered tablecloth and large umbrella near the carved-stone fountain in the center of a vast common area became the central point for our strategy session under the darkening sky. Surrounded by ancient stone buildings, the plans for meeting our guide, Jean-Marie, the following morning were reviewed and finalized. The nearby town of Baume-les-Dames was selected for our rendezvous. From that point, Jean-Marie would escort us across the French countryside and eventually into the village of Frémifontaine where I believed the source of my father's nightmares waited for discovery.

Tank Destroyer passing through Bourg while carrying 2nd Battalion soldiers. (Courtesy of NARA, 180th Infantry Regiment photo collection)

Present-day photo of Bourg house in front of which a tank destroyer carrying 2nd Battalion soldiers passed on September 4, 1944. (Photograph by Michael Reyka on location in Bourg, France)

CHAPTER 3

Baume-les-Dames

My first contact with Jean-Marie occurred several months prior to the start of this journey, after locating his blog during a routine internet search for information associated with the 180th Infantry Regiment's operations in France. He has for many years lived with his wife and family in the small village of Frémifontaine, nestled in the foothills of the Vosges Mountains in eastern France, where the 180th Regiment participated in several intense battles with the Germans and from where my father was medically evacuated in October 1944.

Born in 1941, Jean-Marie was a child during World War II. His passion for the history of the 180th Regiment's activities in this area, and his experience as a non-commissioned officer in the postwar French Army, involving 33 years of service to his country, would serve as a unique resource throughout this exploration into history. Jean-Marie was an infantry heavy weapons specialist (heavy machine guns and mortars) during his time in the French military and therefore possesses a unique understanding of the environment and situations my father experienced while serving with the 180th.

Jean-Marie agreed to serve as our guide throughout the remainder of this journey and introduce us to villagers that lived through both the German occupation and the 180th Infantry Regiment's liberation of their communities. Most significantly, he offered to assist us in becoming acquainted with the village of Frémifontaine in a way that would hopefully promote understanding of the 180th Regiment's, and my father's, actions.

Leaving the ancient city of Besançon shortly before first light, we drove in an easterly direction toward Baume-les-Dames. Upon approaching the center of town as darkness lifted, I was immediately struck by the architecture of the well-preserved old buildings and the narrow streets. Except for the presence of a few late-model cars parked along the curbs and a few modern light posts and road signs, it appeared very little had changed since September 1944. The town was eerily quiet and still, void of people or movement, not even a stray cat in sight. We inadvertently arrived an hour prior to our agreed upon rendezvous time with Jean-Marie and subsequently decided to walk through the narrow streets in the cool early morning autumn air. The silence and the architecture made it seem as though we had again stepped back in time, as if we were the only people alive at that moment.

After returning to our car and making our way to the opposite end of town we pulled into a gravel parking lot near the bridge where a small house converted into a local café had opened for the day moments before our arrival. The comforting aroma of strong coffee filled the air that escaped from the door at the top of the porch steps. A barista behind the counter offered a friendly greeting in French and congratulations for being the first customers of the day. So as not to rely on Larry's interpretation for every interaction, I asked him for the proper way in which to order coffee with cream. Without hesitation and with a sense of new-found confidence, I turned to the barista and repeated, "*Un café au lait, s'il vous plait.*" She responded with a moderately restrained grin, the way in which one responds to a child who just said something cute, and then she spoke to Larry. I had properly ordered a strong cup of coffee with steamed milk—I even said please. But I hadn't pulled off the performance. My thoughts returned to those gas station greetings in Tennessee and my father's attempt to masquerade as a local resident. Larry placed the remainder of our order as we sat near a large window and waited for Jean-Marie's arrival as we sipped the fresh coffee.

In less than ten minutes, I noticed a compact car as it turned into the parking lot. It was the only vehicle seen on the road in town throughout the morning. The little red car was unmistakable from the photograph emailed to me before leaving home. Larry suggested I wait inside and walked across the gravel parking lot as Tara and I watched through the window. Jean-Marie stepped out of his car and smiled widely while reaching out his hand. He appeared to be in his mid-60s with short gray hair, approximately five feet, seven inches tall, and was wearing blue jeans, a sky-blue polo shirt and hiking shoes. Excitement and anticipation overpowered my pledge to wait inside the café and, with no sense of remorse or guilt, Tara and I quickly gathered our few belongings and bolted through the door.

After the long-anticipated introduction to, and greetings with, Jean-Marie, we discussed his plan for the day's events, talked briefly about the history of the bridge over the Doubs River located behind us and reviewed the fighting that had occurred between German and American forces along the river in the autumn of 1944. Jean-Marie spoke little English, so Larry served as the expert interpreter within our small group for the vast majority of conversation. The exploration had officially begun—a retired French military heavy weapons expert leading a French literature professor, a college student intrigued by her dad's quest and drawn to her grandfather's history, and a middle-aged hospital executive/researcher/author still trying to understand his father who had died nearly 35 years before.

Our small group had come together in response to a simple request for information and was positioned to travel the French countryside in search of answers to unknown questions. Understanding my father could only be accomplished by understanding the detailed history of the 180th Regiment, specifically its 2nd Battalion. Beyond that, the specific questions had not been created, which was not consistent with the nature of my personality. My analytical mind typically wants to know what I'm getting into and why I am doing it before I open the door, let alone step through the doorway. In this particular situation, I was following my intuition. Without stepping into the history on the same ground associated with his past, I could not know what influenced my father. The documentation and the veteran testimonials had reached a point where they could offer no additional insight.

★★★

Leading elements of the 180th Regiment crossed the Doubs River into Baume-les-Dames in a northwesterly direction during the early

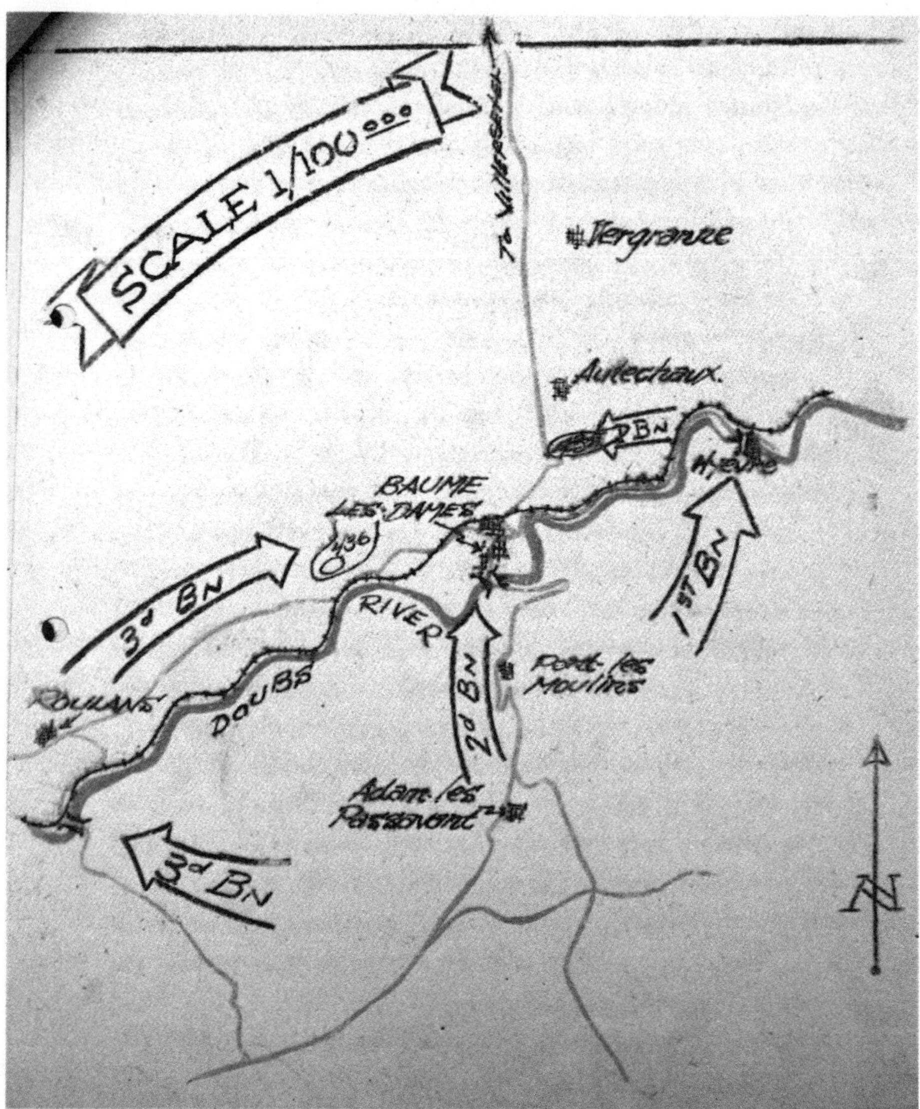

Sketched map overlay of 180th approach to Baume-les-Dames. Sketch located in Headquarters 45th Infantry Division Transmittal of Organizational History, Operations Report of the 180th Infantry Regiment, September 1–30, 1944. (Document courtesy of the 45th Infantry Division Museum Archives. Photo by Michael Reyka on location at museum archives in Oklahoma City, Oklahoma)

daylight hours of September 7, 1944. Many of the pre-existing bridges leading northward to Baume-les-Dames had been destroyed to slow the advancing Americans and assist the Germans in defending the route into the mountains and back into the Rhineland.[1]

The current bridge in Baume is a modern replacement for the original structure destroyed by the Germans and its American replacement. US Army engineers had, however, quickly built a temporary Bailey bridge soon after the arrival of American troops, allowing 45th Division trucks and equipment to safely cross the river. A Bailey bridge is a lightweight steel truss and wooden structure, components of which are transported in sections and assembled in the field by connecting the pieces to form bridges of various lengths, widths, and heights. Although extremely strong when completed, the component pieces are small enough to be lifted by groups of men or small machinery without the use of cranes and heavy construction equipment. Despite their portability, these structures can support the weight of troops, jeeps, trucks, and even tanks.

Bailey bridges were used extensively throughout Europe, and beyond, during the war. While they were intended to serve as temporary bridges, their strength and durability often promoted long-term use. The original Bailey bridge in Baume-les-Dames remained in use until the mid 1970s when it was finally replaced by the current concrete and steel permanent structure. The oldest Bailey bridge in this particular region of France remained in existence, and under daily use, until 2005.[2]

The second most common type of structure used for river crossings during World War II was known as a "Woody" bridge, built completely of wood beams, posts and boards. A World War II-era wooden structure of this type, built by the US Army's engineers in 1944, existed in the village adjacent to Frémifontaine for more than 60 years and received daily use until it was finally replaced in 2008, serving as a testament to US Army engineering design and durability.

Military records provide detailed descriptions of how 180th Regiment soldiers crossed the river during the early hours of fighting near Baume-les-Dames. In the hours prior to dawn, Lieutenant Bridges, from the engineering section, reported the 180th Regiment continued to have difficulty in finding a suitable place to cross the river.[3] An hour after

Lieutenant Bridges made his statement to company command, Captain Franks, from the engineering section, communicated that he had located a bridge and a dam the soldiers could walk across without getting wet.[4]

The Doubs River flows from the northeast to the southwest and, like most rivers, takes many snake-like turns. The 180th Regiment's 2nd Battalion, my father's unit, directly attacked Baume-les-Dames from the south and was the first unit to cross the river and engage enemy troops defending the town. The 3rd Battalion followed across the river at a point downstream from the 2nd Battalion's crossing and attacked the town from a westerly direction, while the 1st Battalion attacked from the northeast.[5]

The Americans moved through the Jura Mountains and the Doubs Valley faster than the enemy had expected; some of the German forces were subsequently left on the wrong side of the river when they destroyed the bridges in Baume-les-Dames.[6] Second Battalion troops were met by heavy fire from flak wagons, tanks and mortars:

> The enemy force defending the town was estimated at 400 to 500, armed with rifles, machine guns and mortars, supported by 10 to 20 tanks and at least two self-propelled 150mm guns. The town was ideally situated for defense, and the Germans held out the first day until surrounded and attacked from all sides.[7]

Second Battalion pushed northward at 6:30 in the morning, with F Company attacking Baume-les-Dames and G Company seizing the high ground to the north of town. Assault companies crossed the Doubs River with little difficulty at 8:47 a.m. while F Company fought their way to the outskirts of town where they were temporarily halted by enemy machine-gun fire, tanks, and 20-mm flak (antiaircraft guns). Seven enemy tanks focused direct fire on 2nd Battalion troops.[8] By late afternoon, the tanks had increased to 11 and were firing point blank into F Company, which had advanced within 75 yards of the bridge. At least one of the tanks appeared to be a Tiger.[9] At 7:00 p.m., battalion and regimental commanders decided to use heavy artillery to silence the tanks and "flatten the town."[10]

H Company Technical Sergeant Jessie W. Fritz, a heavy-machine-gun platoon sergeant, noticed both the gunner and assistant gunner of a heavy-machine-gun squad had been wounded by small arms and mortar fire and the weapon was no longer firing at the enemy. Fritz dressed their wounds and, despite German shells exploding all around his location, he disassembled the weapon and repaired the damage. While firing back at the Germans, he was also wounded. Yet, he continued to fight and advance his machine guns toward the enemy as the Americans advanced into town.[11]

The fighting that occurred in and around Baume-les-Dames progressed throughout the morning of September 8 as 2nd Battalion continued meeting heavy resistance from German forces hitting the center of the 180th's line. Another attempted attack by F Company around 8:00 a.m. was repulsed by German flak, machine gun, and mortar fire. "They were holding desperately in order to give their main forces as much time as possible to get through the Belfort Gap."[12] Second Battalion was under heavy pressure. A French villager reported that he witnessed the Germans taking 20 American soldiers as prisoners. He also reported the presence of five enemy tanks, two 150-mm guns, and 400 enemy troops. G Company reported it was missing 12 men; E Company had 40 men unaccounted for by late morning. Three German machine guns were firing on the battalion troops.[13] By mid-afternoon, F and G Companies were still engaged with enemy infantry, tanks, 20-mm guns, and antitank guns. The Germans began firing heavy artillery and mortars at F Company's outpost.[14] Second Battalion commanders had had enough and, at 8:50 p.m., the order was given: "Take the town of Baume tonight."[15] In response, E and F Companies, reinforced by heavy artillery and tanks, intensified their attack on Baume-les-Dames during the dark predawn hours of September 9. By 4:00 in the morning, they had cleared the town of all but a few German snipers[16] and 2nd Battalion then moved to the high ground north of town and was subsequently placed in regimental reserve.[17] A German prisoner taken during the night said his entire battalion, along with ten Mark V tanks, withdrew prior to the American attack.[18]

My father was assigned to 2nd Battalion's H Company throughout this period. It is difficult to imagine him here as a young man, only 22 years old, in this environment and engaged in such violence. Memories of his behaviors and his interactions with others did not match the descriptions

A 45th Division soldier stands on an M7 Priest self-propelled artillery vehicle. (U.S. Signal Corps photo #7/MM-44–31663/NARA)

associated with the environment or these battles. He was always polite, unassuming, quiet, and rather passive when interacting with others, even those with whom he didn't agree or didn't particularly like. I wondered how the person I knew had dealt with such intense conflict and violence. These weren't simply interpersonal conflicts, disagreements, or arguments. Lives were lost in violent clashes of men, explosions, and bullets. My memories of him involve behaviors typically associated with conflict avoidance, not conflict engagement. Something, somewhere, among this relentless violence involving the 180th Regiment challenged him beyond his ability to cope. But, despite the intensity of violence discussed while visiting Baume-les-Dames, these experiences did not appear to offer the answers to my questions. Something far more intense was responsible.

CHAPTER 4

Rougemont

The main road to Rougemont emptied into a small central open area encircled by two-story stone-and-wood-frame homes as our blue rental sedan pulled quietly into a parking space behind Jean-Marie's little red car along the main road through the village. A brief walk toward the center of town indicated the presence of an outdoor market in process—a Friday morning tradition in this very small village. Jean-Marie immediately began speaking with people along the street in an effort to explain our presence and locate anyone who may have been a resident during the fighting in 1944. Villagers quickly began to take notice and a few showed interest in our presence while others simply stared from a distance. Jean-Marie first approached and spoke with an elderly man who was walking slowly with a cane along the narrow street toward the market area. He seemed to have no interest in our presence. Unfortunately, the man had not lived in Rougemont in 1944 and subsequently continued along the path after a brief moment of dialogue. Resolute, Jean-Marie next spoke with two women who subsequently directed him to a group of three men standing along the street near the corner of the market area at the main intersection. He approached the group; a tall, thin man with silver-white hair, appearing to be in his mid-70s, began to speak freely. He wore a beige cotton jacket, purple-plaid button-down shirt, and carried a pack, all of which appeared to be relatively new and neatly pressed. Engaged and energetic, he listened intently to Jean-Marie's questions.

The man identified himself as François. He had been nine years old in September 1944 when the Americans liberated his village, and had been standing in the street near the main intersection when the first American scout entered his town. Francois recalled the soldier ran along the road and then stopped in front of a house in the marketplace. The soldier was tired, out of breath, and exhausted. He removed rations from his pocket and, after sitting down to rest, began eating. A local woman, who has since passed away, approached the exhausted soldier and offered a small jar of jelly, which he eagerly consumed. Within minutes, additional troops followed. Shortly thereafter, American tanks thundered down the same road and immediately turned to the right as they entered town, just a few yards from where we stood. Francois said of the tanks, "They didn't stop. They just turned and kept going." He spoke clearly with pride and emotion, as if it had occurred yesterday, and finished his description with the statement, "We can't forget the Americans. We are grateful."

According to the 180th Regiment Report of Operations for September 1944:

> The regiment continued to attack on 11 September with the 3rd Battalion on the left and the 2nd Battalion on the right. Company E eventually entered the center section of Rougemont, meeting no opposition.[1]

However, the regiment experienced a strong German presence in the area surrounding Rougemont as it advanced northeasterly from the Baume les Dames region. Company E initially cleared the village but despite the presence of 180th troops on the northern boundaries of town, the Germans sent additional reinforcements to the area via personnel carriers from the northeast[2] where E Company confronted and engaged them in battle as they arrived.[3] Small arms firefights, supported by larger German guns, continued throughout the afternoon and evening hours. Enemy troops used the cover of the dark forests surrounding Rougemont to stage their attacks. The regimental journal recorded that a German prisoner of war reported 270 men and nine machine guns were in the woods and that the soldiers were "home guard troops."[4]

This official Army report, typed in the field of battle, corresponds with François's personal memories. The initial troops he witnessed entering his town were E Company soldiers from the 180th's 2nd Battalion. My father and his H Company heavy-machine-gun squad were frequently assigned to support E, F, and G Companies. It is entirely possible young François caught a glimpse of him entering Rougemont on that memorable day. Sadly, there is no evidence to suggest which rifle company he was attached to at the time, and the combined number of troops in 2nd Battalion was nearly a thousand men. With no manner in which to validate, I simply dismissed this thought as an irrational emotional attempt to find answers.

François excitedly called to a woman walking near us in the market area, the daughter of the woman who provided the jar of jelly to the American soldier, and incorporated somewhat exaggerated hand and arm movements in an effort to entice her into joining us. Despite his sincere efforts, she continued to smile coyly at us from a short distance as he recounted the story and told her of the reason for our visit to their village. Finishing the conversation, François encouraged us to speak with Madame Jacqueline Mallier, a 98-year-old woman who had also lived in Rougemont and managed the local pub during October 1944. The Americans had established a temporary base in Rougemont along the road across from Madame Mallier's family house and she maintained remarkably clear memories of those events. Sadly, her two brothers were both killed at Normandy.

As our small group approached her two-story stone home, Madame Mallier had just come out of the house through the front door, preparing to check her mailbox and completely unaware of our presence. She appeared slightly startled as Jean-Marie offered a cordial greeting. In response, François introduced us. As he explained we were retracing the path of the 180th Regiment, her eyes remained focused on him, in deep concentration. However, once he told her the group included the son of an American soldier who had passed through her village in 1944—a son who was in the process of retracing his father's steps—her concentration broke, her eyebrows lifted, and her eyes filled with tears as she turned her head to look at me. Her face instantly filled with emotion and her demeanor softened. She told us in French, "Just yesterday I received a letter from an American who had been in Rougemont in 1944." Madame Mallier had corresponded with several American soldiers throughout the years following the war. She emphatically invited us into her home to visit and said, "I hope that you get the welcome you deserve in France." Her eyes again welled up as she shared, "This is a great emotion for me."

An active French resistance existed in the village at the time of the fighting and Madame Mallier spoke at length about the group's interaction with the American troops, often involving dangerous covert missions and reconnaissance to identify German troop locations and types of weapons, and proudly shared she had received letters and photographs over the years from both American and British soldiers. I glanced around the small living room and noticed several framed photographs of her family members as well as one of George H. W. Bush protected in a gold-colored metal frame. Madame Mallier realized I was looking at the photos and in response said to me in French, "My daughter lives in Florida, she took me to the White House." She continued to explain that her son lives in Montreal, Canada, but that he had been born after the fighting in and around the town had ceased. Turning toward a credenza along the wall of her living room, she shuffled through a few papers in an upper drawer and retrieved a photograph and letter from George Miller, an American soldier who fought through Rougemont in 1944.

Madame Mallier spoke of the 1st Special Service Force that was operational throughout the Vosges Mountains during the war. Enthusiasm radiated in her words and her face as she talked about the Canadian troops in the area and recalled the moment she asked some of them as they passed her on the street, "Are you American" to which they responded, "No" in French. She smiled and laughed softly as she shared this memory, explaining that hearing them speak French surprised her. A moment later, she lifted her eyes, smiled confidently at us and added, "The Americans arrived first!" She recalled that among the first soldiers to arrive in her town was a soldier named Gerard Halpern. He returned to Rougemont many years after the war, visited with Madame Mallier at her house, and stayed in the area for several days. She recalled that Gerard returned to Rougemont because he longed to see the French countryside once again in response to the vivid and profound memories of this particular time in his life.

Madame Mallier was 32 years old at the time of the American liberation. Her place of business was requisitioned shortly after the 45th Division troops arrived in her village; the local pub was subsequently transformed into a command center. She recalled the Americans had radios and, as a young woman, it was an exciting and emotional experience for her to hear the radio communications and to see all the vehicles, equipment, and soldiers moving about her small village. She shyly commented on the generosity of the Americans and described that some of the soldiers provided cans of beans to the residents and swapped rations with many of them.

One particular memory involves the soldiers taking pills to help them stay awake at night. She indicated the Germans had some as well, but stated, "the Americans had plenty of these pills and even gave some to the villagers." One possible explanation is that they were caffeine tablets to compensate for the lack of rest, sleep, and subsequent fatigue. A Thunderbird soldier later wrote in his memoir, "We were given three big pills called 'pep pills.' We were instructed to take one a day for the first three days … to keep us awake."[5] Coffee and caffeine-enhanced chocolate were commonly associated with American troops in the field of battle. However, amphetamines were also used by both Allied and German personnel during the war to stay awake on the battlefield. Soldiers often referred to them as "wakey wakey" pills. Governments provided them to keep soldiers alert during battle and also to reduce fear and anxiety through the drug's influence on the central nervous system and its ability to produce a feeling of euphoria. In this sense, it was believed the drug might help to reduce the high rates of battle fatigue, now commonly referred to as post-traumatic stress disorder (PTSD). During the war, battle fatigue was estimated to represent up to one third of the non-lethal battlefield casualties. Management of the physical and psychological limitations of infantry soldiers during battle became a critical issue. For this reason, the drug's mood-altering effects, including in some cases increased confidence and aggression, were seen as valuable on the front lines of military conflict. The Germans relied on the drug Pervitin while the Allies relied on Benzedrine. The two drugs were similar in their effects.

My request to take a photograph with Madame Mallier generated embarrassment and she immediately moved her hands to her head, pressing her palms from front to back in an effort to assure her hair was neat and presentable. She looked to Tara for female insight into her appearance and laughed shyly as she prepared to pose for a portrait between the two of us. Tara was struck by her genuine emotion and excitement regarding our presence in her home and our conversations about the war in her village; four strangers stood in her home and she behaved as if we were long-lost friends she had not seen in decades. The war was a powerful segment of Madame Mallier's life. After so many years, she remained thankful and enthusiastic toward the American troops for their presence. Converting the decades-old memories into words brought deep emotions to the surface and she could not contain them. I don't think she had any intention of containing them—she wanted to share them.

When the visit came to an end, Jean-Marie thanked Madame Mallier for her hospitality and for sharing her memories and personal experiences. In return, she thanked me for my father's actions and stated she and the villagers are the grateful ones because they vividly remember what it was like when the Germans arrived. Her sincere and repeated gratitude, and her reference to my father, surprised me. She continued, "We practically became Germans but the Americans came through and kicked them out. The occupation was terrible. They shipped away many people—trains full of men and also children. They shipped them first to Paris and then shipped them off to Germany." Her smile and bright expression faded as she spoke of these unpleasant and painful memories, but they quickly returned as she again recalled her memories of the liberating Allied troops that flooded into her community in September 1944.

As we prepared to leave her home, Madame Mallier hugged and kissed me on the right shoulder—she had intended to kiss my cheek but was too short to reach my face, even as I leaned slightly forward. Her eyes again filled with tears as she said, "It seems like only yesterday." She was visibly appreciative of our visit, of our interest in her memories, and of the personal journey to retrace my father's steps. Madame Mallier stood in her doorway waving, smiling and wiping tears from her eyes as we walked away, back toward the market area in the center of town.

E Company of the 2nd Battalion cleared Rougemont of enemy troops.[6] H Company heavy machine guns supported E, F, and G Companies.

The remainder of 2nd Battalion passed straight through Rougemont before encountering increasing numbers of Germans east of town. Fighting between E Company and several personnel carriers filled with Germans ensued along the eastern edge of town while enemy trucks and artillery were also involved.[7] A large concentration of enemy troops and weapons was concealed in the woods and a German prisoner reported more troops were on the way. Self-propelled artillery guns, 20-mm guns, and machine guns fired on G Company. The more that G Company went into the woods, the more enemy resistance they encountered. Another German prisoner stated they had 270 troops, nine machine guns and several antiaircraft guns. By 7:30 that evening, G Company had taken 100 prisoners, including a dying German major.[8]

I tried to envision nine-year-old François as he stood in awe watching the first American troops move into and through his hometown. I still couldn't grasp the vision of my father within this group of soldiers. While stories of kind gestures and the polite mannerisms of the American troops resonated with memories of my father, the fighting didn't align with anything I witnessed in his personality or his behavior. Although convinced he was indeed present and involved in these situations, I hadn't yet begun to see the connection to the nightmares. The extreme event I had anticipated had not yet been uncovered. Something still didn't fit. Something far more intense and profound than that which Madame Mallier shared with us must have occurred somewhere across the countryside of eastern France in the autumn of 1944 as my father and the remainder of 2nd Battalion liberated a succession of villages on their path northeast toward the German border. Nothing learned so far would be expected to result in a lifetime struggle with PTSD-related behaviors. Perhaps these events represented a cumulative pattern of stressors that reached a threshold—a breaking point.

I pondered the same question that regimental officers wrestled with as they advanced through Bourg—were the Germans retreating or strategically repositioning and drawing the 180th Infantry Regiment into a preconceived trap? The foothills of the Vosges Mountains would be an ideal location because the area acts as a formattable natural barrier. Attacking armies had failed to successfully fight their way across this densely forested rugged terrain time and time again throughout the course of history in response to a variety of natural factors. The mountainous steep terrain and dense forests with few or no suitable roads were not only difficult for exhausted troops but challenging for fighting vehicles to navigate. Establishing supply lines to maintain adequate fuel, ammunition, weapons, and food to support the advance were equally problematic in response to the terrain. In addition, the high elevations introduced mountain range weather such as snow, wind, and frigid temperatures. The elevation of the foothills reaches 1,640 feet and is comprised of dense oak and beech trees whereas the next zone, known as the Montane Zone, reaches 3,280 feet and transitions to beech and fir trees. The next section, known as the Sub-Alpine Zone, reaches over 4,650 at its highest point.[9]

CHAPTER 5

Bonnal—A Crossroad

The 180th Regiment's engagement with German forces occurred at the only road intersection in, and the primary entrance to, the village of Bonnal. As I stood in that same intersection considering how a battle between two powerful forces could have occurred in this tiny community, Jean-Marie stopped a passing mail truck and learned from the driver that the population of Bonnal was a mere 24 people. With no one else in sight and no other vehicles moving about, the scene was again strangely silent, yet incredibly beautiful. Jean-Marie next walked the short narrow path leading to a large old house facing the intersection and eventually approached a woman who cautiously spoke through the kitchen screen door. Despite his most friendly and sincere explanation, Jean-Marie was unable to gain from her or others in the home any firsthand information regarding the fighting during September 1944.

Unfortunately for us, neither the home owner nor any of the other 23 residents of Bonnal had lived in the area during the fighting. The stories were gone, but the history remained in the structures, the roads, and the landscape surrounding this minute village. In addition, the absence of people during our visit allowed the historic structures and images to transport my thoughts to another point in history. When combined with the 180th Regimental S-2 (intelligence and security officer) radio-transcript reports, the experience of 1944 began to form in my visions as the scenery engulfed my thoughts and my imagination. I again began to feel as though we had been transported back to that time; I could almost see the trucks in the distance as they approached.

The 180th's 2nd Battalion had advanced northward toward Bonnal after leaving Rougemont. Following the orders of Lieutenant Colonel Cruikshank (2nd Battalion HQ commanding officer), G Company advanced on the left, E Company on the right, with F Company in reserve following behind E Company,[1] and H Company divided between the three rifle companies. The fighting around Bonnal was more intense than what the regiment had experienced in Rougemont. It began shortly after dark on September 11 as the lead elements of 2nd Battalion approached the southern edge of town.

The Americans initially flushed 20 German soldiers and then sent in artillery barrages in an attempt to encourage more enemy troops to surrender.[2] By first light on the morning of September 12, the fighting had intensified and 2nd Battalion troops were under significant pressure. The Headquarters 180th S-2 Journal for September 12 reported a strong enemy patrol was trying to work its way behind E Company. Several German prisoners of war said a force of 200 was prepared to counterattack and reclaim the town.[3]

As the 2nd Battalion continued its advanced along the main road into Bonnal, trucks filled with German soldiers approached to meet them head-on:

> Three German trucks loaded with infantry came speeding down the road from the direction of Cuse, directly into the path of rear elements of Company E. Colonel Cruikshank, on the spot, ordered his men to open fire and in the fire fight that followed, he personally helped round up nine prisoners. The three German trucks were captured. During the fire fight, Colonel Cruikshank, while trying to make a report to his rear Command Post by radio, had the antenna of his set shot off by sniper fire.[4]

One of the regimental officers reported:

> The enemy employed machine guns, mortars, artillery, and 20mm flak [guns] in an attempt to delay our advance, successfully pinning down Companies G and K just short of Bonnal. Company E then flanked the town on the right, attacking Bonnal from the east. With the pressure relieved, G Company resumed their frontal attack and eventually captured the town, taking 100 prisoners.[5]

German troops later counterattacked from the high ground. Subsequently, a nine-man patrol sent out on the afternoon of September 11 from E

Company's main location found itself in a firefight and killed a large number of enemy troops. After dodging enemy infantry and navigating the dark woods throughout the night, the patrol returned on September 12 at 1:52 p.m. reporting the woods were full of Germans.[6] Contact with enemy troops was often brutal, as described in a report to Regimental S-2:

> One of our C Company boys was wounded yesterday and the Germans went up to him but did not pick him up. Later in the evening a German soldier went up to him and shot him through the chest. This morning, our people found him still out there alive.[7]

An estimated 200 Germans participated in the counterattack designed to recapture Bonnal during the early morning hours of September 12. A radio report from 2nd Battalion to the Regimental S-2 indicated, "G Company is catching hell now. They [Germans] picked off 6 men out of one platoon. We are getting some mortar fire."[8] Fifty minutes later, the battalion reported, "We are having a lot of trouble. There is a big group [of Germans] between Companies E and G."[9] The road was busy with enemy motorcycles, heavy trucks, and armor moving in both directions. Second Battalion estimated that two companies of Germans were fighting between Bonnal and Pont Sur. Shortly before 10:00 a.m., 2nd Battalion radioed to the regimental commanding officer: "Company E is completely disorganized. There is quite a gap there. A good many Germans have worked in there."[10]

Jean-Marie pointed with his outstretched arm in the direction of the high ground the Germans continued to hold to the northeast of Bonnal throughout the early stages of the battle, providing them with a strategic advantage. Despite the advantage, the Germans eventually retreated under the relentless pressure applied by 2nd Battalion forces as well as their concern for becoming surrounded by all three of the battalion's rifle companies.

G Company seized and guarded the Bonnal bridge as the Germans retreated, finding it to be in good condition with only a few roadblocks and no evidence of mines or explosives.[11] Regardless, the engineers that cleared the roadblocks warned the men of continued dangers. The regimental S-3 (operations and mission-planning officer) reported, "They told us to warn our boys not to monkey with the branches of the trees used as roadblocks. Some have been found to be booby-trapped."[12]

Building on its successful resistance against the German counterattack, the momentum of the 180th continued and all three battalions forged ahead to the northeast. Second Battalion, supported by tanks from the 1st Tank Platoon, protected the left flank of the regiment.[13] As the fighting progressed toward Pont-sur-l'Ognon, F Company encountered increasing numbers of enemy troops, including an estimated two companies of Germans supported by five tanks. Nevertheless, the determined soldiers of F Company captured 260 Germans and killed just as many during the fighting.[14] By 5:04 p.m. on the 12th, a platoon on the left of 2nd Battalion's lines was fighting in Pont-sur-l'Ognon, while F Company was entering the town on the left flank.[15] Despite the heavy fighting and violent clashes, by 6:38 p.m., 2nd Battalion troops secured Pont-sur-l'Ognon and the town eventually fell under 180th Regimental control, although F Company continued to receive tank fire from across the river.[16] Prisoners from Germany's 1000th and 1021st Regiments indicated that the 111th Regiment, with air-corps attachments, was also fighting in the area but less than 200 men remained in the unit. It was believed German troops were withdrawing to the northeast and digging in.[17] With these small towns liberated and secured, the 180th Regiment continued its relentless advance to the north and northeast toward the foothills of the Vosges Mountains.

We walked up a dirt driveway in an attempt for a better view of the high ground to the northeast to gain a better understanding of the disproportionate fighting within this tiny village. As we stood on the path imagining the German troops positioned across the clearing on the hill, a French military jet abruptly appeared overhead at a high rate of speed and at very low altitude, so low it appeared to be dangerously close to the treetops. Although I found the event to be symbolic, Jean-Marie smiled confidently and said it was a common occurrence in the region. I struggled to believe such a tiny, peaceful, quaint, and beautiful village was the location of such brutal fighting in the autumn of 1944. But, why should this town be any different than any other French community that lay in the path of the retreating Germans?

I had stopped fighting the disparity between my memories of the quiet and gentle man I knew my father to be and the violent history of

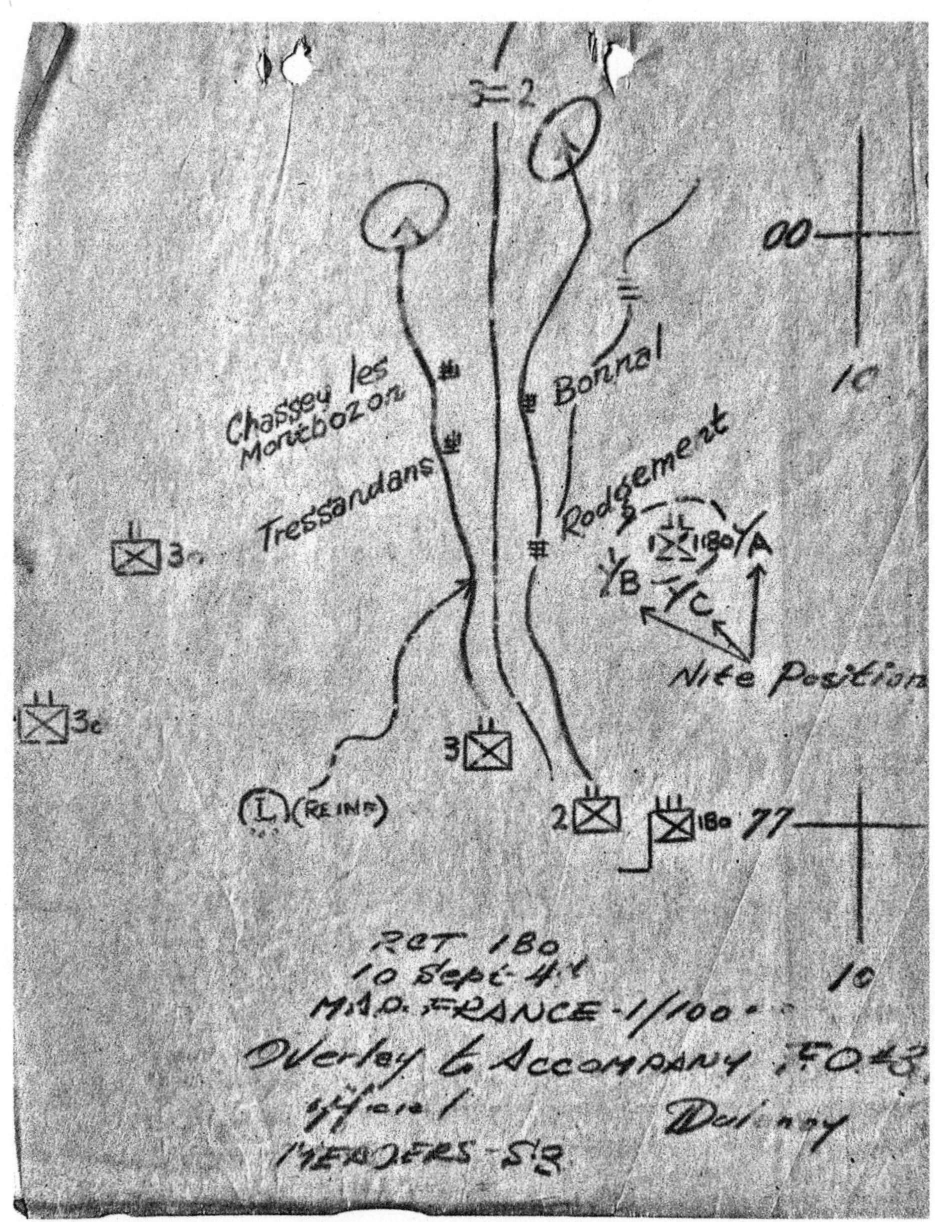

Sketched map overlay of 180th Infantry approach to Bonnal on September 10, 1944. Sketch located in Headquarters 180th Infantry S-2 Journal, September 1944. (Document courtesy of the 45th Infantry Division Museum Archives. Photo by Michael Reyka on location at museum archives in Oklahoma City, Oklahoma)

this region. Perhaps he wasn't always a quiet and introspective person. As with Rougemont, an isolated event here in Bonnal was not going to provide answers to my questions. I looked over my right shoulder at Tara standing near a monument at the side of the road intersection. She was trying to understand the purpose of the unusual rock formation that resembled an eight-foot-high and 20-foot-wide prehistoric lava deposit, with irregular pitting across the entire surface, and countless craters resembling the petrified remains of broken bubbles. A three-foot-high smooth ceramic statue of the Virgin Mary stands atop the strange rock formation and a small statue representing Saint Bernadette Soubirous kneels below at the entrance to a small grotto. An iron fence with a gate encircles the grotto across front of the structure. The monument was commissioned in 1903 by Jules Truchot, owner of the Bonnal Castle, through a bequest that included the gift of the monument and 4,000 francs for its maintenance as well as that of the family tombs behind the village church.[18] My father and 2nd Battalion troops no doubt viewed the same structure during the fighting in this small village. Tara lifted her eyes and, in silence, gazed down the road 2nd Battalion had used to approach the village. I knew she was trying to make sense of this as well. It seemed the more I learned about the 180th Regiment's actions, the less I understood about my father. Something more intense than what caused the scar across the side of his neck happened to him in eastern France.

CHAPTER 6

Villersexel

We followed Jean-Marie's small, red car into the village of Villersexel and proceeded directly through the main sections of town to the high ground and the even smaller rural village of Fougerolles, where Monsieur Robert Grosjean, a mechanic and restorer of vintage American military vehicles, lived and worked. His face showed quiet excitement in response to our presence, and this unique opportunity to share his skillful work with a group of Americans on a World War II-related quest for understanding. The hillside property was scattered with workshops, barn-style structures, vehicles, and machines. Monsieur Grosjean's curly blonde-and-gray hair was mostly hidden under a weathered baseball cap. His thick sideburns and matching bushy mustache, both of which extended to his jawline, matched the thick hair reaching out from under the cap. Silver wire-rimmed glasses, a cotton green-and-white plaid button-down shirt, dark-blue work pants, and black work boots that appeared to have received a great deal of daily use over an extended period of time, complimented his rugged physical appearance. In this seemingly cluttered landscape of tin buildings and sheds filled with metal, grease, oil, tools, and vehicles in various stages of restoration, there was order and purpose. Monsieur Grosjean was aware of every element, its purpose, and its individual history. This was his place, his passion, and his home.

We stood outside a large sheet metal, stone, and wood barn filled with wartime-era vehicles, many of which he had skillfully restored to their original operational state. A Sherman tank involved in the August 1944 45th Infantry Division landing in southern France sat prominently in front of the main barn doors. According to Monsieur Grosjean, approximately fifty thousand Shermans were manufactured during the war and his tank was one abandoned in southern France as the troops moved northward from the beachhead. He explained that, prior to his restoration efforts, the tank was originally powered by five 6-cylinder Chrysler gasoline engines, arranged in a semi-circle, totaling 30 cylinders, and producing approximately 370 horsepower.[1] Chrysler called the unique engine the A57 Multibank. This M4A4 Sherman had a crew of five men and could reach speeds up to thirty miles per hour. The Sherman was the most widely used US tank during the war. Monsieur Grosjean's had been meticulously restored, complete with paint, decals, numbers, and 50-caliber machine gun with attached ammunition box. Shovels and netting were carefully attached to its back and a spare wheel to its left front. The number "614698" appeared in white paint on the front center and left rear. I thought of the photo that shows my father riding on the back of the tank destroyer through Bourg. I then climbed onto the tank, walked alongside the main gun turret to the back and sat down in the same location where he had been photographed. This was obviously a different vehicle, but it didn't matter. It landed on the beaches of southern France along with the 180th Regiment in the August heat of 1944.

Monsieur Grosjean's expertise with steel began when he worked in a metal and die factory at the age of 14. His knowledge and skill continued to expand through his experience as a truck driver for more than 35 years, working out of local mills and factories. Inside the barn we found a restored US Army jeep, complete with a canvas roof and camouflage netting rolled across the hood near the windshield. Large white markings were stenciled onto the side of the hood, and the front bumper next to an American flag decal. The dust and dirt that had accumulated on the metal and on the tires from sitting in the barn, the restored paint, decals, and letters made the jeep appear as if it had been driven into the barn directly from the battlefield in 1944. Monsieur explained that almost 650,000 jeeps were made during the war by several companies, the most prominent being Willys–Overland, which produced more than three-hundred fifty thousand of the MB version.

In the center of the barn sat a small Army green lightweight motorcycle. With two small wheels no larger than those found on a child's wooden wagon, a tubular frame and handlebars, and a gas tank slightly larger than the barrel beneath a St. Bernard's collar, it resembled a child's scooter, not a military combat operations vehicle. Nevertheless, it was designed for that very purpose. The Cushman Model 53 Airborne Infantry Scooter was developed for use by paratroopers during World War II and was parachute-dropped from transport aircraft. The Cushman Company made 4,734 of them for the US military beginning in 1944. The scooter included a 4.6 horsepower, 1-cylinder gasoline engine and could reach speeds up to 40 mph with a range of 100 miles.[2] Monsieur Grosjean said the parachutes were attached directly to the 200-plus pound scooters. The bikes often sustained structural damage to the wheels or frames when they landed on the ground because they were designed and built without suspension. For this reason, many were simply left where they had landed in fields across Europe.

To the right of the tiny Cushman Model 53 Airborne Infantry scooter, with its front grill pressed against the back of the barn wall, sat a WC-54 ¾ ton 4×4 field ambulance. Built by Dodge for the US Army, these were the most widely used ambulances throughout the war. The vehicle bodies were made of steel panels and plywood sat on a metal chassis. Specifications include four-wheel drive, a four-speed gearbox, leaf-spring suspension for added comfort to the wounded being transported, and space for seven sitting wounded or four stretchers. From 1943 through 1944, WC-54 ambulances were equipped with four stretchers, 12 large olive-green blankets, a set of splints and a camouflage net. These vehicles were designed for transportation, not for rendering medical treatment. Like all of Monsieur Grosjean's vehicles, it was covered in a fine layer of dust and dirt, giving the appearance he intended the vehicles to be seen this way to recreate the image of wartime service. His ambulance included the shovel, ax and pickax attached to the passenger side. The olive-drab vehicle included a red cross in a large white square on both sides. A faded medical insignia could be seen behind each side door. This is no doubt the type and model of ambulance that transported my father from the aid station at Frémifontaine to the 27th Evacuation Hospital on October 10, 1944. The ride was likely bumpy and uncomfortable, despite the improved suspension and wider wheelbase from the earlier WC versions.

Parked on a dirt path along the side of the barn was a fully operational M3 half-track personnel carrier. The M3 was an armored vehicle designed with wheels in the front and steel tracks in the back to transport infantry troops, evacuate wounded soldiers, and haul supplies. The sides and rear doors were made of light armored steel for protection against small-arms fire. Manufactured primarily by the White Motor Company and introduced in 1941, over forty thousand were produced and used throughout many theaters of operation during the war. The half-track's White 160AX 6-cylinder engine provided the 17,650-pound vehicle a maximum speed of 45 mph.[3] The M3 had a Browning 50-caliber machine gun mounted above and behind the passenger compartment and two additional mounts located on the rear compartment inner-hull sides for mounting 30-caliber machine guns.[4] Monsieur Grosjean's M3 had been meticulously restored. The 50-caliber machine gun was in place, a spare gas can was mounted near the passenger front door, an ax was in its mount under the edge of the passenger door, shovel and pickax in place under the driver's side door, and full canvas cover with straps and buckles in place across the top. Monsieur Grosjean opened the rear steel doors to reveal welded bench seats on either side of the transport compartment. A 30-caliber machine gun lay on the right bench, presumably removed to install the canvas top. Above and behind the passenger seat was a steel turret that held the 50-caliber machine gun with its attached ammunition can. The presence of a turret indicated this model was a later version of the M3. The initial 1941 design for the 50-caliber used a pintle (steel post or pin) gun mount, which was replaced by the "pulpit" M49 mounting design. This revision also included a third 30-caliber machine gun mount. Vehicles with this specific arrangement of weapons were referred to as M3A1s.[5]

The engine and all of its components appeared to be original, with only a few new electrical wires confirming we were not actually living in 1944 as we stood next to the impressive vehicle. The master restorer opened the driver's door, climbed into the seat, and started the engine. With a wide grin and an expression of personal satisfaction, he watched through the open door as we reacted to the low roar of the engine.

The sheet-metal barn walls and the ground around the half-track seemed to vibrate in response to the sound of the engine thundering to life. I imagined the M3A1 in battle, moving alongside the 180th's Second Battalion infantry soldiers as they advanced across rugged terrain. The roar of the engines would have blended in with the sounds of the tanks, artillery, machine guns, rifles, the relentless rain, and the voices trying to communicate over these encompassing sounds. The troops must have eventually gained the ability to decipher sounds during armored advances and distinguish between American and German vehicles without seeing them. I wondered how 2nd Battalion soldiers felt when they realized the roar of a distant engine was in fact a German vehicle.

★★★

Men of H Company, 180th Infantry Regiment, 45th Division, try to repair a French-built Peugeot 402 recently acquired from the Germans in southern France on August 17, 1944. (U.S. Signal Corps, 111-SC 268083/NARA)

The fighting continued to build throughout the early autumn days of 1944 as the remainder of 2nd Battalion continued advancing toward the Vosges Mountains and the German border. German troops had been well prepared to fight here, as evidenced by reports that a self-propelled gun and a large, towed weapon were seen in Villersexel. Several 180th Regiment troops identified the towed weapon as a 76-mm antitank gun with significant supplies of ammunition. In addition, German soldiers were seen taking away American prisoners.[6] Additional reports suggested German troops were located in the wooded areas northwest of Villersexel and that the bridge leading out of town had been destroyed.[7] German prisoners picked up from 5th Company of the 111th *Panzergrenadier* Regiment, 11th *Panzer* Division, reported they had rocket guns, mortars, machine guns, and 50 soldiers southwest of Villersexel.[8]

Fighting lasted throughout the afternoon and into the late evening. According to 2nd Battalion officers, "F Company captured 260 PWs [prisoners of war] with about that many dead. One of our PWs reports that there are 2 Companies with about 200 men each and 5 tanks in support in the town of Bevegue."[9] The Germans had been expected to forcefully defend the high ground north of the river but they withdrew without significant fighting. In their hasty retreat, they left behind a 105-mm artillery piece, nine vehicles, six machine guns, 24 rifles, four 81-mm mortars, and 4,000 rounds of small-arms ammunition. Forty-six German prisoners were taken in the area south of Villersexel.[10]

Throughout the advance northward from village to village and in the forests surrounding them, the distance between 180th Regiment troops and enemy soldiers was so small Amercian patrols could hear German conversations and see activity among enemy troops through the darkness. A patrol from 1st Battalion reached a stream junction at 2:45 a.m. on the 16th and after hearing German voices decided not to cross because even the smallest splashes would have drawn fire from the German machine guns located on the north bank. Units of the 180th attempted to follow the right fork of the stream and advanced only a few yards before being spotted and fired on by a machine gun. They were so close to the enemy at this point that they saw a German soldier light a match in the darkness in front of them.[11] When elements of the 3rd Battalion reached Étroitefontaine in the afternoon hours of September 16, on the heels of the retreating Germans, they found the town's water supply had been intentionally polluted,[12] likely an attempt by enemy forces to poison thirsty Allied troops and subsequently slow their advance.

On September 16, the French resistance (*Forces françaises de l'Intérieur/* French Forces of the Interior, FFI) group number 42, stationed in Frémifontaine, 60 miles to the north of Etroitefontaine, was ordered by its regional leadership to gather existing weapons and supplies and report to the region of Fontenay. Their intended mission involved attacking a German supply depot to capture additional weapons, of which the FFI was in short supply. The group had been expecting a delivery of weapons via parachute drop, codenamed *Prefecture*. However, the drop never materialized. In response, they decided to attack the German depot and take what was needed. Armed with a couple of rifles, pistols, and revolvers captured during a local fight several years earlier in 1940, the group proceeded with the intended plan. However, the larger-than-expected number of Germans found at the depot upon arrival convinced the FFI group it would be unsuccessful. Georges Fortier, Jean-Marie's father-in-law and a member of the group, was known for his skills as a sharpshooter. Armed with a French rifle, model 1886–93, he had intended to offer covering fire from a small knoll along Route 420 during the assault. Fortunately, he didn't need to use the weapon because he later noticed in horror that none of the rifle cartridges were capable of firing from his rifle. The entire supply of ammunition he had been given was defective, which would have prevented him from supporting his comrades had the need presented itself.[13]

According to the 180th Infantry Headquarters Field Order dated September 18, 1944, 2nd Battalion marched from Villersexel, starting at 1:00 p.m. on the 19th, to a new assembling area north of Rougemont. The regiment's passwords for the 19th were "Task" and "Baloney."[14] I remember my father using that word on several occasions during my youth. When someone said something that seemed unbelievable, he simply said "baloney." It was likely a common term associated with his generation, or maybe I was on to something. I quickly recognized my insight was merely another irrational emotional reach intended to validate his presence in, and connection to, this history of the 180th Regiment. Perhaps it suggested I finally believed he had indeed been involved and engaged in this progressive fighting to a level that influenced his life. The conflict avoidance, emotional stonewalling, and introspectiveness that I witnessed in his personality may in fact have been the direct result of events that occurred across France. These presumed personality traits were potentially defense mechanisms brought on by profound feelings of distress that he couldn't process at the time of their occurrence. Feeling emotionally overwhelmed by things that can't be discussed openly or rationally can cause a person to simply "tune out." Perhaps this is what I interpreted as introspectiveness. Over time, this can lead to stress-related health problems, such as heart issues, cancer, depression, and fractured relationships. My father had experienced all of these health conditions by mid-life. Instead of attempting to explain the situation by continuing to focus on the man I knew, I began to explore how he may have perceived the events as they occurred in the moment. From this perspective, I hoped to learn something specific to his behavior and his outlook on life overall. I hoped to find logical answers to some of the questions that had accumulated throughout my childhood and adolescence and, quite honestly, well into adulthood.

CHAPTER 7

The American Cemetery at Épinal—Sacred Ground

The autumn sun was well beyond its high point in the sky as we gradually proceeded to the town of Dinozé and the American Cemetery at Épinal, where Monsieur Roland Prieur, the recently retired superintendent of the cemetery and a personal friend of Jean-Marie, had agreed to meet.

The entrance to this sacred ground includes a circular driveway and a large, majestic cut-stone building with a center passageway that leads to the burial sites and the seemingly endless spread of white-marble crosses carefully spaced across the bright-green lawns of the cemetery. At the opposite end, an American flag flies quietly at the top of a tall flagpole, watching over the eternal resting place of American soldiers. As we stood at the entrance to this strangely beautiful place, Monsieur Prieur arrived and extended an enthusiastic and respectful interest in the nature of our journey. He had returned to the cemetery only a few times since retiring, primarily for the purpose of attending scheduled ceremonies. Given his lengthy tenure as curator, he had limited his appearances out of concern frequent visits would make it difficult for his successor to build his own legacy.

Located on a plateau in the foothills of the Vosges Mountains and overlooking the Moselle River, the French gifted these 54 acres of land for the purpose of establishing a cemetery. As long as it remains a cemetery, it will remain American property. Although the acreage itself was a gift, Roland clarified that everything on the site was erected and funded by US taxpayer money. He quickly emphasized, "This is money well spent!"

The 45th Infantry Division liberated this area on September 21, 1944. Two weeks later, it was used as a temporary cemetery in response to the increasing numbers of American troops killed throughout the region. Over several years immediately following the war, the American Graves Registration Service, through repatriation, assisted in moving the temporary graves to permanent resting places. Families were authorized to request their loved ones be returned to the United States or remain in a final resting place on French soil.

Five cemeteries associated with World War II are located across France, each of which has a large memorial structure positioned at the entrance. The memorials include a museum room on the left and a chapel on the right. The American Battle Monuments Commission both designed and constructed the cemetery at Épinal, including the memorial, the chapel, the visitors' building, the paths, the sculptures, and the landscaping. Roland stated this permanent cemetery, including the stone memorial, was completed and dedicated in 1956.

The memorial is a large rectangular white-limestone structure with a central open passageway. Carved into the south face on the left are images of US soldiers fighting toward the center passageway of the monument. An eagle flies above them, talons forward toward the direction of their fight. Images of angels facing the center and embracing fallen soldiers are carved into the north face on the right. An archangel floats above them, a torch pointing toward heaven in one hand and the other hand reaching for the soldiers. The image is intended to represent the survival of the spirit. Inscribed in the stone above the arch are the words, "I bear you on eagles' wings and brought you unto myself." The overall structure is 81 feet long, 35 feet wide, and 36 feet tall with an open-air covered portico extending through the center from front to back.

As we quietly entered the structure's central arch, Monsieur Prieur said, "This is called the Wall of the Missing—it records the names of those soldiers missing in action." The impressive walls are 16–18 feet tall and the small letters of the names are so numerous they fill the majority of the walls' surfaces. Inside the west wing of the memorial is a large map of the European operation, beginning with the southern France amphibious landing of VI Corps. The entire map was constructed with small pieces of colorful glass tiles, forming an overall mosaic 14 feet high and 54 feet long. Inside the east wing of the memorial is a chapel accessible through two large oak-and-glass doors. Carved into the limestone wall above the altar is a representation of the Angel of Peace. The chapel pews are made of dark teakwood.

According to Roland, the 5,257 soldiers buried at Épinal remain because of individual choice. They are not forgotten—they are here because either the family, or the soldier himself, expressed a desire to remain on the foreign soil where the life had been lost. Sixty-nine graves at Épinal contain the remains of unidentified soldiers. As we walked around the cemetery grounds, I noticed numerous headstones with the inscription, "Here rests in honored glory a comrade in arms known but to God." So many soldiers that couldn't be identified created an uneasy feeling. I wondered about the reasons, from missing dog tags to massive mutilating trauma, making either tags or features unrecognizable. Each of the graves at Épinal is marked with a marble headstone, imported from Italy. The headstones are designed either in the shape of a cross or a Star of David and include the soldier's name, rank, unit, date of death, and state of origin. Roland emphasized that the markers require meticulous maintenance and cleaning—almost every day someone takes a bucket and scrubs some of them.

More than a final resting place, the cemetery represents the gratitude felt by the French people of this region. A nearby road bears the name of Duffy Street in honor of two American brothers killed in the area—one in 1944 and one in 1945. John Duffy was a first lieutenant with the 79th Infantry Division, 27th Infantry Regiment. He was killed on January 7, 1945. Edward Duffy was a private with the 45th Infantry Regiment, 180th Infantry Regiment. He died on September 12, 1944, fighting near Villersexel and Pont-sur-l'Ognon.[1] Extensive fighting occurred throughout the regiment's location on that day. First Battalion was in regimental reserve on September 12, so Edward most likely had been assigned to 2nd or 3rd Battalion when he was killed. The Germans had built numerous roadblocks and had placed countless mines, supported by 40 tanks, during the night of September 11/12. Engagement between the 180th and the Germans was already active at the first light of day. Many of the German troops were from the 111th *Panzergrenadier* Regiment, 11th *Panzer* Division.[2] Although the specific circumstances involving Edward's death are unknown, he was apparently involved in significant fighting at the time of his death.

The Duffy family traveled from the United States to Épinal for the dedication of the street in 1998. Several of the local families continue to place flowers on the Duffy brothers' graves each year and subsequently send photographs of the floral memorials to the family. While it seems profoundly tragic that these brothers lost their lives in the same war and are both buried in the same location on French soil, the occurrence is more common than one would expect. In 14 different areas throughout the cemetery at Épinal, brothers are buried side by side.[3]

As we walked across the meticulously manicured lawns of the cemetery, it became apparent great care and attention had been given to this sacred ground. The marble crosses are so perfectly aligned that a person could rest a rifle along the side of a cross at the end of any row, fire a round to the other end of the row, a distance of approximately 100 yards, and not hit another cross between the two points. The precision is impressive and humbling. Roland stated, "That was hard to do because we had to measure in height and distance from side to side and also the angles in every direction." As we walked slowly and respectfully along the rows of markers, differentiated only by the inscriptions carved into the face of the white stones, it became apparent that even in the differentiation offered by the inscriptions, common themes existed.

The vast majority of the dead buried here belonged to the 45th, 36th and 3rd Divisions, and many belonged to the 180th Infantry Regiment—my father's unit. When I asked Jean-Marie if any H Company soldiers were buried in this sacred place, he immediately walked to the cemetery office to review the records. Several moments later, he returned and led us toward a marble cross in the right section of the cemetery. We walked to row 29 and counted the markers until we reached marker 51. The inscription read, "Andrew Cepar, Sgt., 180th Infantry, November 4, 1944." I stood and stared at the marker, wondering if my father had known him. Certainly, they had seen each other, and likely interacted with each other to some extent. Since Andrew Cepar had been a sergeant in H Company, his rank suggested he probably had not been a recent replacement in the autumn of 1944. Therefore, he and my father had likely fought together across this region following the beach landing in August. The two had been in the same towns we would visit over the next few days, and they presumably fought together during the brutal fighting at Frémifontaine on October 6 and 7 where all three rifle companies of 2nd Battalion, with their H Company attachments, were surrounded multiple times by the enemy in hand-to-hand fighting. The H Company morning report for October 17 indicates Sergeant Cepar was evacuated from the Frémifontaine sector and transferred to the 11th Field Hospital of the 120th Medical Battalion. Had they been friends? Had they played cards together in foxholes and shared letters from home?

Memories of my father's poker buddies and their monthly card games returned to the forefront of my thoughts. The group rotated homes for each of their card games and once a year they met at our house. We lived in a turn-of-the-century, three-story, center-stair colonial in a suburb of Cleveland. An enclosed vestibule opened into a large foyer with 12-pane glass-and-oak double doors separating the dining room. The doors were always open, unless there was a poker game. I'd peer through the lace curtains on the glass doors a few times before being directed upstairs to bed. There was never very much to see, except a lot of snacks and food and a few liquor and soda bottles on a small table in the corner. My bedroom was directly above the dining room. I remember intensely listening in an attempt to interpret their muffled jokes and laughter. Some of the card games involved players rapping on the dining-room table with their knuckles, the faint sound to which I drifted off to sleep.

We walked quietly across the cemetery grounds as the sun continued to set closer to the surrounding mountaintops, and I noticed a strange phenomenon. As the shadows behind the perfectly straight rows of crosses continued to lengthen against the lush green autumn grass, they appeared as soldiers, packs upon their backs, positioned behind each of their own crosses and standing at attention in this hallowed place. I felt a sense of comfort as I quietly acknowledged this thought. While still staring at the shadows, Roland approached and asked for my thoughts as they related to the cemetery. In response, I pointed at the shadows

Present-day photo of Épinal Cemetery grave markers—the shadows suggest images of soldiers standing behind their grave markers. (Photo by Michael Reyka on location in France)

on the grass in front of us and described their image as soldiers standing behind their resting place markers. Roland stood in silence, also staring at the shadows. Without shifting his gaze, and in a low thoughtful tone, he replied, "Yes. I had not noticed that." He stared for several more moments, deep in thought, before turning to look at me.

We walked away in silence and returned to the wide granite steps just inside the main entrance to the cemetery, turning at the top of the steps back toward the graves and the thousands of perfectly spaced markers. From our vantage point on the top steps, we gazed across the immaculately maintained and peaceful grounds to the tall flagpole at the far edge of the cemetery overlooking the river. The new superintendent, who recently replaced Roland after his retirement, approached the distant flagpole and began to lower the American flag, a ceremony performed each evening at precisely 4:30 in the afternoon. When the colors were retired and the cloth secured in the protective arms of the superintendent, we thanked Roland for his time and his insight and left this very special and sacred place in search of the field where my father had recovered from his respiratory illness in a tent hospital near the village of Xertigny.

CHAPTER 8

Xertigny—The 27th Evacuation Hospital

Prior to us arriving in France, Jean-Marie assisted in making contact with the Épinal Historical Center in an earnest attempt to confirm the exact location of the 27th Evacuation Field Hospital during October 1944 when my father was treated after leaving H Company. On September 6, a month before the start of our journey to France, I received an email offering such confirmation:

> After questioning several people in the commune who were alive at the time, we can assure you that an American field hospital in fact existed there. It was set up in the place called La Regingotte on the road linking Xertigny and Bains-les-Bains. In 1944, there probably were, according to the information gathered, one or perhaps two, houses. It was a rather sequestered plateau. The tents were set up out in the open and on their tops were red crosses to identify them. The American military installation was lower down, hidden in the woods. Several people of Xertigny remember it.[1]

Early evening marked our arrival to the outskirts of Xertigny. A mixture of dirt and gravel formed a short path wide and long enough for both cars to safely leave the road. A more prominent private driveway led to several newly constructed houses a distance ahead—at the 2 o'clock position. A car pulled in behind us and Jean-Marie assumed it was his contact—a local real estate agent who was familiar with the area and who had gathered information at our request related to the site of the hospital. She indicated the local residents had undergone five years of deprivation under German occupation until the Americans finally arrived with supplies. The field hospital's doctors and staff had the habit of using a portion of something and then saying to the locals, "Go share this with the other villagers." The villagers took anything offered to them, including partial loaves of bread, bandages, and clothing. She indicated that the Xertigny villagers' most bitter memories of war relate to the middle of June 1940 when German forces completely destroyed the center of town. They demolished the City Hall and killed 31 villagers, including the chief of the local resistance. His body was found in the wreckage. The townspeople resisted for the rest of the war. Still, not everyone participated. A small number of French across the region disguised themselves as French resistance fighters but were in reality Nazi collaborators, which caused local families to worry and carefully limit the trust they offered within their own community.

The real estate agent recalled stories that some of the American soldiers responsible for liberating Xertigny were "Indians." One of the local farmers owned a mule that delivered a colt during the liberation and some of the American soldiers gave it a Native American name. The local story certainly appears credible, given the 45th Infantry Division was originally an Oklahoma National Guard unit that included Native Americans.

She pointed to several small recently built one-story houses in a field on the hillside in front of us and stated that the American hospital had once been located where the houses now stand. Disappointment filled my thoughts and my enthusiasm deflated like a ruptured playground ball after an overzealous kick from an older schoolmate. Seeing these three new houses on such a historic site was discouraging. As we talked with the realtor through French and English translations, a woman, appearing to be in her mid-forties, came out of the nearest house and approached the group. She asked somewhat cautiously, "What are you doing here pointing at my house?" Jean-Marie explained our purpose and our hope that we would be able to locate the American tent hospital that had been in Xertigny in October 1944. He explained that our real estate contact believed the hospital had existed where the woman's house now stands. Appearing relieved by our purpose, the woman appeared less defensive. "No. It wasn't here. It was on the next field over, behind the neighbor's farmhouse and across the field up on that hill," she said as she pointed across a cow pasture and beyond a thin line of trees. She then called to a teenage boy who had been quietly standing near the front corner of her house, also wondering why our group had gathered in his front yard, and asked him to take us to the location. Excitement quickly returned and we immediately walked with the teenager up through the yard. Larry, Tara and I followed him through the row of trees, stepped over a wire fence, marched across the pasture, exchanged greetings with several massive, perplexed, cows, crawled under another wire fence and rose to immediately find ourselves at the edge of a lush green hilltop field. The grass was ankle high, which allowed us to walk freely across the field and stand in the center, providing a 360-degree view of the French countryside. It was incredibly beautiful. The boy pointed and stated in French, "Between the wood pile and the corn field—that's where the tents were." I turned to Larry for a translation, who stated, "He said that's what his grandmother has always told him—and she would know because she was there in 1944. She still lives in the farmhouse over there," pointing to our left in the direction of the main road.

On September 28, 1944, the hospital staff arrived at this rural location after traveling approximately one hundred miles from the village of Mouchard. Their medical equipment and supplies arrived shortly after. One nurse recalled, "We loaded into trucks and went on our way in the dark and rain, arriving at our hospital area at Xertigny late that night. Familiar rain and mud greeted us. We crowded together in a ward tent to keep warm and dry. Neither was possible that first night."[2]

The field rests on the top of a gentle hill that slopes downward at equal grades in all directions. It was the perfect spot to place an Army tent hospital. During the fighting in this region during 1944, "The hospital could be seen for miles around and looked distinctly American in the midst of the French provincial communities."[3] Evacuation hospitals were designed to be located near the front lines to allow easy and timely access for injured and sick soldiers. The locations were intended to be seen by all forces. Conversely, from this hilltop position the distant sounds and sights of battles raging throughout the countryside would have been heard and seen by everyone present. One nurse commented, "The guns of the armies fighting in the Vosges Mountains rumbled steadily. Patients could identify enemy planes as they passed over us."[4]

I walked to the center of the field and tried to imagine the medical tents assembled across the grass. I tried to feel the autumn air and hear the sound of the rain on the tent fabric. It was cold and damp when the hospital first opened for operations in 1944. The staff only had discarded French and German stoves to heat the tents, as the more-efficient US pot-bellied stoves did not arrive until several weeks later.[5] I imagined the rows of Army cots, glass IV bottles hanging from metal poles, green woolen blankets, nurses and physicians attending to bandaged patients. The ward tents had at that time been arranged in an end-to-end fashion so the resulting wards could accommodate up to 75 patients.[6] I could almost hear the sounds, visualize the activities, and see the faces of the nurses and physicians. I looked up across the field at the beautiful panoramic views. This is what my father had seen during the days he spent here at the 27th Evac Hospital, if he had been permitted beyond the canvas tent walls and if the rain had stopped long enough. I was fortunate to experience ideal weather conditions during our visit. My father was not so fortunate during the early days of October 1944 and the six days he spent here. A nurse serving with the 27th Evacuation Hospital wrote:

> It rained each day in downpours or drizzles. Water-soaked canvas leaked and patients were covered with rubber sheets or their cots were moved to avoid the dripping spots in the tent ... the continued dampness and lack of sunshine made everyone wet and cold.[7]

Despite the rain and cold, the soldiers were grateful to be out of the open environment and thankful to have a cot on which to sleep, as opposed to a water-filled foxhole.[8] In view of the unpleasant weather and the endless stream of casualties that began pouring into the hospital within days of opening on September 30, it is doubtful the hospital staff was able to take in the beauty of the French countryside. Within the first few days after opening, the tent hospital was filled to capacity.[9] Throughout the month of October, it averaged 1,000 admissions per week.[10] Colonel Charles Pueston, Medical Commander of the 27th Evac Hospital while stationed at Xertigny, wrote in his report:

> Two months spent at Xertigny were extremely busy ones. The three combat veteran divisions of the Seventh Army, the 3rd, 36th, and 45th, were engaged in the battles for the Vosges Mountains and were taking part in some of the most severe and costly fighting of the battle for France. The heavily wooded and mountainous terrain, the incessant rain and cold and a well-dug-in and determined enemy combined to produce severe and heavy casualties and extreme fatigue among our troops. Utter exhaustion and suffering from exposure seemed more marked at that time than were evident in the colder weather to follow. Although we were operating on a 900-bed basis the hospital was filled most of the time and operating rooms never were inactive. During the month of October nearly one-half the battle casualties among all American troops in France were sustained in the 7th Army.[11]

A dirt and gravel path used by ambulances during the tent hospital's operations in October 1944 remains intact along the edge of the field. A large two-story building with stucco-covered walls, an arched entranceway and a clay tile roof sits at the intersection corner where the path meets the main road. The old structure was presumably present at the time of the war and was most likely used as a marker for ambulances and other vehicles. I imagined wounded soldiers passing the structure when they arrived via ambulance. At the point where the path and the road met, I noticed it appeared to be a legitimate intersection resembling a paved country road. However, just 100 yards up the path into the field, the distinction faded and disappeared, suggesting the utility of the road was at its height in 1944 and it fell into disuse soon after. A hospital nurse confirmed this assumption in her original notes:

> The 36th Engineers had constructed an excellent service road into the hospital area which greatly aided the placement of equipment. No truck was permitted off this road. This point is emphasized because such care in the prevention of mud plays a most important role in the future efficiency and comfort of the hospital.[12]

Where the dirt and gravel road ended up at the edge of the field, it transformed to the right into a long narrow raised area resembling the remnants of a man-made path approximately 75 yards in length and five yards wide. During our visit, the path was covered with weeds, mulch piles, and short cut logs intended to be used as firewood to heat the farmhouse. The raised path now serves to keep the logs elevated slightly above the mud and grass. But, according to the teenager, the Americans originally constructed the raised area after bringing in large amounts of gravel so the ambulances didn't create ruts or become stuck in the soggy, muddy fields. A nurse recalled in her notes, "We were proud of our hospital area in Xertigny. Army engineers and our own men worked hard to make gravel paths and roadways through the mud."[13]

From over my left shoulder, I faintly heard Larry talking in French with the teenage boy near the edge of the field, and I recalled something he had said a short time earlier—something pertaining to his grandmother telling him over the years that this was the location of the American hospital. Walking over to where they stood near the raised path covered in cordwood, I asked if his grandmother was present at the hospital in 1944. The teenager replied in French, "Yes. She was a young girl. She still lives in the house—over there." He pointed to the farmhouse and cluster of farm buildings near the road, not far from where we stood. I must have appeared a little stunned because he then asked, "Do you want to talk with her? She's home."

In response, we walked together down the weathered path connecting the field to the main road and followed a short gravel driveway to the farmhouse. At her grandson's request, a woman, appearing to be in her early 80s, walked through the kitchen door and approached our group as we stood in her yard. Still wearing her kitchen apron and drying her hands on the cotton fabric as if it were a towel, she walked toward us with cautious, purposeful eye contact and introduced herself as Madame Jacqueline Pierre. With the demeanor of a calm investigator, she somewhat strategically asked for the dates my father had been in the hospital, and when I stated October 10th through 16th, 1944, she shrugged her shoulders and acknowledged that the hospital had indeed been operational in her family's field in October after setting up the tents in the final days of September. "He would have been here," Jacqueline said confidently. Jacqueline became less guarded after determining that my answers supported the legitimacy of our presence on her farm and she subsequently proceeded to share her memories.

Jacqueline was 14 years old at the time. As she described the hospital structure and the placement of the various tents, Jacqueline recalled that the local villagers came to the hospital to visit the patients and staff on Saturdays and Sundays. French soldiers received treatment there as well, but the villagers simply had interest in the American visitors who seemed markedly different from them. One of the hospital nurses wrote in her report, "Sundays were holidays to the French peasants. They thronged through the hospital area in larger numbers than we had ever encountered before. We felt that we might have been a circus, and we were in a sideshow on display."[14]

Although Jacqueline worked part-time during the week in the Xertigny mayor's office at the time, she also worked on the family farm. Fondly recalling her interactions with the nurses and doctors that worked at the hospital, she proudly stated, "We cooked food for them. They liked our chickens—my mother cooked chickens for the doctors and nurses." I asked Jacqueline, through Larry's interpretation, if any photographs of the hospital existed that she could share with me, but she had none and explained that "there were no photographs taken—no one was allowed." She pointed to the path I had walked earlier and explained that the trucks and ambulances had driven up and down the path all day and all night. "There was always activity." Standing in the yard, Jacqueline recalled her memories with clarity as if the hospital had been active in recent months. Her face showed comfort, happiness, and pride as she described the hospital, the staff, and her family's involvement with the activities of the facility. She was deeply reflective yet open to our presence and transparent with her thoughts, memories, and emotions.

Jacqueline said, "The Americans were advancing faster than expected, so the hospital had to pack up and move. When they left here, they set up in a place called Baccarat."[15] Every couple of weeks after the hospital moved from Xertigny, some of the staff routinely returned to visit with Jacqueline and her family. She fondly recalled that two of the doctors were from Chicago and said they had struck up a friendship with her family in response to the kindness and hospitality shown by her parents. "After they left, they sent back a package of coffee." They also brought with them during subsequent visits, or sent later, shirts and other things the family didn't have.[16] She recalled, "There was a gazette in the village. Information about the hospital was printed in it to keep the villagers informed." The hospital remains a vivid memory for the villagers, and it serves as a common topic of discussion today just as it had during the autumn of 1944. I noticed Jacqueline had become deeply introspective as she shared her memories. She paused between statements and stared past me at the field while smiling in silence. It was as if she had returned to that place and time in her mind, the resulting emotions comforting her in some manner. We were merely fortunate bystanders to this personal connection between past and present. It has been said that time heals all wounds. As the decades pass, people tend to remember more of the good times and less of the bad. What I witnessed in Madame Pierre was not simply the sharing of a good memory—it was something much more profound. She was transported before my eyes to a distant place that provided great personal comfort.

After half an hour of talking in the yard, we bade farewell to Jacqueline and walked toward the main road after thanking her for accepting us and welcoming us onto her farm and into her memories. In turn, she said, "Thank you," which caught me by surprise. I paused and instinctively made eye contact—she was still partly immersed in 1944. Her face radiated the same peaceful joy that I noticed in Madame Mallier's face during our visit to Rougemont. The hospital had been a dramatic experience in her life, one that had created a lasting effect. Perhaps her experience was strangely different from that of my father. Each had been influenced in significantly different ways by the same events. They may have passively caught a glimpse of each other on this small hilltop field. If not, Jacqueline had certainly been in his general presence while he recuperated on this family farm—whether or not she was aware. This was not an emotional reach—such as attempting to align a battlefield password with my father's speech patterns—this was real. A sense of comfort slowly moved through me. Jacqueline stood in the yard waving and displaying a warm grin that reflected the comfort these memories still provided after nearly seven decades. Her head was tilted slightly to the side in a relaxed manner—the way my father often appeared in photos when he was happy and smiling and the way he appeared on the back of the tank destroyer. Despite the trauma and tragedy of war that raged across this beautiful countryside from town to town and from village to village, a strong sense of joy and gratefulness existed in her voice. Jacqueline spoke

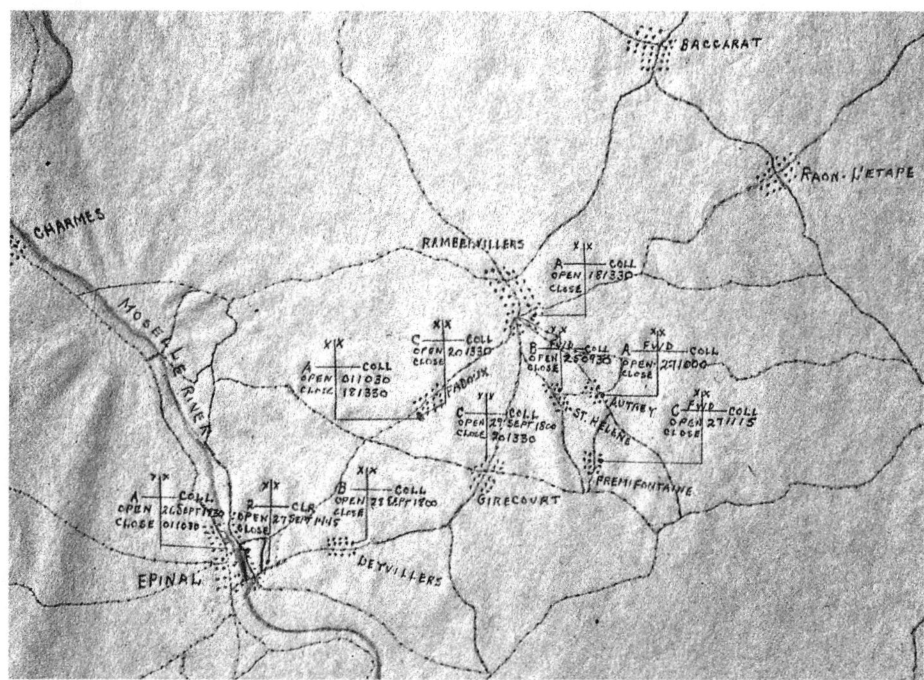

Sketched positions of medical stations and dates of operation. Sketch located in the Clearing Company, 120th Medical Battalion, 45th Infantry Division, A History of the Company in the French Campaign, October 1944, Overlay #31 October 1–31, 1944, Europe Road Map 1:200,000, Sheet No. 62. (Courtesy of NARA. Photograph by Michael Reyka on location at NARA)

of the compassion, kindness, and generosity of the Americans. As we reached the main road and I turned to look at her one last time, I took note of the address displayed on the rural mailbox at the edge of her yard in the event that a follow-up correspondence would be beneficial.

The autumn sun had finally set on the French countryside as it slipped behind the hills as we left Xertigny and drove along the winding country roads through the Vosges Mountains to the woodland chalet where we would stay throughout the remainder of our visit. By the time we reached the house, nestled on a hillside among dense tall pines, the forest was quite dark and the sky was filled with stars. There were no electric lights within sight, which made finding the door locks rather challenging by the light of a cell phone. It was not until the following morning that we gained our first views of the exterior and its quaint architectural beauty. Opening the door to the small front porch as the morning's first light poured through reminded me of Dorothy opening the door of her house that crash landed in the Land of Oz. The sun was barely rising behind the rolling hills in front of the chalet and a hazy mist covered the lush green hills and towering pine trees. A small stray cat quietly emerged from a hedgerow to briefly greet us before proceeding with his morning stroll. Watching the sunrise and sipping coffee on the uncovered porch of this mountain chalet in the Vosges Mountains, I wondered how we arrived at this place. To some degree I felt that I was "winging it." I briefly considered that perhaps my father was pondering the same thing for different reasons in the autumn of 1944. What am I doing here?

CHAPTER 9

Épinal—The Fortress City

Once again up and on the road before sunrise, the journey continued. Jean-Marie rendezvoused along a quiet street in the outskirts of Frémifontaine, where we left his car in a small parking lot and drove together in our rented sedan toward the ancient city of Épinal. The air was crisp and the sky was bright blue. Conversely, regional weather during the same week in 1944 had at that time set a ten-year record for excessive rain and cold temperatures.[1] The rains had begun to fall consistently and progressively throughout the end of September by the time American troops reached Épinal. "These showers were harbingers of the wet and dreary days that were to follow."[2] This made the relentless advance of the 180th Regiment even more difficult in response to surging rivers, flooded fields, and muddy roads. The miserable weather conditions also made fighting more difficult as the Germans slowed their retreat and intensified their defense. One historian summarized the exhausting progress achieved during September 1944:

> The routing of the enemy from Southern France ended in September. The first confusion and their subsequent unbalanced reaction to the fury of the 45th's advance was finally absorbed by the realization that they must now dig in and defend while they had fighting room—or be thrown back to their own Siegfried Line. Naturally, the German High Command chose the foothills of the Vosges, and the rivers that formed natural barriers to an attacking force. Every kilometer that the Division advanced toward the Moselle River was won only after strong lunges against the determined Germans, and frequently the same kilometer was secured only after beating back a fierce counterattack.[3]

The 180th Regiment launched its attack on Épinal during the afternoon of September 21; 2nd and 3rd Battalions met heavy active German resistance as they approached the river. "It was defended by three battalions of [enemy] infantry, reinforced by artillery, mortars, and dual-purpose anti-aircraft guns."[4]

The city had been fortified long before the start of the war:

> Epinal [*sic*] became a fortress city after the Franco–Prussian war when the French, realizing the need for bulwark against German encroachment, constructed a defensive line which ran southward through Toul, Verdun, Nancy, Epinal and Belfont … while Epinal's defenses were designed primarily against attack from the east, they were nevertheless of a type that could be used if the city was attacked from any direction.[5]

Divided by the Moselle River and protected from attack by high stonewalls on both sides of the water, this rather large city served as a center of roadways and military communications for the Germans prior to the fighting in September 1944. This was the first large metropolitan city my father and his battalion liberated after landing in southern France. The fighting up until that point had primarily involved rural countryside, small villages, and towns. Épinal, however, brought new challenges, risks, and dangers to the American troops.

The 180th's three battalions approached Épinal from the west and northwest. All approaches to the city were heavily mined, including the roads, the streets, and the riverbanks; at least one of the bridges leading across the river had also been wired for detonation.[6] The Germans had even mined some of the trees in the forest[7] in an effort to slow the advancing American troops. At the fork in the road atop the hill overlooking Épinal, the 180th's 2nd Battalion advanced to the left and the 3rd Battalion advanced to the right as the troops approached the city, according to Jean-Marie's extensive research.

Based upon his knowledge of warfare, as well as his familiarity with this area and German military tactics, Jean-Marie suggested the road to the left, taken by 2nd Battalion, was likely mined and included as many roadblocks as possible to slow the American advance. Official Army records support Jean-Marie's assumptions. Radio-report transcripts from Headquarters clearly indicate roadblocks were located every

100–200 yards, and the two railroad passes at the bottom of the hillside were partially destroyed and mined with railroad cars over them.[8] Roadblocks were covered by enemy machine gun and rifle fire.[9]

The 2nd Battalion, "encountered severe heavy automatic fire while clearing the roadblocks, mines, and wire entanglements at the approaches to the western part of town."[10] Intense fighting occurred in the forested area on the outskirts of Épinal, a place later referred to as Bois de L'Homme Mort (Dead Man's Wood).[11] George Fisher, in his detailed history of the 180th Regiment, wrote of the same location:

> About 3,000 yards north of "The Woods of Dead Men," our Second Battalion advanced eastward on the Uxegney–Epinal [*sic*] Road to a blocked and mined railroad underpass at the northwestern entrance to Epinal. Many roadblocks were cleared out and mines were everywhere. During the night of the 21st & 22nd, both battalions held their positions and received heavy concentrations of German artillery, tank, and rocket fire.[12]

The first American soldiers killed at Épinal lost their lives as they advanced along the streets of Chantraine, on the opposite bank of the Moselle, on September 23. Although unable to verify the exact cause of death associated with these two men despite extensive research, Jean-Marie continues to believe they were killed by artillery fire because the direct small-arms fighting occurred further down the hill along the banks of the Moselle on that particular date. Three parallel streets lead down to the river and converge in somewhat of a funnel shape in the same general area at the bottom of the hillside several hundred yards from the water. Jean-Marie believes the battalion's companies most likely moved down all three roads simultaneously. From any of these roads, looking toward Épinal, one can see the ruins of an ancient castle high upon a hill across the river. German observers were certainly posted in the castle ruins, given its location on the highest ground in Épinal, with a clear view of the approaching Americans.

Located approximately halfway down Jean-Charles Pellerin Street, a bronze plaque marking the spot where the two soldiers were killed is displayed on the front of a two-story street-front house. These unfortunate soldiers, whose lives ended on this narrow hillside street, were members of the 2nd Battalion—my father's unit. Looking at the castle ruins in the distance created an uncomfortable feeling. I could almost hear and see the artillery shells falling on the unsuspecting Thunderbirds. I assumed the soldiers were focused on the windows and rooftops lining both sides of the narrow winding streets as they searched for German snipers, unaware of the strategic threat associated with the castle ruins far off in the distance.

Where the three roads merge at the bottom of the hillside, the battalions crossed a trench and a set of demolished railroad tracks that run in a north and south direction. The 180th S-2 (intelligence and security officer) report indicates infantry troops advanced to 300 yards east of the tracks but were driven back by enemy forces, while another patrol advanced 400 yards past the railroad tracks before being driven back by German machine-gun fire originating from the houses near the river. The 3rd Battalion reported, "We are still getting some sniper fire in front of us. They shoot even at the aid men [medics]."[13] One of the underpasses at the bottom of the hill had been destroyed, and the other was not large enough for the American Sherman tanks to pass through. Both roads leading away from the area of the railroad tracks into the city were mined.[14]

After crossing the tracks, lead elements of the 3rd Battalion continued straight ahead and followed the road a short distance toward the city. As they approached the Sadi–Carnot Bridge spanning the Moselle, the troops immediately recognized that the extensive damage caused by German demolition efforts, as well as active enemy artillery and small-arms fire, would prevent them from crossing. In response, they followed the road along the railroad trench and moved approximately 500 yards downstream, turned left toward the river, and advanced several blocks. There, they found the ruins of an old bridge the Germans had also demolished in advance of the 180th Regiment's arrival. However, battalion officers decided the ruins could be crossed by infantry soldiers, since large sections of debris remained above water.[15] The road leading from the west across the bridge is referred to as Avenue de la Loge Blanche. Jean-Marie explained the original bridge was named the "White Balcony Bridge" for the corner house on the west end of the bridge that prominently displayed a white balcony. When the structure was rebuilt years later following the war, it was renamed "The Patch Army Bridge" in honor of General Alexander Patch.

Throughout this section of Épinal, the Moselle is approximately fifty yards across and bordered by vertical stonewalls extending 10–15 feet high and measuring two feet thick.[16] When lead elements of the battalion approached the site of the destroyed bridge, they determined that troops would be able to wade across the river if the enemy forces on the opposing banks could be weakened. The heavy weapons company fired mortars at the enemy machine-gun nests as advancing troops reported via radio, "There are plenty of Germans on the other side."[17] A large portion of the bridge, essentially its entire center section between the two innermost supports, had collapsed following the German demolition, but could still be used as the largest sections remained well above the water line. When the attack started, German forces opened fire with carbines, machine guns, and artillery as 180th Regiment soldiers waded, swam, and climbed across the debris in the river.[18]

The first troops crossed the bridge ruins by leaning ladders against the various sections of concrete and debris, while the rest waded across.[19] The battalion was under heavy enemy fire throughout the entire time required to cross the river. It was reported that, "In more than one instance the soldiers scaled the walls by forming pyramids of themselves."[20] Additional soldiers lowered themselves with ropes to cross some sections of the fallen bridge as German machine guns and mortars fired in the darkness.[21] The water level across the river was three–four feet deep at the time of our visit and fairly consistent all the way across (flat river bottom) but had been slightly deeper during the same week in 1944 due to the heavy rains. According to battalion radio reports from October 1944, the river was six feet deep at this location.[22] The majority of soldiers were not that tall, which suggests their efforts involved swimming more than wading. Drowning became an additional threat and stressor to exhausted troops. After covering the initial waves of the advance across the river, machine gun squads followed to ensure effective support of the riflemen. Machine gunners would certainly have carried the weapon, its tripod or multiple ammunition cans across while trying to avoid the deep water and swift current.

Enemy troops were in position along the east side of the river, atop the high stonewall that lined the edge of the water. The German 1st Police Company was in place along the wall in Épinal. This unit contained elements of the *Ordnungspolizei*, the uniformed police of Nazi Germany, but was not a formal company or numbered military unit. The German 1st Marine Company was positioned on the east side of the bridge at Golbey. German foxholes lined the wall in ten-foot intervals while machine gun and mortar strong points were located at the bridges.[23] The 3rd Battalion continued fighting for the bridge and, despite this fortification of enemy troops, "Firepower and guts" are attributed to the battalion's success in pushing back the Germans.[24]

After 180th Regiment troops entered Épinal and secured the crossing point, engineers built a Bailey bridge across the river over the remains of the White Balcony Bridge. Nearly all of the 45th Division trucks and armor used it to cross the Mosselle into Épinal.[25]

As the 3rd Battalion fought its way into the city, the remainder of 2nd Battalion troops continued their attempts to cross the Moselle. At 9:10 on the evening of September 22, E Company entered the water and received a German mortar barrage and small-arms fire from across the river for its efforts. By 9:50 p.m., the battalion had still not found a suitable place to cross. A radio report indicated the water was six feet deep and 75–80 yards across and that mines were everywhere.[26] Efforts continued into the night; at one minute after midnight on the 23rd, Lieutenant Luger reported to Captain Turner:

> E Company patrols report Germans dug in on the east bank of the river. When patrols tried to cross below the point attempted earlier, they got to the other bank but were fired on by S/A [small arms] and mortars. Could not stay and pulled back across the river. No casualties. Will keep probing for a chance to get across. Report many Jerries [Germans] on the east side of river with tank or anti-tank support.[27]

During my conversation with Jean-Marie, he shared that local accounts had previously been unable to pinpoint the exact location of 2nd Battalion's eventual successful crossing of the Moselle. However, he had developed a theory, based upon his military experience and the historical information available to him. Jean-Marie escorted us to the location he

Soldiers of the 40th Engineer Regiment work on the Moselle River Bridge (White Balcony Bridge) in Épinal to prevent debris carried by high water from destroying the structure. (U.S. Signal Corps, 111-SC 233024/NARA)

believes represents the initial unsuccessful attempt by E Company to cross the river near the Saut le Cerf Bridge.[28]

We left our car near the west end of the bridge, across from an overgrown field along the road at the edge of the river valley. Following a narrow but well-worn dirt path through the forest, we eventually made our way to the bank on the west side of the Moselle. While standing in the water looking across to the opposite bank where elements of the 2nd Battalion may have first attempted to cross, I imagined the sights and sounds that battalion soldiers might have experienced nearly seven decades prior. Wading through the cold water, knowing that enemy machine guns and rifles were hidden in the woods less than fifty yards in front and pointed directly at them, must have been extremely frightening for these men. If you've ever tried to walk through chest-deep water, even in a pool, you can imagine how vulnerable they must have felt. They could not move quickly and they could not conceal themselves while crossing. Ducking under the surface wouldn't stop a bullet. The men were easy targets. Their only option was to keep moving and keep advancing toward their goal—behavior consistent with the motto of the 45th Infantry (*Semper Anticus*).

Near this attempted initial crossing site, the remnants of rough concrete foundations can be seen on the bank, which were most likely poured with the intent of supporting a temporary bridge. The other end of the bridge was likely intended to attach at a large rock outcropping that can be seen on the opposite bank. Jean-Marie suggested the Army engineers often assembled bridges in the easiest way possible. Therefore, a rock outcropping was preferable because it saved time and effort and provided a stable land anchor. A canal exists just beyond the river. Although not often mentioned or discussed in detail within military journals or publications, Jean-Marie indicated the canal forms a half-circle facing to the west around this section of the city. The canal banks are nearly vertical, serving as an effective natural barrier to tanks and trucks and, therefore, another significant obstacle to the advancing Americans.

Where the 2nd Battalion successfully crossed the river, however, the water is wider and deeper than this location. Local accounts failed to identify the area associated with the successful crossing, but historical documents provide a rather clear image:

> At the northern edge of Epinal [*sic*], along the Moselle, lies the little factory town of Golbey. Just south of Golbey, the Uxegney–Epinal highway crosses the Moselle into eastern Epinal proper. On the south side of the highway near the river is a brick factory building. The bridge over the Moselle at that point had been destroyed.[29]

During the morning hours of September 23, Colonel Robert Dulaney, the regimental commander, left his vehicle at the 2nd Battalion defensive line and walked to the site of the demolished bridge near the factory building in an attempt to select an appropriate location for the 2nd Battalion's crossing of the Moselle. He selected the factory building as his command post and then proceeded to the destroyed bridge. The Germans placed significant amounts of small arms and tank fire on all of the roads leading to the bridge:

> Through that heavy fire, Colonel Dulaney walked calmly onto the demolished bridge to determine the practicality of using it as a means of crossing. He was exposed during all of this time to observation and fire from a pillbox on the far side of the river. Finding the bridge too badly damaged, he continued his reconnaissance of the river line and selected a suitable crossing site. He directed that our Second Battalion cross at that point.[30]

Jean-Marie has concluded this activity occurred at the Republic Bridge. His research indicated:

> The Second Battalion began crossing on October 23rd near le Pont de la Republique and eventually took the high ground and conquered the east bank of the Moselle River near the destroyed bridge du Saut le Cerf [*sic*]. Companies F and G crossed near the Republic Bridge and Company E some hundred yards to the north of this same bridge.[31]

Jean-Marie is certain the 2nd Battalion crossed near the Republic Bridge in part because of a French newspaper article that reported several American soldiers testifying to their crossing the Moselle near the gas factory, which was located at that spot. In addition, he pointed out that when the map contained in the 180th Regiment operations report is examined closely, a faint pencil line can be seen drawn across the Moselle at this location, as well as another pencil line marking the location of the 3rd Battalion crossing point at the White Balcony Bridge.

During the afternoon and early evening hours on September 23, after an extensive search, 2nd Battalion, led by F Company and followed by G Company, eventually waded across the river and then advanced to high ground approximately half a mile northeast of Épinal. E Company later forded the river and took up positions on the left flank of G Company.[32] There were no stone walls in this area, as there were at the 3rd Battalion's point of crossing. However, crossing the river at any point was still extremely difficult against the heavily defended city. "The cold and swift water was hip deep in some places."[33] My father presumably crossed at this point. As a member of a heavy-machine-gun squad, he would have certainly been carrying the gun, the tripod, or multiple cans of ammunition while battling the cold, swift current.

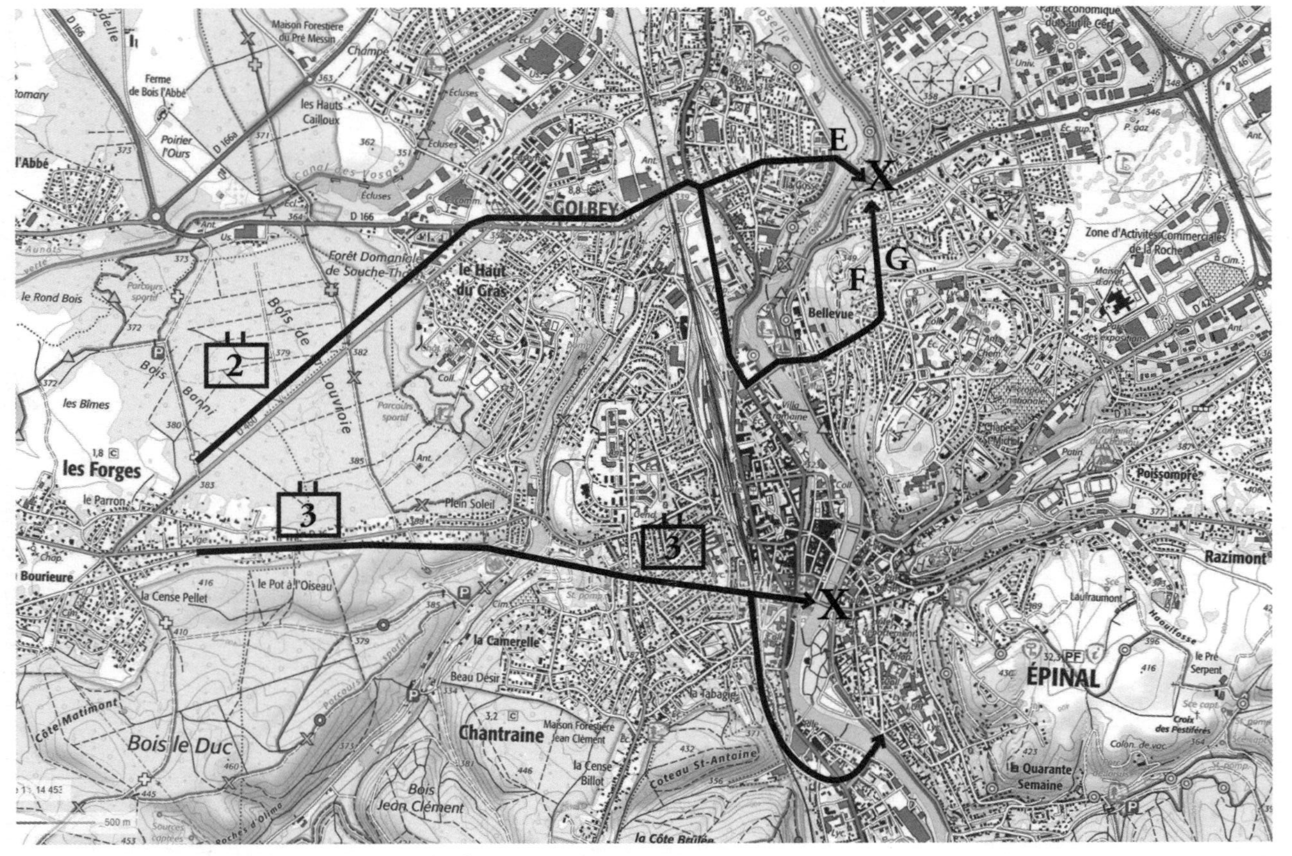

Map of the 2nd and 3rd Battalion approach to Épinal marking both the unsuccessful crossing (marked with an "X") as well as the successful crossings of the Moselle River. (Map and markings courtesy of Jean-Marie Siret)

Colonel Dulaney's observation post next to the bridge drew a great deal of artillery and sniper fire, but served as an effective vantage point from which to observe the actions of the 2nd Battalion. "Dulaney watched until Lieutenant Colonel Chester L. Cruikshank had all of his troops on the other side of the river. As Company G drove eastward through the town, it swung to the left and paralleled Company F, thus presenting a two-company front."[34] The well-prepared German forces that held and bitterly defended Épinal against the 180th Regiment's advance included a large number of SS troops. Prisoners captured from the 5th Company of the 19th SS Police Regiment said their battalion had 250 men. Their mission was to hold the city at all costs.[35] However, "The 'SSers' never were particularly fortunate in their brushes with the

Signal battalion soldiers repair phone lines along the Army-built bridge across the Moselle River in Épinal after high, raging waters disrupted the lines. (U.S. Signal Corps, 111-SC 233027/NARA)

45th Infantry Division."[36] A patrol from F Company engaged in a firefight and captured a prisoner who said a German general was in town.[37]

Throughout the day on September 24, 1944, the infantry troops of the 180th Regiment's 2nd Battalion continued to hold the high ground to the northeast of Épinal.[38] After engineers had completed construction of the Bailey bridge across the Moselle, tanks, trucks, and armor subsequently rushed across to assist the infantry.[39]

German presence in Épinal was significant. Each of the rifle companies from the 180th Regiment's 2nd Battalion met heavy resistance involving large numbers of enemy troops. "The house-to-house fights were bitter … slowly, under continuous fire, the units worked their way forward … clearing each point of steadily increasing resistance and fighting the swift current of the rain-swollen river."[40] Despite the enemy's preparations and well-fortified positions, the 180th Regiment eventually overpowered them. American artillery and mortar fire kept the German mortar squads pinned in their foxholes, causing them to run out of ammunition.[41] On September 25, French Forces of the Interior units reported large groups of Germans preparing to leave the area and retreat to the northeast.[42] Others that apparently couldn't retreat decided to surrender under a white flag.[43] German prisoners taken from the *Panzerjäger* Regiment said their unit had been in Épinal for ten days, had no kitchens, received only cold food, and described morale as being low.[44] This situation may have provided a slight advantage to the American forces.

Located to the east of Épinal in the autumn of 1944 was a mix of cultivated meadows and thick forests consisting of tall, straight pine trees and groves of dense leafy trees.[45] After liberating Épinal from enemy occupation, the 180th Regiment continued relentlessly across this rural terrain toward the French–German border. All three battalions fought their way northward through numerous towns and villages in pursuit of the retreating Germans:

> The enemy's use of artillery, mortar, and automatic-weapons fire increased accordingly as the division progressed toward the mountains … strong counterattacks by enemy forces became daily occurrences. Villages and houses were fortified for use as strongpoints and defenses. Many of the French villages along the way were seized only after the heaviest and bitterest fighting, which virtually destroyed the towns.[46]

On September 27, the 2nd Battalion was again on the front lines. They passed through the 1st Battalion to liberate the village of Girecourt, with G Company advancing and liberating Destord and E Company liberating Gugnécourt. A nighttime German counterattack forced E Company to withdraw from the village. But, after reorganizing to the west of town, E Company again liberated Gugnécourt the following day by forcing a German retreat to the northeast. F Company advanced in a southeasterly direction from Destord and liberated Nonzeville and Pierrepont under small arms and heavy artillery fire. G Company passed through Pierrepont earlier in the day and attacked toward the north of Grandvillers.[47]

I stood along the riverbank and reflected on the crossing. As a member of H Company, my father was assigned to a Browning water-cooled heavy-machine-gun squad which supported E, F, and G Rifle Companies as they engaged in this brutal close-contact fighting. He must have been exhausted and terrified and the stress had likely begun to affect his physical health, even if not obvious to him. The gun and tripod together weighed more than one hundred pounds. He either carried the gun, the tripod, or multiple cans of ammunition through the water, across the river, and through the streets of Épinal under heavy enemy fire. At the time of his enlistment, he weighed 153 pounds, stood five feet, nine inches tall, and had a chest circumference of 37 inches; his weight was slightly less upon discharge from the Army. Carrying heavy weapons and ammunition would have required considerable effort. He was consistently on the move as the regiment forged ahead across France. My presence in this region offered the ability to blend the historical reports with the actual terrain, creating a powerful image of his experiences, although almost seven decades after the events had occurred. This presence provided greater appreciation for the physical obstacles and challenges associated with the grueling advance of the regiment and the determination of the soldiers and officers. Why hadn't I seen some reflection of this determination in his personality during my childhood? The man I knew didn't fit this scenario. He wasn't a fighter. He wasn't assertive. And, he wasn't what I would consider to be a driven individual. Rather, he was quiet, introspective, and complacent with his environment. Despite the fact he seemed generally unhappy throughout my later childhood and young adult years, he seemed unwilling or unable to do something about his situation. How could he have demonstrated the determination and personal drive to fight his way across France while constantly under fire from enemy guns, grenades, mortars, and tank shells and yet seem powerless against social determinants? I was once again perplexed and felt I had lost ground in this journey to understand him. What role did this intense and sustained fighting play in his outlook and his character in the decades that followed the war? What could have been hidden in his subconscious that changed how he related to the world around him? Advancing through the dark forests, through frigid waters, while under hostile fire from buildings, windows, roadblocks, and bunkers must have been terrifying. Once again, I quietly hoped the next

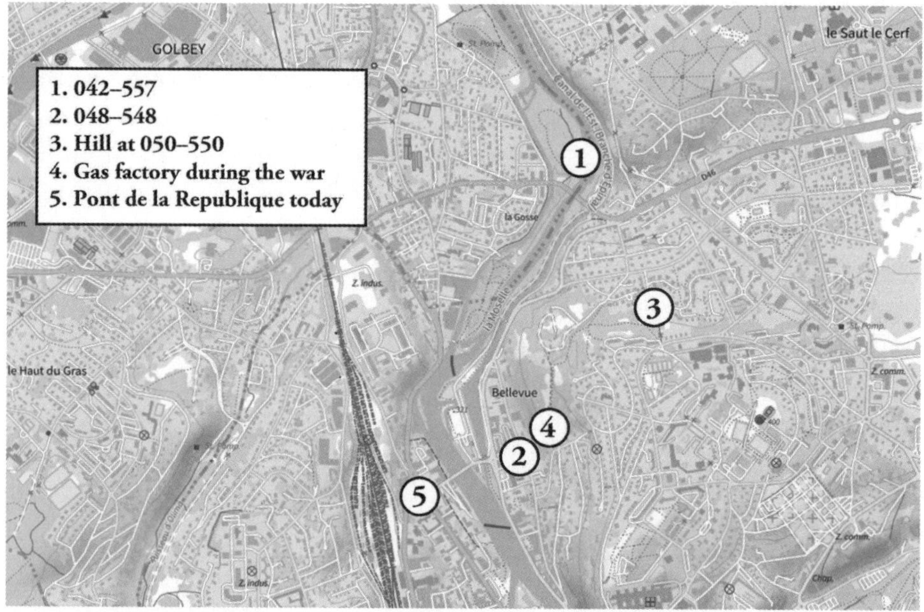

Map showing placement of 2nd Battalion troops at Épinal. 1) The first unsuccessful attempt by E Company to cross the Moselle River near "Post du Salt le Cert" at location 042–557. We visited this location and stood in the river. 2) The approximate location where F & G Companies crossed the Moselle River at 1550 hours. The location is 048–548. 3) The location of the hill reached by F Company at 1706 hours. (Map and markings courtesy of Jean-Marie Siret)

town might offer additional insight into this stubborn mystery as we continued across the French countryside with its brilliant fall colors and golden fields of harvested hay.

★★★

Autumn was a special time for fishing. My father somehow became interested in salmon after becoming aware of the annual salmon spawning run up the Rocky River west of Cleveland. The river was located a few miles from our home. It forms the spine of the Cleveland Metroparks in that region of Ohio. During high school, I occasionally joined my father on Saturday morning fishing trips to the river. When I first started salmon fishing with him, I was in ninth grade and entering that awkward transition between middle school and high school when friends often become more significant than family. Consequently, my best friend, Marc, often joined us. At that time, the fords that crossed the river were the preferred fishing spots. There were three of them. We often focused on

Pre-World War II postcard with photo of the Republic Bridge. (Courtesy of Jean-Marie Siret)

the second and third fords, for no particular reason obvious to me (then or now). They were old concrete structures elevated slightly above the water line that spanned the banks and allowed vehicles to cross the river. A gap approximately two feet wide existed in the center to allow the current to pass without covering the length of the concrete surface. There must have, at some point in time, been wooden planks across the gap to prevent tires from dropping down into the water but they were long gone by the time I had started to visit the fords—rotted and washed away by the current. When the water was low, the concrete surface remained above the water line, and subsequently dry, allowing safe passage. When the water was high, the current covered the ford with a few inches of rushing water. During the rainy season, the ford could not be seen whatsoever. Only the presence of a unique change in the pattern of the water surface over the gap provided an indication of its presence. In my youth, I recall wondering why the fords were there, because there weren't any visible roads at either end, just forest or overgrown brush along the banks. Apparently, nature had consumed what man had once created. Photographs of the broken and semi-submerged concrete sections of the White Balcony Bridge across the Moselle reminded me of those fishing trips to the fords across the Rocky River.

Our efforts to follow the path of the 180th Regiment, and to retrace my father's footsteps across eastern France during the autumn of 1944, led us away from the fortified city of Épinal, continuing our advance to the northeast. The fighting in this area was quite different from that which the 180th soldiers experienced along the streets of the city as the environment dramatically changed back from narrow urban streets and buildings to farm fields, groves of trees, sections of forests, and small rural villages.

CHAPTER 10

Girecourt

The 180th Regiment's path northward across the sprawling countryside toward Longchamp and Vaudéville eventually led them to Girecourt. Elements of the regiment advanced to the small village of Deville while the remainder followed the road to Vaudéville on September 26, 1944, where it encountered small-arms resistance, and rather quickly passed through the village after clearing it of scattered enemy troops. Small, but intense, firefights defined the interactions between opposing forces throughout the region, often characterized by hand-to-hand fighting. The first four soldiers leading the advance reached a barn at the edge of town and were cut off by 20 Germans. All but the right flank of the company, which was held up by a squad of heavily armed enemy troops firing from a farmhouse, advanced into the village. First Lieutenant William W. Gunn advanced on the house and threw several hand grenades into the window before firing his M1 rifle into the structure. Several German soldiers were wounded or killed and several surrendered.[1] This pattern of close fighting continued until eventually clearing the town of all enemy troops and establishing a 180th regimental command post in Vaudéville.

The towns and villages in this area of France are located close to each other, often separated by only one or two miles. The few roads connecting the villages were heavily mined during the fighting in 1944 and, as a result, much of the regiment advanced across wet and muddy fields and open countryside as opposed to following the existing road surfaces, thereby avoiding the hidden explosives.

After traveling along a narrow gravel road that divided pastures and low rolling hills, we eventually entered the village of Dompierre as our small group continued to trace the steps of 2nd Battalion. American soldiers and vehicles entered the village along either side of the same path in the autumn of 1944, immediately turned to the right, and continued their advance without stopping to rest in response to the intensifying German resistance ahead of them. This pattern of constant fighting is reflective of the relentless progress associated with the 180th Regiment troops. As such, H Company soldiers repeatedly set up the machine guns, picked them up and moved them forward, set them up again, continuing the cycle day and night. They may have carried the weapons more than they fired them as they moved between these small rural villages. Nevertheless, any lengthy periods of time spent defending a particular position would have involved additional action from the Browning water-cooled heavy machine guns. The daytime physical stress of constant movement and the nighttime emotional stress of defending the position, knowing that the machine gun was a primary target of enemy troops, would have been both physically and psychologically exhausting.

As the 180th Regiment approached Dompierre on the afternoon of September 26, soldiers encountered several dozen Germans and several vehicles moving along the main road into town.[2] An hour later, 40–50 additional enemy troops on foot, five large trucks and several other vehicles were reported moving east toward Dompierre.[3] German troops, hidden in wooded areas along the roadsides, used machine guns against the approaching 180th soldiers, and heavy tank and artillery rounds fell in four-minute intervals.[4] Second Battalion passed through the 1st Battalion and captured Girecourt approximately six miles east of Épinal—and then established its command post in a large white brick-and-stucco castle-style structure on the outskirts of town.[5]

We paused along the road 20 yards from this grand two-story structure. Ten windows decorated the side facing the road. Twelve-foot-wide cylindrical towers, with windows stacked above one another, stand prominently at each corner and extend up to the roof edge of the main structure. Each tower had a round pointed roof, a metal cone cap, and a lightning rod. Several dormers atop the main structure protruded from the slate-gray roof, suggesting the presence of a large attic. Four tall masonry chimneys extended through the roof in various locations and a small slate-tile-and-metal cupola sat in the center of the roof at the highest point. The structure was impressive, and one could easily understand the thought process involved with 2nd Battalion's selection as its command post.

Continuing with our pursuit of the regiment's history, we entered the town of Girecourt, just as the 180th had done in 1944. After a few turns along quiet streets, Jean-Marie slowed the car and parked in front of an old majestic house along the main road to speak with long-time resident, Pierre Triboulot, who was waiting in the driveway. Pierre's blue-and-orange, long-sleeve plaid shirt, burnt-orange wool sweater vest, green rubber boots and green wool newspaper-boy style cap with plaid fabric accent under the brim presented the traditional image of an older French farmer. He appeared extremely pleased to see us and spoke rapidly with an excited voice and a bright expression. Although holding a cane, he was quite spry and energetic for a man in his early 80s. Pierre spoke extensively about the German occupation and the liberation of his village. His memory seemed exceptionally clear, which is understandable in view of the fact these events had such a dramatic and traumatic effect upon his life. He initiated our conversation by sharing with us several prominent memories.

Pierre had just turned 15 years of age when the Germans arrived in his town. He recalled:

> The first two Germans that came into town were killed by villagers. The Germans were mad. In revenge, a German knocked on my neighbor's door and when he opened the door the German shot him. The German soldiers came into town in large numbers after that. We could hear them walking and marching because of the nails in their boots.

During the war, German troops wore boots with hobnails in the soles. The short, thick-head nails were driven into the soles of boots to improve grip in muddy ground. Pierre recalled experiencing mixed emotions about the invading Germans. He was a child and didn't understand how to process what he was witnessing. He told me, "The Germans were nice guys on their own. But put two together and they became bastards because each one thought the other would turn him in for being nice." The invading troops confiscated food and other essential items from local villagers. Pierre said, "The Germans came in and ate the way a dog would eat a bone. They were very hungry." He paused for a moment and then quickly turned his head and said in an excited tone, "I saw the church steeple blown up—I saw it from my front yard. American artillery did it." Both American and German forces often targeted church towers because of their favored use as vantage points for snipers and observers. Following Jean-Marie's encouragement to proceed with the planned tour of a specific location near the edge of town, the focus of our engaged and excited conversation shifted to driving directions.

Pierre joined us while we drove through town to the sprawling countryside surrounding the village, and eventually followed along a dirt road leading into a wooded area on the edge of a large field. Pointing and speaking in his consistent energetic tone from the front passenger's seat, he said, "We were liberated at 3:00 in the afternoon. The Americans were walking across the field toward us in the direction of the woods but the Germans were in the woods hiding and waiting. It was an ambush. A lot of Americans were killed in this trap." Regimental documents support Pierre's statement. Around 10:00 in the morning on September 27, 2nd Battalion reported to the Regimental S-3 (operations and mission-planning officer) that Germans were dug in along a tree line across a field.[6] Pierre indicated the Germans had been hiding in the woods for several days as the Americans zig-zagged across the fields and along the roads from village to village. Both Jean-Marie and Pierre agreed that the Americans advanced along a wide front and that because of this they simultaneously advanced through, and liberated, multiple villages throughout the area.

Pierre directed us to the specific place where he had been injured and his brother killed by a landmine following cessation of the fighting. As we approached the location in a secluded wooded area, we crossed a small bridge that spanned a narrow stream. The bridge is one of the few in this area that survived the war. Jean-Marie acknowledged that he was baffled as to why the Germans had allowed this particular bridge to remain intact. There didn't appear to be a specific reason for their inaction.

It was a small bridge over a narrow stream; perhaps they determined it was insignificant in their attempts to slow the Americans' advance.

Pierre shared a graphic memory of the bridge as we crossed, stating:

> I was about 15 feet away from an American jeep when it hit a mine and blew up. The jeep was crossing the bridge. It made a big fireball that lasted a few moments. The shoe of a soldier flew up in the air spinning and hung there in the air momentarily. There were two soldiers in the jeep.[7]

Pierre shared that the mines in this area were strategically located on both sides of the dirt road. The Germans often cut down large trees, several yards away from the edge of a road, and let them fall across the path, forcing the Americans to walk and drive around the fallen sections of the trees where mines had been planted.[8] The tree stumps were often left sticking up out of the ground several feet to several yards high to serve as obstacles to trucks and other military vehicles.

The fallen-tree roadblock in this particular location was placed slightly around the bend in the road and a short distance beyond the bridge. According to Pierre, the Germans watched from their hiding place along a trench in the woods 100 yards beyond the bridge while the Americans struggled with the roadblock and the mines. The trenches were already in place at the time, designed and created by villagers to divide communal forests. The Germans, however, used them for defensive purposes. Pierre continued:

> One of the villagers went to see what was going on and didn't come back for three days. The Germans had been holding him. On the third day they stood him up against the wall of the cemetery and shot him. Shortly after that, an American artillery shell came in and the Germans ran back into the woods. By the next morning the Germans had left the area.

While standing in a wooded area several yards from the road, Pierre paused for several moments, as if making an association in his mind or recalling a specific memory. He then said, "My brother stepped on a mine here and was blown up in the air fifteen feet."[9] Wiping tears from his eyes, Pierre was momentarily unable to speak, overcome by the memory of his brother and the vision of the explosion that killed him in late September 1944. He and his brother had been collecting firewood. They had an ox with them to assist in dragging the large sections of trees out of the forested area but his brother stepped on the mine while attempting to reach a fallen tree branch. Pierre had been standing nearby and felt the rush of the blast, causing him to lose his balance and fall forward into the crater created by the explosion. The left side of his face was injured by hot shrapnel, leaving him scarred with nerve damage and limited function of the facial muscles. Pierre abruptly shifted his thoughts and described how he watched an American engineer locate German mines. In his words, "They used a long stick with a disc at the end. When it beeped, the soldier took out his knife and dug out a big anti-tank mine. He disarmed it and set it up on the wall. He did this many times."[10]

Upon returning to Pierre's house, he quickly left the car and went to his garage, emerging a few moments later with several rusted and corroded pieces of metal. Speaking in French with an excited tone, he held out his hands and gestured for me to take the objects. I turned to Larry and asked him for an explanation in English. "He wants you to have them. It is a German 'pop-up' mine that he dug up himself many years after the war. He found it near the spot where his brother was killed." Jean-Marie inspected the artifacts and acknowledged that they appeared to be severely rusted wartime-era relics. Pierre talked constantly in French and he frequently pointed in various directions to indicate the locations of the events as he described them. Again shifting the focus of conversation, he said the Americans had set up their post office in the right side of his house, indicating "The American payroll came through town. Millions of dollars came through here—all the way up to the German border."[11] During a momentary break in our conversation, he eagerly agreed to pose for a photograph and without hesitation quickly removed his cap, threw it to the ground behind him and ran his hand over his head to smooth his thin hair before smiling at the camera.

Pierre bade us farewell, waving from the driveway as we drove away from his house. The rusted metal components of what was once the "pop-up" land mine rested in my lap. This was an intimate piece of Pierre's personal history yet he selflessly offered it to me as a parting gift. He had clearly enjoyed his time with us and seemed to embrace the opportunity to share his powerful memories. I wondered why Pierre seemed so excited and why he opened up in such a transparent manner to strangers from halfway around the world—people whom he would never again see. Throughout our interaction, Pierre reminded me of an excited adolescent eagerly describing to his best friend every memorable detail associated with a recent adventure. While his personal adventure and the associated memories were certainly not pleasant, his desperate need to share them created the connection between us.

Pierre wanted to tell his story. Perhaps he wanted someone from outside of his life and from outside of his small community to know and understand what happened. He may have wanted the world to know. For whatever reason, he trusted me with this information and with the relic. Pierre wanted to talk about his pain, his personal loss, and his trauma associated with the war. My father, in contrast, chose silence and secrecy. Pierre watched his brother die, he lived with his own facial paralysis from a German landmine, and he observed death and destruction all around him as a young teenager. Perhaps my father's experiences were far worse or more extensive in their duration, so much worse or extensive that he could not bear to bring those memories back to the conscious mind. This was his secret, and this was the reason for his silence, his introspective demeanor, and his subtle sadness. It was also the reason for my journey.

Pierre continued to wave and smile as we rounded the bend in the road and headed for Gugnécourt, the next stop on our journey and the site of yet another flashpoint in the perpetual fighting:

> The 180th Infantry captured Dompierre and entered Girecourt without significant opposition, then advanced into Destord, which it was forced to defend immediately against strong counterattacks supported by increased artillery fire. The enemy opposed the 180th Regiment's approach to Gugnecourt [*sic*] with heavy concentrations of small arms and mortar fire and a sudden crescendo of artillery fire, then counterattacked in force sufficient to cause elements of the 180th already in the town to withdraw for reorganization.[12]

The relentless combat showed no indication of losing intensity. Rather, it was increasing.

CHAPTER 11

Gugnécourt

Villager statements and local stories indicate E Company liberated the village of Gugnécourt after running into numerous roadblocks and heavy German resistance during its advance on the town in the autumn of 1944.[1] Official military records support the local stories. Jean-Marie's research determined the Americans ran into the 19th SS police regiment in Gugnécourt, reportedly there to keep their own troops from retreating. The regiment gathered and combined different disorganized elements from retreating German units with the intent of leading the eventual counterattack on Gugnecourt. A German roadblock was located at the edge of town near the walled cemetery and in the direct path of 2nd Battalion companies. This roadblock, as well as many like it, was not merely intended to serve as a physical obstacle to slow the American troops, it was also designed to cause severe physical damage and kill American soldiers. According to a report from the engineers recorded in the 180th Regiment S-2 Journal at 7:40 p.m. on September 26, a total of 26 trees were taken out of roadblocks; 17 of them were booby trapped with twelve 4" × 1" blocks of TNT, tied to the limbs and trunks of the trees. This man-made explosive is a solid pale-yellow nitrogen compound known for its devastating effects on objects and individuals. The engineers also found a boobytrapped roadblock that had five "potato-masher" grenades with 12 packets of TNT powder strapped around each of the grenades. After clearing all the roadblocks, 2nd Battalion troops advanced into Gugnécourt behind tanks, with a line of infantry approximately 150 yards across. Progress was difficult as weather continued to create miserable conditions—it remained cold and rainy throughout the advance.[2] F Company stopped at the roadblock, turned left and traveled north along a dirt road parallel to the cemetery wall, most likely because the 179th was already positioned up ahead in the next town to the east.[3]

As we stood near the Gugnécourt Cemetery gate at the point where a German roadblock was once located, a local resident, Monsieur Rivot, and his adult son walked toward us from his house on the corner of the intersection and asked what we were doing in the middle of the road. After explaining the reason for our presence and the purpose of our journey, he was eager for the opportunity to engage in the discussion and offer insight associated with his personal memories of October 1944. He recalled, "An American tank hit a mine on the street corner and blew up [at the site of the roadblock across from the cemetery wall]. The tank was towed out the following morning and taken away for repairs." He pointed toward a metal wheel that decorates his yard, allegedly from the tank destroyed in front of his house.

Consistent with many of the stories shared along our journey, Monsieur Rivot's family experienced both physical and emotional wounds and subsequent scars associated with the fighting. He shared that his brother was in the window of their family home watching the Germans as they ran away from the advancing American troops. "The Germans were doing a low crawl so as not to be seen." The intersection in front of their house had been heavily mined by the Germans; when some of the American artillery landed along the road it detonated one of the mines. While watching the retreating Germans through the presumed safety of an upstairs window, his brother received shrapnel wounds to his arm when a mine exploded. The small size of these rural villages promotes close communities and supportive social bonds between families. Monsieur Rivot described how a childhood friend was killed during the conflict. "An American pilot mistook a hay wagon for a German truck and a father and son were killed in the attack. The Germans had been disguising their trucks to look like farm vehicles to hide from American airplanes." He paused for several moments, turned, stretched out his arm in the direction of town and said, "The Germans blew up the Gugnécourt church tower."

I began to notice a pattern in the villagers' behavior when they shared their memories. After eagerly describing specific intense memories, a brief pause always followed. It was almost as if the emotional intensity of the memory caught up with their words; after the pause, the person changed the subject to something less personal. He turned toward me again, smiled, and said, "I was given chewing gum. The Americans spoiled us." Perhaps in a similar manner my father's memories were likely too painful to ever bring to the surface after returning home.

The fighting in this area continued across a wide front and involved all three of the 180th's rifle companies along with their H Company attachments. German soldiers fought hard as they continued to withdraw to the east and northeast. The commanding officer of 1st Battalion reported to the S-3 (operations and mission planning) officer, "We just received heavy shelling. We're getting tank and mortar fire. There are a lot of Germans all around this place. That stuff is coming from the northeast and to the east of us we can see lots of Germans."[4] Third Battalion reported receiving heavy flak and tank fire, and a platoon from K Company initiated an attack that was driven back by accurate German artillery fire.[5] Second Battalion reported fighting near Destord and encountered enemy tanks south of Gugnécourt while chasing the Germans from foxhole to foxhole.[6]

During the fighting from village to village across the region, in the rain, mud, and cold temperatures, the heavy machine gunners of H Company were just as engaged as the riflemen throughout both night and day. Private First Class John Puckett, a heavy-machine-gun ammunition bearer, crawled forward through heavy enemy fire during the German counterattack through Gugnécourt and killed several Germans, including a sniper, who were firing on his machine-gun squad. Puckett was eventually wounded by a German grenade but managed to crawl back and tell his squad the location of the enemy. Rather than report to the aid station to address the grenade fragments, Puckett joined his squad in a firefight with the enemy. He was last seen moving forward and firing a rifle toward the enemy. It was initially believed he was subsequently captured[7] but later confirmed that he was killed in battle on September 28 at the age of 22.

During this same German counterattack, Private John T. Kayda, assistant gunner of an H Company heavy-machine-gun squad, fought intensely against the advancing Germans. He became the main gunner when his squad was ordered to move to a new location while attached to E Company. As the Germans closed in on him, he continued to fire his machine gun until he ran out of ammunition. Instead of surrendering, he drew his pistol and continued firing at the overwhelming number of German riflemen until he was eventually killed by a hand grenade. However, his valiant efforts allowed his squad members to move to new positions and prevented them from being encircled and captured.[8]

Private First Class Horace D. Dodd, squad leader of another H Company heavy-machine-gun squad attached to E Company, encountered a similar fight. Dodd's squad had become surrounded during a German counterattack and, rather than surrender, he ordered squad members to remain with their machine gun until their ammunition had been exhausted. Once out of ammunition, the men withdrew to the edge of town and continued to fight as riflemen.[9]

Ammunition supplies at the front line continued to be a challenge. Private First Class Felix P. Rudy of H Company continued throughout the night to fire his heavy machine gun from a position near the edge of Gugnécourt. When his ammunition began to run low, he had his assistant gunner take over the machine gun while he crawled through the intense fire to obtain additional ammunition—not once, but twice. On the second return trip, he encountered several Germans, but managed to fight his way through them and successfully supply his squad with the additional ammunition.[10] Involved in this same fight was H Company's Sergeant Desmond C. Palmer, whose heavy-machine-gun section had been hit hard by the advancing Germans in and around Gugnécourt. As the enemy closed in on his squad, Palmer single-handedly held off the advancing troops long enough for his men to successfully relocate the machine gun. After all of his comrades were safe in their new positions, he crawled through 25 yards of enemy fire to rejoin them.[11]

Despite the hard fighting and determination of E Company riflemen and the attached H Company machine-gun squads, the German counterattack throughout the night forced the 180th to withdraw to the west of town and reorganize its forces. However, the withdrawal was brief, as the two companies counterattacked the next morning in an effort to recapture Gugnécourt.[12] Tanks from the 191st Tank Battalion supported E Company during the morning fighting. Upon seeing the tanks, the Germans responded with automatic fire, forcing the armored vehicles to close their hatches, to "button up." When the hatches are closed, it is more difficult for the tank crews to see the battlefield. Sergeant Andrews of Pittsburgh, Pennsylvania, went forward to the leading tank and pointed out German machine-gun positions to the tank gunner despite heavy enemy fire. The tank used its 75-mm gun to silence three or four German positions and moved forward into the town with E Company riflemen following closely behind.[13]

Without doubt, my father was involved in this fighting and he experienced the same challenges. No able-bodied soldier would have been spared front-line action during this battalion-wide fighting. Second Battalion led the fighting in this area as the lead column, followed by 1st Battalion and then 3rd Battalion. It was supported by C Company of the 191st Tank Battalion, C Company of the 120th Engineering Battalion, C Company of the 83rd Chemical Battalion, C Company of the 645th Tank Destroyer Battalion, and an artillery company[14] as they fought through Girecourt, Destord, Gugnécourt, and Grandvillers during the final days of September.

Second Battalion alone took many German prisoners during those subsequent days of fighting from village to village. The battalion captured 11 east of Girecourt, 49 on the road to Destord (including one German officer), seven to the east of Gugnécourt, and eight in Destord.[15] Throughout September, and leading up to the battle at Frémifontaine, the 180th Regiment captured 1,383 Germans, 150 of which were officers. From the time of its original landing on the beaches of southern France on August 15, 1944, through the end of September, the 45th Infantry Division had advanced more than 600 miles.[16] On September 28, only two towns remained along the 180th Regiment's path to the village of Frémifontaine and the foothills of the Vosges Mountains. The events that followed in these small rural towns indicated the enemy had decided to slow its established pattern of retreat to the German border and prepare to defend its homeland.

After finishing the roadside conversation with Monsieur Rivot, we backed up 100 yards from the dirt path where we had stood along the edge of the cemetery and proceeded to the first legitimate road north as we continued to follow the overall route of the 180th Regiment, advancing toward the town of Destord.

The sun was getting low in the sky and the shadows were long across the road and the fields as we reached the edge of town. Army records indicate the 180th Regiment encountered only light resistance in Destord, but it served as a strategic hub to reach other nearby villages. Jean-Marie suggested that practically the entire 180th Regiment passed through Destord in late September 1944, which indicates my father had been in this small town and likely walked the same road where I stood quietly imagining the sights and sounds of 1944. My thoughts began to play like short movie clips, the images becoming less foggy with each new community we visited. A pattern was developing. I first focused on the physical scenery in front of me, and then the vision of tired and weathered troops appeared in the movie clip playing in my mind. They were always moving in my visions—walking forward, running under German artillery, or firing at the enemy from any cover they could find (trees, rocks, or structures). I could sense fear, determination, tenacity, and exhaustion. Interviews with veterans had already established that most of them were in fact scared to death. Each man fought off not only the enemy but the constant fear of traumatic wounds or death. Passing through and liberating individual towns did little to reduce the emotional intensity because the next town to be cleared of enemy troops was always just a few miles ahead. As evening approached, we too passed through Destord and proceeded to the next rural village liberated by the 180th Regiment's 2nd Battalion—Pierrepont.

CHAPTER 12

Pierrepont and Grandvillers—Little Stalingrad

The exhausted but determined American soldiers of the 180th Infantry Regiment arrived in Pierrepont during the final days of September 1944. Fortunately, the bridge leading into town had not been destroyed[1] and therefore the regiment's trucks and armored vehicles were able to cross without delay during their relentless advance. I walked across the bridge and again envisioned H Company machine gunners taking the same steps nearly seventy years earlier. They had been engaged in this constant fighting for weeks and no doubt knew the adversities and dangers that waited across the bridge. Given the terrain, the increasing presence of German troops, and the short distances between villages, machine-gun squads likely carried the weapon, tripod, and ammunition as opposed to riding in trucks. Their services were needed constantly on the front lines as the rifle companies continued their advance against increasing enemy resistance.

German armor, specifically tanks, presented formidable threats to American infantry. On September 28, at 12:25 in the afternoon, an American observation airplane reported at least one German tank in Pierrepont[2] in addition to enemy infantry. According to Jean-Marie, the 180th immediately encountered the waiting German troops when the first elements of the regiment arrived in Pierrepont and subsequently engaged in widespread small-arms firefights throughout the town as additional Thunderbirds arrived. The 180th S-2 Journal supports his statement. E Company's commanding officer (CO) reported to the regimental CO, "The town is strung out and all I could do was place strong points on all

An abandoned example of the much-feared German 88-mm gun is inspected by a pair of 45th Division soldiers in the Grandvillers area on October 13, 1944. The sighting equipment and breech block are missing, which was typical of German behavior when abandoning artillery pieces. (U.S. Signal Corps, 111-SC 195443-S/NARA)

sides of the town. Just after dark the Germans attacked us. I judge there were 150–200 of them … they were trying to get out."[3] At the same time, F Company was on the move toward Pierrepont and encountered a company of Germans along the road, 50 of which retreated after the Americans attacked. German troops began systematically surrendering in response to 2nd Battalion's antiaircraft fire directed into the woods. E Company received heavy shelling from the north.[4]

The close fighting in and around Pierrepont continued throughout the day and well into the night on the 28th. At the onset of the fighting, 2nd Battalion sent a patrol east of town toward the main highway where it was stopped, after advancing only 300 yards, when the Germans opened fire.

Approximately 40 Germans with machine guns slowed the advance until American tanks responded.[5] Second Battalion officers later reported, "Our people are on the edge of those woods and we are shelling the woods now. There are plenty of Germans in there. The Germans have been in front of F Company all day and were shooting into them with tanks."[6] By nightfall, the regiment was positioned at the edge of the woods where the Germans had taken shelter and was relentlessly shelling the forest in an attempt to flush them out. G Company focused on clearing out the town and then rejoined E, F, and H Companies as the momentum continued and the fighting spread from village to village.

The villages are so close to each other throughout this region that the three battalions of the 180th were simultaneously fighting in several villages as the troops moved across fields and over hills. As fighting began to slow in one village it was just beginning in the next. Troop advancement was so rapid and progressive that reconnaissance often relied upon limited information obtained from patrols of small squads intended to draw fire and expose the German positions, and from assumptions made during brief conversations and interactions. There was little time for anything more.[7] The Regimental S-2 Journal indicates that by late afternoon Pierrepont had been successfully liberated. However, heavier and more brutal fighting was yet to come in and around the next village a short distance to the east, where the Germans had set up strong lines of defense around Frémifontaine and were waiting in force within the cover of the dense, dark forest.

Just beyond the bridge leading into Pierrepont, on the right side of the road where the 180th crossed into town, stands an old barn that still bears the scars of the fighting. It was built in 1940 and its walls remain covered by the original stucco finish. Chips and gouges in the stucco caused by shrapnel are visible across the surface of the structure. The 180th Regiment passed directly by the barn as it entered Pierrepont and immediately turned left along the road toward the village of Frémifontaine.

While continuing our journey, we walked across the bridge, made the same left turn at the barn, and stopped at the first house on the left side of the road. The two-story dwelling belongs to Monsieur Thomas, who had been meticulously painting his front doorway prior to our unannounced arrival. Jean-Marie approached and explained our reason for visiting his village. He appeared intrigued and listened intently, stopping to wipe his hands and set down his paintbrush. This had been his family home during the fighting. He recalled from his childhood memories that an artillery shell had landed 20 yards from the barn and subsequently killed a horse standing just inside the barn window. He shared, "When the shells started to fall, my father said, 'To hell with the cows, we need to get out of here.'" Since they had no cellar, the family went to another house a short distance up the road in order to seek shelter from the escalating violence.

Monsieur Thomas recalled, "There was a German soldier in the house located just across the bridge. He had a machine gun and he was holding up the Americans. They sent out a squad to surround him and kill him." He pointed and described the scene as if it had occurred only yesterday. As he continued to describe the events associated with late September 1944, he said to me in French, "Your father must have passed directly in front of our house." I turned to look down the road and process the structures within my view as well as the emotions. It felt strange to stand along this narrow road where he walked many decades ago. The cool air and colors of autumn would have been similar to those that embraced my senses. I stood deep in thought for several moments and then realized Monsieur Thomas was looking at me with a subtle smile. He seemed to understand. I was beginning to connect with villagers in a way I could not explain, nor fully comprehend. Perhaps a more accurate statement would be that they were connecting with me. The realization was more associated with intuition and a growing sense of "knowing" than a conscious, quantitative historical recount. These villagers had progressed through decades of emotional processing, subsequently developing some form of personal and social understanding that allowed them to cope, heal, and move on with their lives. Each villager seemed to comprehend I was attempting to reach a similar place in an effort to understand someone very special to me. I wrestled with a new question. Why had my father not been able to progress through the same healing process as these villagers? The answer may involve the concept of community.

Men of my father's generation were conditioned to believe they needed to be tough and stoic and appear invulnerable. Sharing personal memories of emotional trauma with family or friends who were not associated with the traumatic events creates a sense of vulnerability and the potential for judgement, rejection, and social isolation by those who simply don't understand. In response to apprehension and fear of these social traps, soldiers returning from the war elected to suffer in silent pain rather than risk additional emotional distress. French citizens living within these small villages and towns openly shared common memories, emotions, and traumas of war as authentic components of the social structures within their communities. They worked together to rebuild their villages, their infrastructure, and their lives. Families, friends and neighbors all shared in the experience and subsequently assisted each other in the process of healing across decades and across generations.

In order to process the intensity of the fighting, I stepped away from the group as Jean-Marie and Monsieur Thomas continued their discussion while I momentarily focused on one single day in this overall conflict. Second Battalion had fought hard and accomplished a great deal in the course of this one day. Early on September 28, F Company left Destord and advanced to the southeast toward the town of Pierrepont. During the advance, the company captured the village of Nonzeville late in the morning after engaging in small-arms fighting with enemy troops. Before the day was finished, the Americans had captured Pierrepont under heavy German artillery fire and small-arms fire.[8]

Expanding this assessment of a single day into multiple days, weeks, and months, I pondered the ability of the officers and soldiers to maintain this intensity and the all-too-real threat to life. How were they able to continue functioning within this relentless drive while fighting enemy troops each step of the way? How had they managed to cope in those moments and continue performing their jobs? With each town and with each discussion along our journey, I became increasingly amazed, humbled, grateful, and saddened. These men accomplished so much, and at such personal expense, much of which would remain with them throughout the remainder of their lives in the form of emotional

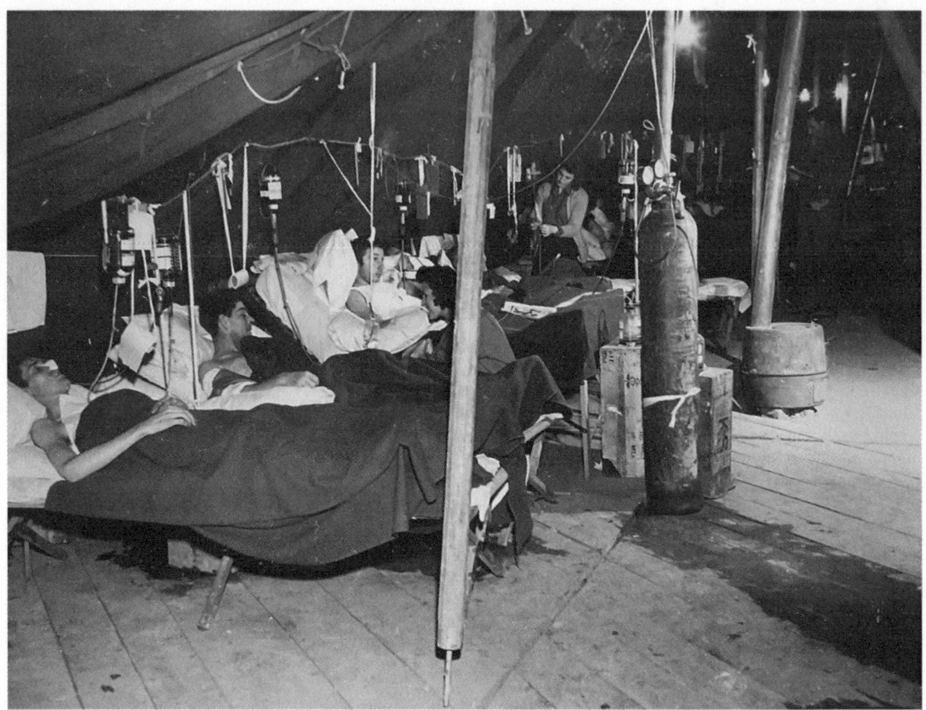

Wounded Seventh Army soldiers rest in beds in the post-operative ward of the 10th Field Hospital in Grandvillers, France. (U.S. Signal Corps, 111-SC 233020/NARA)

scars or nightmares. Many of the villagers who shared in those same memories as the returning soldiers were half a world away, never to be seen again following the war. Such traumatic and profound experiences over such an extended course of time must have taken a great toll on the human spirit.

Our continued advance eastward in the direction of Grandvillers remained consistent with the strategic plan to end our day's journey before the fall of darkness. Jean-Marie solemnly said the Americans had nicknamed the town of Grandvillers "Little Stalingrad" because so many had died there in the autumn of 1944. He shared that people in this region were all keenly aware the village of Frémifontaine is where the fighting between American and German forces became so intense and brutal in October 1944 that the survival of any of the two opposing

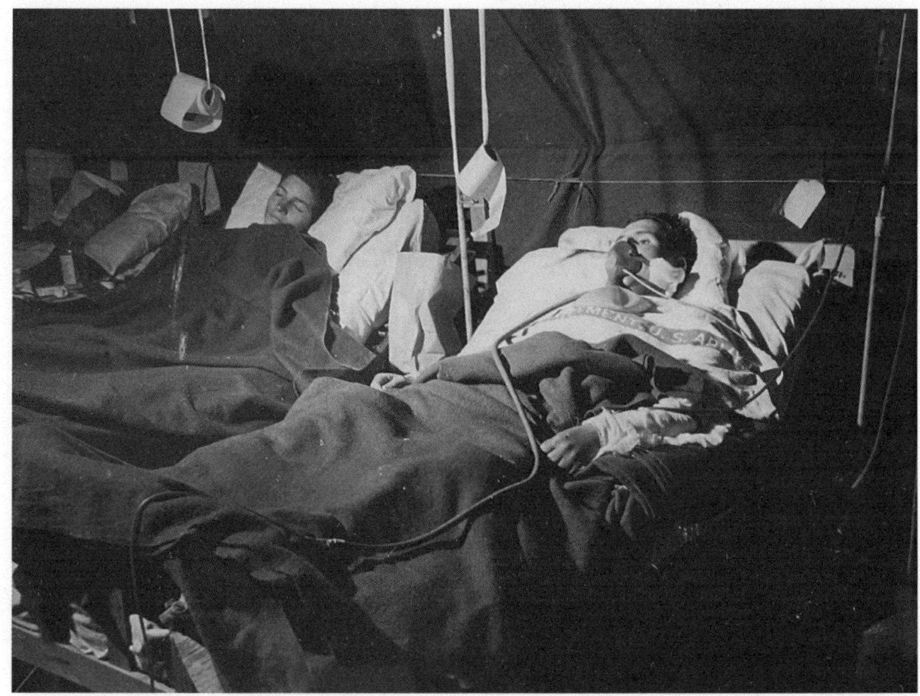

A wounded soldier of the Seventh Army receives oxygen in the post-operative ward of the 10th Field Hospital in the Grandvillers, France area. (U.S. Signal Corps, 111-SC 233021/NARA)

forces remained in question. Grandvillers was the immediate predecessor of this heavy fighting, the difference being primarily associated with a much shorter period of time.

Located slightly more than two miles from Frémifontaine, the fighting in Grandvillers represented the beginning of the German effort to dig in. This was undoubtedly the point where the building blocks of my father's nightmares began to arrange and fortify. According to the 180th HQ Field Order for September 29, 2nd Battalion along with its attachments was ordered to continue its attack at 6:30 in the morning with the objective of assisting the 179th Infantry in capturing Grandvillers. The order came directly from the 180th Regimental Command Post located in Girecourt.[9]

In the predawn hours of October 1, the 179th Regiment's 1st Battalion launched its attack on Grandvillers, meeting strong enemy resistance from within the town and from the high ground located to the east that significantly slowing its advance.[10] Four hours after the assault began, regimental command reported to the 180th's 3rd Battalion commanding officer. "They are not even as far as the crossroad where the north road enters the town. The Germans have been reinforced by a Pz [*Panzer*] outfit and they are having a hard time."[11] At 6:00 the following morning, both 1st and 3rd Battalions of the 179th attacked the town but again met heavy resistance from enemy infantry, mortars, machine guns, tanks, and artillery. The wooded paths leading into town were heavily mined and the enemy troops defending the area proved to be "more tenacious than any yet met."[12]

After extensive fighting throughout the entire day on October 2, the enemy was eventually pushed out of the town after American tanks and infantry attacked house-by-house, destroying structures and charging strongholds in close fighting. As the Germans retreated to the forests east and southeast of Grandvillers, the fighting moved from houses to densely wooded areas. Enemy troops were dug in and well camouflaged in the dark forests but the 179th and the 180th Infantry's 2nd Battalion continued to advance with the assistance of accurate mortar and artillery fire laid down in heavy concentrations.[13]

The fighting in and around Grandvillers was exceptionally intense and often hand-to-hand, lasting for more than two days. The Americans sustained many casualties and deaths from heavy artillery barrages. Large numbers of German and civilian deaths occurred as well.[14] Near the center of town stands a large and impressive granite memorial dedicated to the end of World War I. The monument sits high on an elevated bank supported in front by a wide six-foot-high arched stone retaining wall. The face of the monument, on all four sides, is riddled with chips, gouges, and scars caused by the fighting here during World War II. Jean-Marie believes the damage on the monument was primarily created by artillery fire because, he explained, artillery shells usually explode upward, unlike mortars and bullets. It is ironic such an impressive monument, built in tribute to

Grandvillers granite memorial dedicated to the cessation of fighting associated with World War I showing extensive damage from World War II. (Photo by Michael Reyka on location in France)

the end of hostilities associated with World War I, would actually acquire a more prominent legacy in response to the damage caused by a subsequent world war in the same location.

Official 180th regimental reports confirm that September involved a significant increase in casualties and brutality. The medical system treated 366 soldiers wounded in action as opposed to 118 during enemy contact in August. The operations report indicates, "Among those killed by German snipers were three medical aid men, each shot through the head while going to the aid of wounded Americans. At the time of death each wore the Geneva Red Cross brassard on his left arm."[15]

We drove along the road from village to village through the beautiful French countryside, passing the small village of Nonzeville in the distance just over a slight rise approximately four hundred yards from the main road. The 180th Regiment's 2nd Battalion assisted in liberating Nonzeville in late September 1944 after repelling resistance associated with small-arms fire and German attacks involving mortars and at least one Mark VI tank positioned in the village.[16]

According to the regimental S-2 (intelligence and security officer) reports and company-specific morning reports, H Company remained briefly in Nonzeville while in reserve, after the town was cleared of enemy troops. Although 2nd Platoon and 2nd Section's 81-mm mortar squads remained on the line fighting alongside F Company against heavy resistance near Brouvelieures, the rest of H Company converted to company control and received hot showers and hot food. The men were given, "Hot meals with doughnut girls serving doughnuts for dinner."[17] They watched movies in a makeshift theater assembled by the battalion chaplain and enjoyed a well-deserved rest, away from the fighting and briefly sheltered from the weather.[18]

H Company was in battalion reserve on the 2nd, 3rd, and 4th of October. The long overdue rest and nutrition received would be needed in the days that followed. My father and his comrades could not have anticipated the intensity of the fighting they would experience in the dark forest near Frémifontaine a few days later and just a few miles away. On October 5, H Company received orders to move back on the line and relieve 3rd Battalion at Frémifontaine.[19]

I reviewed my notes, which filled most of the pages in the legal pad I had carried throughout the afternoon, as I began to think about the following day when I would experience the highlight, or piéce de résistance, of our lengthy journey across the French countryside, the village of Frémifontaine, where my father experienced what could be considered the fight of his life, at least up to that point in time. Based upon everything I had learned, the fighting that occurred around Frémifontaine held the secret I had been searching for throughout my journey across France.

The French Resistance were also active in the Vosges in the fall of 1944.

Jean-Marie shared with me an FFI action order written prior to the battle and signed by "George." Evidently, the FFI groups wished to maintain their secrecy in case the Germans intercepted local orders. The order directs any and all FFI groups already assembled, whether armed or not, to take immediate action wherever possible to harass the enemy by cutting down trees, cutting telephone lines, knocking down communication poles, and changing or relocating road signs. Groups that were armed were ordered to conduct ambushes against enemy vehicles and capture their weapons. Groups were strongly encouraged to conduct such activities as far away from populated areas as possible so as to avoid German reprisals in the towns and villages. The order also directed that, upon the arrival of the Allies, the road signs were to be replaced and the communication lines repaired.[20]

A resident of Frémifontaine, Madame Moulin, explained that, prior to the advance of the Allies, the Germans, who were holding numerous prisoners of war from the "Commonwealth" at Épinal, decided to move them to Saint-Dié. Commonwealth soldiers during World War II represented various countries, including Australia, Canada, India, and others. The columns were not very well guarded and numerous prisoners were subsequently able to escape along the journey, thanks to the favorable terrain and poor weather conditions. Those who successfully fled the column hid in the forests that lined the length of National Route 420 and waited for the American liberation. The inhabitants of the nearby French villages, who knew where the prisoners were hiding, secretly provided them with food during this period of time. For example, the owner of the mill at Frémifontaine was able to detour some flour for the benefit of those hiding in the woods.[21]

Tank approaching Frémifontaine in late September 1944, with hatch open but commander peering out from a safe position. (Photo courtesy of Jean-Marie Siret)

In the final days of September, the 180th Regiment found itself in position to advance in an easterly direction toward the village of Frémifontaine.[22] On October 1, just before H Company began its rest period in Nonzeville, 2nd Battalion of the 180th Regiment along with its attachments received fateful orders that would thrust my father and the rest of E, F, G, and H Company into a horrifying battle with disastrous consequences. Field order #48 instructed 2nd Battalion to clear Frémifontaine of enemy resistance and provide reconnaissance for a stream crossing. This order would prove to be life changing for the men of 2nd Battalion.

The village of Frémifontaine sits in the foothills of the Vosges Mountains, terrain known for its impenetrable dense and dark forests. The heavy fog and mist of October 1944 clung to the ground between the pine trees and added to the 45th Division soldiers' challenges. Enemy troops were often mere yards away from unsuspecting Thunderbirds. One soldier later wrote:

> The mere snapping of a twig underfoot could cost a man his life. It took immense sangfroid, nerves of iron, to creep up on enemy positions, footsteps soft in the pine needles beneath towering fir trees. Without a compass, men would get lost for days. Every tree was a possible German strongpoint and every bush could shield a machine gun.[23]

The soldiers were on edge every moment and primeval fears became a common bond among them. "Men felt they were being watched at all times."[24] The fear, the mist, and the darkness pressed the imagination to the level of terror. Raindrops, and the steady dripping from tree branches in the darkness, sounded like enemy footsteps within feet of the soldiers.[25] The mind constantly struggled to differentiate between human and natural noises in an effort to stay alive. The silence was often just as deadly for the troops that patrolled softly and cautiously at night as they moved through the forest where the lowest pine limbs often touched the ground. Under these branches, "The enemy would dig in, cover their holes, and wait for Americans to creep past, then jump up and fire at them from behind."[26] Sleep was impossible, even in the total darkness.

My father was one of these soldiers and he no doubt felt the same tension, anxiety, and fear as he wondered whether he would survive the next few minutes. I don't recall ever seeing him in a state of heightened anxiety or fear, not even when I witnessed him experiencing a mild heart attack in our living room. During that event, I watched him in his chair from my vantage point at the top of the stairs, assessing his subtle discomfort through his wincing expressions, furrowed brow, and occasional rubbing of his chest, and then secretly telephoned my older brother and our family physician. When I said, "Dad, Dr. Woods is on the phone and wants to talk to you" he replied softly, almost to himself, "Damn it," and then folded his newspaper and walked to the telephone. My brother arrived a few moments later and drove him to the local emergency room. In response to the evolving event, he simply appeared quiet and perhaps slightly annoyed and frustrated—maybe even sad. But, in the forests near Frémifontaine, he must have been terrified along with

Infantrymen of the 180th Regiment advance across French farmland near Frémifontaine on October 4, 1944. (U.S. Signal Corps, 111-SC 271460/NARA)

every other soldier. According to an Army physician, "There aren't any iron men … the strongest personality, subject to sufficient stress over a sufficient length of time, is going to disintegrate."[27]

As the sun continued to set and the countryside slowly became gray and hazy, we ended the day and returned to the hillside chalet hidden in the dense pine forests of the Vosges Mountains for a restful night's sleep. In the morning, our journey would take us to the village of Frémifontaine and into the most frightening experience that changed a man for the remainder of his life.

CHAPTER 13

October 10—Frémifontaine

My mind was filled with a mix of emotions as we left the peaceful hillside farmhouse just after dawn on October 10. My secret hope involved finding a village relatively unchanged over the course of time—a time warp that would help me in this quest for understanding. During the autumn of 1944, slightly more than 300 people were living in Frémifontaine. At the time of this personal expedition, there were 403. This relatively unchanged population, as well as the large number of historic buildings, barns, sheds, and houses, would facilitate the achievement of our objective in uncovering my father's hidden experiences as an H Company soldier of the 180th Regiment.

Located in the township of Brouvelieures, Frémifontaine is part of the district of Saint-Dié-des-Vosges and the Department of Vosges within the Region of Lorraine in eastern France. Its name translates to "beautiful fountain" in recognition of the large circular stone fountain located near its center. The small village was peaceful and silent as our sedan navigated the early morning mist and followed road signs leading to the 45th Infantry Division monument, up narrow, winding streets to Le Chaudpoil, a wooded area on the edge of the village. Jean-Marie stood at the crossroads near the granite memorial. He was leaning back against the bumper of his little red car, arms folded and smiling widely, as we stepped out of our vehicle and onto the pavement of the road junction in front of the monument. It was clearly an emotional moment for Jean-Marie. He shared with me that this was the first time the son of a 180th Regiment soldier had made the journey to visit the 45th

Division memorial in Frémifontaine. Jean-Marie had been the inspiration and the driving force in the creation and placement of this monument, with the engaged support of community, government officials, and local leaders. His father-in-law worked for the French resistance during the war and supported F Company of the 180th Regiment's 2nd Battalion during the fighting in this region. His name was Georges Fortier. Of the five FFI members who worked together with Georges's group, three were captured, two of which later died in captivity. Georges and one other fighter were able to escape their German captors. According to Jean-Marie, "It was a hell of a mess in Frémifontaine because of the German counterattacks. It was very difficult for villagers to know what was happening at any given moment and to which unit because of the constant battling back and forth." He noted that at one point the 180th Regiment was forced to completely evacuate the village after being pushed out under heavy German aggression.

I turned toward the monument and walked slowly along the narrow, curved gravel path that led up the short slope to the granite memorial, consciously immersing myself in the moment and trying to notice every aspect of my surroundings. I secretly wanted time to slow down so I didn't miss any hidden clues, messages, or insight into the past. The familiar thunderbird emblem could be seen from a significant distance away, displayed prominently on the front of the gray granite surface. A bronze plaque below the emblem expressed the undying gratitude of the local villagers.

Through my peripheral vision, I noticed the abruptly brightening sky behind the monument had begun to illuminate the morning mist of the forest and the otherwise gray and damp air. Crouching down to read the plaque, I heard Tara call to me from the road junction behind me. "Do you see that?" Without turning, I replied, "See what?" Her sincere tone caught my attention. "You need to look at this, Dad. Come here, look at the sun!" I reluctantly stood, turned away from the monument and walked back down the gravel path to the road where Tara stood. As the two of us faced the monument from the vantage point of the road junction, the view appeared no different than it had when we first arrived at the structure—hazy and gray. "It's gone," she said in both disappointment and astonishment. I looked at her camera and smiled at the image she

Michael Reyka upon viewing and experiencing the 45th Infantry Division monument in Frémofontaine for the first time with rays of early morning sunlight illuminating the moment.

had captured several moments earlier. The sun's rays had briefly burst through the clouds and the dense trees at the very moment I knelt in front of the memorial. The intense light momentarily poured onto the granite monument at the instant she had snapped the photograph. And, just as quickly, it disappeared after I walked away.

Jean-Marie quietly watched as we became familiar with the monument and the surrounding grounds. Visibly pleased and proud of this very special place, he approached and presented to me a written first-person testimonial from a woman who had lived in Frémifontaine during the battle but who had since passed away. She described an event during the early stages of the battle for Frémifontaine that Jean-Marie believes was consistent with events described in my journal and the previous research that led to this overall journey. That specific event, described by a 180th Regiment soldier, now has a location—Frémifontaine. The villager's experience involving the fighting around the village church, and described by the soldier, is presented later in this chapter.

After thoroughly exploring the monument and its immediate surroundings, we returned to our sedan and drove to a community park on the edge of the village. A granite plaque honoring the local French resistance fighters displayed on the side of a park building marks the location where two F Company soldiers were captured during the early days of October 1944. The resistance movement was formally known as *Les Forces françaises de l'intérieur,* but more commonly referred to as FFI. The group provided not only direct fighting ability, but also passive resistance against the German occupiers. Jean-Marie provided several written testimonials and shared stories that offer specific examples of passive villager resistance.

In the two weeks preceding the arrival of the American troops, German soldiers moved throughout the village, frequently making unwelcome requisitions of local livestock in order to feed their hungry troops. Out of resentment, the villagers devised ways to keep food away from the Germans. In one instance, several local families collaborated in killing and butchering a pig during the night in order to prevent the German soldiers from eating the animal they had requisitioned for the following morning. The pieces of meat were lined up in a large tub and hidden for several days between the mattress and the wooden slats of the bed where an elderly grandmother allegedly slept. This credible lie, involving the old woman sleeping, prevented the house from being searched. Similarly, one of two horses located on a local property near the edge of town had been requisitioned. The villagers chose to give to the Germans the nastier one of the two animals, which subsequently kicked and fractured the leg of a German artillery company soldier as he attempted to attach the horse to a cannon. In response, the Germans grabbed the other horse and made a quick retreat across the field with the artillery piece in tow. In another instance, a group of villagers protested vigorously during a fodder requisition. They tried to discourage the Germans through outright resistance but were ultimately unsuccessful. It was only under the threat of a weapon pointed at them and the statement, "*Vous Arbeit,*" meaning "you work," that the villagers went back to their homes and their kitchens under fear of deportation and forced labor. One villager shared, "We didn't stop making fun of a German soldier, who had drunk too much and had difficulty climbing back up to La Raplye, until he became angry, raised his rifle to his shoulder and pointed it at people while shouting threats at them."[1]

Monsieur Albert Begel lived in Frémifontaine and worked at a local sawmill. Beginning in mid-September of 1944, a German observation post had been established at the back of Begel's house near the window that faced toward Dracourt and Bonnehet. The spotter was replaced each day and was equipped with either a field telephone or radio, Begel couldn't be certain from his vantage point. Unnerved by this undesirable presence in his house, Begel had the burning desire to give the intruder a "whack" with his shovel and then drop the body down a well. His wife, however, became aware of his intentions and was able to discourage him from carrying out the plan in response to her fear of German reprisals.[2]

Like other inhabitants of the village, the father of Madame Moulin, unobserved by the Germans, restocked supplies for whom he referred to as several "Indian soldiers" that escaped from the Germans' prisoner compound. The soldiers successfully hid in the surrounding forests outside of town throughout September 1944. Jean Thiriot had developed a unique way of assisting the escaped soldiers. He was employed at the Frémifontaine mill and, on his way to work each day, left a bag filled with food at the foot of a large tree. When leaving the mill each evening, he picked up the empty bag and carried it home. Although he repeated this procedure numerous times, he never caught a glimpse of the Indian soldiers that benefited from his generosity and the risks associated with his actions. Then, one afternoon when picking up the empty bag, he had the pleasant surprise of finding with it two small wooden birds that had been carved and decorated in gratitude for his kindness. Jean was likely either referring to Native Americans from the 45th Division when he made reference to the prisoners, since all three of its regiments fought in this general region, and the 180th Regiment had the most significant presence in Frémifontaine, or to Commonwealth soldiers referenced earlier. Although Jean has since passed away, the two hand-carved birds remain in the possession of his family. The Germans continued their relentless search for the escaped prisoners throughout the region over an extended period of time. Madame Moulin recalls they questioned villagers in the upper part of Frémifontaine in regard to the whereabouts of the escaped prisoners. During the course of this questioning, piles of straw and fodder were frequently tested with bayonets, probing for the presence of soldiers or resistance fighters who may have been hiding inside.[3]

Jean-Marie's detailed descriptions of the basic troop formations throughout the multiday battle effectively linked the existing landmarks with the history, creating vivid images through the narrow winding streets of Frémifontaine and the surrounding fields, forests, and hills. He pointed out that the Germans occupied the high ground east and northeast of town during the first week of October 1944. Much of Jean-Marie's local knowledge had been obtained through conversations with villagers and family members. His passion for the 180th Regiment, his love for this small village and his respect for his father-in-law who fought here

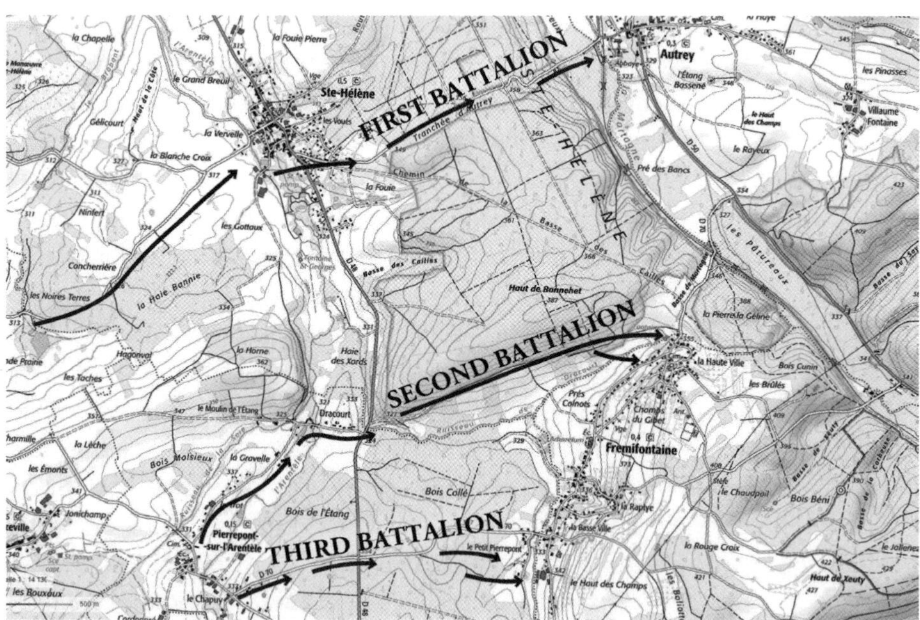

Map with drawings indicating 2nd Battalion's approach to Frémifontaine. (Map and markings courtesy of Jean-Marie Siret)

alongside the Americans served as the motivation that led to his expertise regarding this little known, but significant, battle, a battle that could have changed the course of history had the 2nd Battalion failed.

When the 180th approached Frémifontaine, 2nd Battalion was positioned in the center of the advance during the first few days of October. Jean-Marie believed the 2nd and 3rd Battalions crossed each other at some point during the early stage of the liberation of Frémifontaine after the battle was well underway. Based upon years of field and document research, his theory involved the 2nd moving to the right and the 3rd moving to the left on their way up the hillsides at the edge of town. Meanwhile, 1st Battalion was positioned slightly over two miles to the north fighting in the village of Autrey.

Enemy resistance was quite heavy as the two battalions approached Frémifontaine. According to regimental commanders, "Mined roadblocks covered by fire and well emplaced infantry, using artillery and mortars, contested our advance … narrow trails and thickly wooded forests restricted the use of our heavy armor, while extensive mines and booby traps, as well as natural terrain features delayed all our advances."[4] The continued unfavorable weather conditions contributed to the regiment's difficulties as the rain and fog slowed the progress through dense woods.[5]

The troops continued to fight in cold and wet weather conditions as the regiment methodically moved into the foothills of the Vosges Mountains on October 1. The rain continued falling with increasing frequency and intensity. The foothills were "covered in many places with deep and dark forests, in some of which, even on days filled with sunshine, there was always a semi-twilight. The Germans skillfully concealed their positions in these forests so that every step that a man took was taken with the risk of being cut down by hidden weapons."[6] The artillery tree bursts in these forests were devastating to the troops. Shrapnel and timber exploding together in the air was extremely dangerous. Even though the troops covered their foxholes with logs and branches to protect themselves, the overall conditions contributed to perpetual stress among them. "The continuous cold rain seeped into the slit trenches and throughout the rest of the Vosges fighting, made living very miserable."[7]

Soldiers at the 45th Division command post in the Rambervillers, France area carry a cot with personal belongings and equipment out of a flooded tent after heavy rain. (U.S. Signal Corps, 111-SC 233026/NARA)

As this historically significant battle began to develop on October 1, the regiment maintained positions around Frémifontaine in an area that stretched from Autrey in the north to the lower periphery of Frémifontaine in the south, a distance of more than three miles. With 1st Battalion in the vicinity of Autrey, the 2nd Battalion to the west of lower Frémifontaine and the 3rd Battalion to the south of the 2nd Battalion on its right flank, the regiment presented a broad battle line.[8]

Jean-Marie led us to the jump-off point of the 180th Regiment's 2nd and 3rd Battalions where the troops initiated their attack on Frémifontaine. "Jump-off" is a term used by the military to indicate the start of a planned attack. According to Jean-Marie's research, half of 2nd Battalion advanced down the road and the other half moved across the field. "The 180th Infantry Regiment, supported by armor, cleared one viciously defended roadblock only to come up against the enemy

Soldiers at the 45th Division command post in the Rambervillers, France area inspect damage caused by flooding after a 24-hour downpour of rain. (U.S. Signal Corps, 111-SC 233025/NARA)

positions on the high ground east of Frémifontaine which effectively halted the advance."[9]

In advance of the 180th's attack, American artillery targeted Frémifontaine in an attempt to weaken the enemy's resistance. A German infantry outfit had dug in across the fields around the house of Louis Delaite at 8 Rue de la Bonne. They were preparing to pull out of the area during cold rain on October 1 in response to the advancing 180th Regiment troops when American artillery arrived and took a heavy toll on them, virtually annihilating the unit before it could leave. The German officer commanding the unit had been billeted in the Delaite house prior to the barrage and was subsequently killed by shells that landed in front of the house while he was attempting to return to his men. The inhabitants of the house across the street had become accustomed to seeking shelter in their basement during the fighting because it was the last remaining one to be considered safe. The structure has since been destroyed, but at the time it was located directly across from the Morel family house. The American artillery barrage set the house on fire, forcing the occupants hiding in the basement to flee to the Delaite house. Louis Delaite and his younger sister, Odile, were late in arriving and were escorted by a German soldier during the barrage. They crossed the threshold of the doorway at the same moment a shell blasted across the facade of the house above their heads. However, the explosion remarkably failed to cause any injuries. Louis and Odile immediately went to hide with the others already safe in the basement; the German soldier returned to his post. The shell that hit the house had been aimed at a small window in the attic where a German machine gun had been set up in preparation for the Americans' arrival.[10]

Monsieur Marcel Demangeon recalled that, on October 1, a German machine gun, having been set up in the wooden shed attached to the Demangeon house, fired continuously on the American positions in the Bois Collet (Collet Woods). To protect themselves, the crew of four had assembled a rampart using bags of recently harvested potatoes. One well-aimed American artillery shell destroyed the corner of the shed, the machine gun, the crew, and the harvest of potatoes, to the great despair of the Demangeon family.

In the written work of Jean Laurain, regarding the liberation of the Vosges by the American VI Corps, he mentions that German soldiers attempted to infiltrate toward the positions of American tanks. Marcel Demangeon contributed first-hand information to the story. Two American tanks had become stuck in the mud as they attempted to cross the Roseaux Stream between the Demangeon and Doridat houses in

Frémifontaine. Even though immobilized by the mud, their gun turrets could still operate. In response, soldiers from a German *Panzerfaust* squad tried to destroy them on three separate attempts (the *Panzerfaust* was a single-shot, portable antitank weapon designed to fire a warhead about thirty-five to fifty-five yards). Their efforts were in vain, however, as each assault was repelled by bursts of American machine-gun fire that killed the infiltrating Germans.[11]

According to the 180th Regiment S-3 (operations and mission-planning officer) radio transcripts, one of the tanks described by Marcel hit a German mine shortly before 8:30 in the morning, resulting in a damaged track. The other tank became stuck in the mud later in the day as it tried to go around the disabled one blocking the road. Lieutenant Cobbs from the tank battalion sent a T2 recovery vehicle (based on the M3 Lee tank) to the scene in an effort to pull the disabled tanks out of the mud but it and the tanks were under heavy enemy machine-gun fire throughout the day. By 8:00 p.m., complete darkness had set in and the tank crews were facing increased German aggression. Despite the defensive measures observed by Marcel, the crews eventually abandoned their vehicles. The Germans subsequently converged on the tanks, booby trapped one and burned the other before leaving. When questioned by the regimental commanding officer, Cobbs replied, "Well, there was no sense in staying there because it is going to take at least 2 or 3 T-2s [*sic*] to get them out."[12]

Roadblocks had become a common obstacle for 2nd Battalion as it continued its advance toward Frémifontaine from the west, proceeding along the road toward the village. Another formidable German roadblock came into view slightly beyond the second curve, which required the troops to slow the advance and subsequently become easier targets for German snipers and machine gunners. Elements of the 3rd Battalion took the wooded path, as opposed to the road, in response to the enemy roadblock. Second Battalion moved straight toward Frémifontaine and followed a path through the woods. It was a well-marked path in 1944 that followed a small stream all the way into the village. It is not marked on any official maps because it was simply a wooded footpath that has long since become overgrown with brush and trees. The entrance is

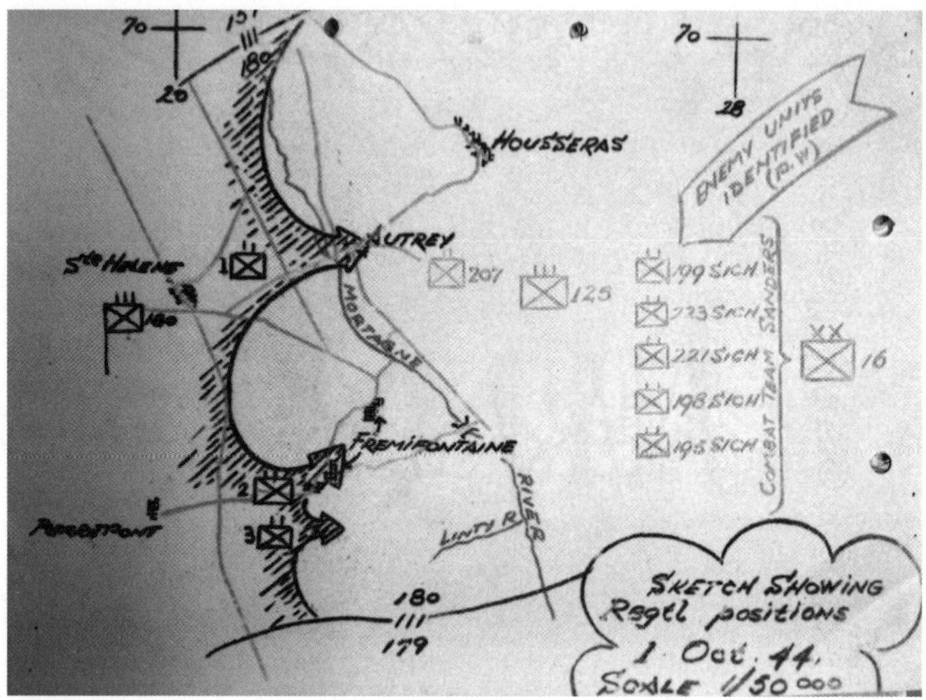

Military map and overlay courtesy of Jean-Marie Siret. Overlay also reviewed in Headquarters 180th Infantry, Report of Operations, October 1944 at the 45th Infantry Division Museum archives. (Photo taken on location in France by Michael Reyka)

slightly more than a mile from Frémifontaine. Twenty-five years ago, an American GI returned to visit the battlefield around Frémifontaine and showed this route to Jean-Marie, stating that he and other 2nd Battalion soldiers had walked it in 1944 as they entered the village.

Second Battalion experienced steadily increasing German resistance and intensifying combat as all three rifle companies and their H Company attachments approached Frémifontaine on September 30. The 180th Regiment S-2 (intelligence and security officer) journal recorded the detailed movements of battalion troops. At 5:21 in the evening, 2nd Battalion reported to the Regimental S-3:

> F Company is jumping off again. This is the 3rd time they jumped off. They have one platoon going around to the left of the road and the other coming around to the right of it. They are getting fire from the hill mass to the right

> of the town of Frémifontaine ... F Company is getting a pretty heavy barrage. They have a by-pass now so that the tanks will go with them.[13]

Second Battalion continued its relentless pressure against the enemy and at 9:05 p.m. reported to the S-3:

> F Company had a hell of a fight out there. We got the tanks up there and they are in the outskirts of town. They are still moving. Jerry [Germans] tried to go around on the left flank but we quieted that down, and we are moving out again. I believe we will get that town.[14]

The fortified German troops were dug in on the high ground east of town and used strategically placed machine guns to suppress the approaching American forces.[15]

The 180th Regiment's advance into Frémifontaine on October 1 was made in frigid rain.[16] Despite the German resistance and the terrible weather conditions, all of F Company had advanced into town by 8:45 on the morning of October 1. However, German artillery and tank fire received from multiple locations continued to harass the company as it trudged through the mud and mist. The tank rounds fell at the village crossroads, all around town and in the woods to the west of town. They were thought to have originated near the towns of Housseras and Grandvillers.[17] The authorized strength of a rifle company during World War II was 187 enlisted men and six officers. However, the intense fighting during the first few weeks took a tremendous toll and the average strength of the rifle companies throughout the month of October was reduced to 121 enlisted men; the company officer strength reduced to three later in the month.[18]

Both American and German artillery and tank fire fell consistently in and around the Frémifontaine throughout the early days of October. The first heavy artillery barrages to fall on the village were fired by the Americans in advance of the 180th Regiment infantrymen in an earnest attempt to weaken the German resistance and save American lives.

Madame Pernot (née Demangeon), who was nine years old and living in her family home in Frémifontaine during the battle, confirmed for Jean-Marie the testimony provided by her sister. She recalls that, on October 1, when the initial American artillery shells began falling in front of her family's home, everyone in the house wondered fearfully what was happening, except for a few Germans that had been eating breakfast in the kitchen. They seemed to immediately understand that American troops had arrived because they left their food and quickly jumped out the kitchen window in an effort to return to their positions on high ground behind the Demangeon house. The family took cover behind the "water stone" in the kitchen, a term used to describe the large stone sink common to rural farmhouses throughout the Vosges Mountain region.[19]

Madame Balland recalled that a German soldier was "blown up" by an artillery shell in front of her family's house at 14 Rue du Calvaire. All that remained at the site of impact was a rifle and a single shoe. After the shock of the moment had passed and the family members realized what had happened, Monsieur Henri Balland quickly grabbed the rifle, which appeared to be brand new. The weapon today decorates the fireplace of a local house in the French countryside.[20]

Jean Alix lived at 38 Rue des Tilleuls in Frémifontaine during the autumn of 1944. On October 1, during the first American attack in the lower section of town, a shell from an American tank breached the facade of the family house, killing a German officer who was billeted in one of the bedrooms.[21]

Madame Lucie Begel recalled that, prior to the start of the battle, on September 29, young German soldiers dug trenches and set up a battery of several machine guns behind her family house. The weapons were directed toward the town hall. However, the Americans neutralized the troops during the night of October 1/2. At the time, it wasn't possible for Madame Begel to determine whether the German soldiers had been killed or taken prisoner, but she remembers having heard extensive yelling and gunfire in the darkness outside her bedroom window.[22]

During the course of a German artillery bombardment in the upper section of Frémifontaine, a shell punched through the chimney along the side of Madame Begel's house and into the fireplace but miraculously failed to explode. After the shelling ended, and as soon as some brief semblance of calm was restored, Lucie's father removed the dangerous projectile from the interior wall of the fireplace. He had fought the Germans during World War I and was subsequently somewhat knowledgeable regarding artillery. The shell had been damaged from the impact and seemed, in his opinion, not to contain an explosive charge because of its failure to detonate. After disassembly and upon closer inspection, he noticed that in place of an explosive charge the shell contained a piece of paper. Written in French with pencil were the words, "Sorry. This is all I can do for you." Lucie's father believed a French worker forced into factory labor had most certainly sabotaged the artillery shell.[23]

Madame Alice Delaite lived on a small farm at the time of the battle. As with most of the farmhouses in the Vosges area, the family house was equipped with a large sink located near the door and under the kitchen window. The sinks, as with Madame Pernot's home referenced earlier, were made of stone, often sandstone. The stone sink offered a place to take cover against artillery fire. An American soldier stationed near the house had recognized the shelter offered by this large stone. Alice recalled that during episodes of German harassing artillery fire in lower Frémifontaine, the soldier frequently rushed inside her house to take cover behind and under the sink until the barrage ceased.[24]

Georges Fortier lived at 18 Rue du Calvaire during the extensive fighting. In a written testimonial, he spoke of the circumstances that brought about the death of his neighbor, young Hubert Begelle, on September 29. Hearing the sounds of cannons getting closer to the village of Frémifontaine, Henri Balland and Lucien Guidat advised the villagers to dig trenches around their houses in which to hide from the cannon fire. The two had lived at La Raplye during World War I and subsequently developed this survival tactic. In response to this advice, villages expanded the concept and constructed temporary shelters near the top of the Creuse by digging long trenches and placing barrels in the ground, eventually covering them with dirt for added protection against shrapnel. According to Fortier, this excavating did not escape the observation of reconnaissance planes that flew over the village 48 hours prior to the onset of the battle and the area soon became a target. After a few initial artillery shells, a large bombardment fell on La Raplye at the very moment Hubert Begel was attempting to move his cattle out of the barn. Hubert was practically cut in half by the shrapnel from an artillery shell. Georges Fortier aided Hubert in his final minutes and gave him his last drink.[25]

In a written testimonial titled "The test of the buried barrel," Frémifontaine's anonymous resident author described the events that occurred on the same day Hubert Begel was killed. Marcel Balland wanted to test the level of protection offered by the buried barrels as the shelling began but while doing so an artillery shell landed approximately three yards from the barrel. Marcel was dazed by the impact of the explosion and he immediately began running in an effort to get into a basement with other villagers who had already taken shelter there. He appeared white with fear and was heard praying out loud for God to give him courage as he ran to safety.[26]

The fighting continued throughout October 1 and into the next day with very little sustained progress gained by advancing American troops. The regiment began to realize the German resistance had markedly intensified throughout the vicinity of this small village. An enemy patrol attacked F Company in strength with bazookas, machine pistols, rifles, and grenades as it advanced on Frémifontaine[27] while German artillery and mortar fire relentlessly fell on the company's troops entering the village.[28] The 3rd Battalion commanding officer who requested military police assistance with prisoners reported the soldiers were tougher than those encountered in previous weeks.[29] A German soldier captured from the 1316th Engineering Regiment, part of the German *Wehrmacht*, reported that the 2nd Company of the 221st Regiment arrived on October 1 and was digging in with 75 men, three machine guns, and 12 rockets.[30] The 221st Regiment was part of the *Sicherung* (security) division that functioned primarily in the rear areas during World War II. Its presence on the front lines suggests the Germans were accessing all available resources in the fight against the US 180th Infantry. German troops were hidden in houses and basements and their heavy weapons were hidden in the surrounding woods and orchards, a French farmer living near Autrey and an FFI member both confirmed, also reporting the presence of three 75-mm antitank guns shooting at the 180th Regiment from a cherry orchard.[31] Third Battalion faced numerous tree roadblocks, machine-gun nests, and enemy tanks as it approached. The German

216th Infantry Division was dug in and additional enemy troops from the division had been arriving from their previous positions in northern France. After taking several of them prisoner, regimental command reported, "They are younger and better than most PWs [prisoners of war] we have been getting lately."[32] As tough as it had been for the 180th Regiment, it was about to get far worse.

The 1st Battalion had been stubbornly fighting several miles to the north in the village of Autrey. The 157th Regiment eventually relieved the 1st Battalion on October 5, allowing the unit to advance south through the woods toward Frémifontaine and join the 2nd and 3rd Battalions already fighting a well-entrenched enemy force in the village. Three 1st Battalion patrols were sent ahead, one of which went in the direction of Hill 385.[33] This particular hill was located on the southern side of the Route D-50 and D-70 intersection. As the battalion approached the outskirts of town, it stopped at Hill 385 after encountering heavy German presence and subsequent intense fighting. C Company squads advanced 100 yards into the woods near the hill and engaged the enemy forces that had consolidated there in response to the 180th's advance.

The dirt and gravel forest road originally followed by 1st Battalion between Autrey and Frémifontaine to Hill 385 appeared to remain well-traveled as we retraced the unit's steps. Despite the passage of nearly seven decades, we found ourselves in the same spot where the battalion emerged from the woods into a clearing near the base of the hill, and where battalion soldiers formed a defensive line behind the edge of the tree line. American foxholes remain just inside the edge of the woods at this location. Jean-Marie had found various military and personal artifacts associated with the battle—including cartridges, ration cans, and weapon magazines—in some of these foxholes.

Weather conditions continued to work against the 180th on the morning that reconnaissance elements from C Company advanced toward Hill 385. "The rain which had been falling in sheets all morning diminished to a heavy drizzle, which, together with rolling fog, slowed the advance of our troops through the dense and dark woods."[34] As the small group of advanced elements from 1st Battalion approached the hill, they encountered more resistance than had been anticipated. Additional patrols were sent out ahead of C Company's main force in an attempt to determine the extent of German presence in the area. At 5:40 in the afternoon on October 4, the commanding officer communicated to regimental headquarters, "My two squads are back at Company C. There are more Germans than I have men in C Company. The fight first started on the right and then to the front and finally to the back of them. They fought their way out and finally got back."[35] The following day, elements of the 1st Battalion continued their efforts to take the hill, supported by tank destroyers, mortar, and artillery fire.[36] During the fighting at this infamous hill, known locally as Colline Pierre la Geline, an additional FFI group of approximately twenty-five men, was engaged alongside the Americans. The unit sustained significant losses during the fighting. Statements gathered locally have been unsuccessful in definitively determining the origin of this particular FFI group. But, following the combat, a woman who lived in Thaon, came to identify the body of her brother. It is therefore assumed the FFI unit may have originated from that nearby village.[37]

The railroad tracks near Frémifontaine supported powerful locomotives and served to bring in the large vehicles and many of the supplies necessary to support the German counterattack. Jean-Marie and local residents recall stories of the Germans using these tracks during the initial days of fighting in early October, which effectively resolved the mystery of the train sounds described in the original 180th regimental reports reviewed at the National Archives during my initial research. Radio transcripts indicate initial confusion around the presence of these tracks. At 9:00 p.m. on October 5, the Regimental S-3 asked:

> This sounds funny, but did anybody report something like the rumble of a train out there? Well, 3 Companies of ours report that they can hear sounds like the rumble of a train to the East of them on the track. They know that it can't be a train, but it sure sounds like one. They have a PW down there who says (and swears to it) that it is a secret weapon.[38]

Second Battalion reported to the S-3 that they could hear a train out in front of their position and the sound of many vehicles moving about. In addition, they conveyed having captured an enemy soldier who reported 150 Germans in his company and that they were ordered to initiate a counterattack at dark. Villagers recall the trains traveled primarily at night in response to Allied air superiority during the day. The Germans quickly unloaded the train cars and moved supplies and equipment directly to the front lines, including ten German tanks (a villager reported this to Jean-Marie several years prior to our visit). Two of the ten tanks were eventually destroyed during the fighting at Frémifontaine.[39]

Monsieur Charles Balland had been an agent of the Société Nationale des Chemins de Fer Français (SCNF, the French national railroad) during the war and he was present at the Frémifontaine train station during the arrival of German reinforcements at dawn on October 6. He recalled the ten tanks and infantry reinforcements were immediately directed toward the combat zone. Most of the tanks drove up the hill near the Frémifontaine mill. He remembers there was a great deal of yelling over the engine noise as the tanks were directed into battle.[40]

According to Jean-Marie, a small group of French fighters were killed near the top of Hill 385 at the site of the current memorial marker. After drinking together in the village, they had become somewhat intoxicated and subsequently decided to climb the hill to fight the Germans.

The Americans lost a tank destroyer while capturing Hill 385 after a German antitank shell struck the armored vehicle. Local accounts support the story and suggest the fatal shell came from the area near the current high-voltage electrical tower to the east of the village. The armored vehicle was attached to 1st Platoon, 1st Company, 645th Tank Destroyer Battalion, and had been assigned to the 45th Division during the attack on Frémifontaine. A soldier, who had been running communication wire near the site, witnessed the attack and described it to Jean-Marie on a return visit several years prior to our visit. The tank caught fire immediately after being hit. Local accounts in the village suggest one crewmember climbed out and two were burned alive inside the vehicle. One of those unfortunate soldiers is buried in the American Cemetery at Épinal.[41]

The lineman who witnessed the event was John B. Reeves. After joining the 180th Infantry Regiment as a 19-year-old replacement on

September 30, he served as a lineman with Headquarters Company. John wrote the following memory in a letter to Jean-Marie:

> One day one of our companies was on attack and Clarence Rimby and me were laying a line following them. We had a tank with us that day and the tank was hit by German fire setting the tank on fire. The tank was less than 100 feet from us. The hatch of the tank opened and one man got out but was on fire. The second man got to the hatch opening and fell back into the tank. With the exception of the one that was on fire the rest of the crew burned in the tank. We were told that there were three or four burned. Medics reached the burning man almost within 2 or 3 minutes and was working on him as we moved on. The smell of human flesh burning was terrible. Our advancement was repelled and we withdrew.[42]

Jerry Morgan was the A Company Commander for the 645th Tank Destroyer Battalion from Anzio, Italy, through to the German surrender and the end of the war in Europe. He participated in the fighting at Frémifontaine. In a written testimonial provided to Jean-Marie, Jerry described his memories of the fighting near Hill 385 and the destruction of this particular tank destroyer. Morgan explained that the loss of Howard Atterbury and his crew remained an intense memory and an extremely vivid image in his mind:

> A platoon of Tank Destroyers of A Company of the 645th Tank Destroyer Battalion was attached to the 180th Infantry of the 45th Division to support the advance elements of the attack. At about mid-morning on a day around the middle of October of 1944 the infantry had just entered the woods along a well-defined lane leading eastward from the point where the attack began. Atterbury's Tank Destroyer was slowly following the advance elements and as he entered an open space on the road, an 88mm German Antitank Gun, situated in a concealed position on the Tank Destroyer's right front on a small wooded hill at a distance of less than 100 yards, scored a hit in the thin side of the Tank Destroyer. The enemy round caused the ammunition inside the vehicle to explode and the fuel was ignited immediately. I was about 25 yards directly to the right of the Tank Destroyer and at the time saw no one escape from the vehicle. This is not to dispute John Reeves statement about one man getting out. Because of the flames coming out of the vehicle and the obvious fact that there was little chance that any of the crew [survived], I turned my attention to how to overcome the antitank gun. Small arms fire became quite heavy and before we could take any action against the antitank gun, they had withdrawn from their position very shortly after they had fired at the Tank Destroyer.[43]

A 45th Division engineer points to where a shell from a German Mark IV tank penetrated a Sherman medium tank and killed two of its crew while fighting in the La Salle, France area. (U.S. Signal Corps, 111-SC 231956/NARA)

Monsieur Pierre Grenott, a resident of Gugnécourt, recalled seeing several damaged armored vehicles around Frémifontaine immediately following the battle. Pierre was 18 years old at the time. He and others were collecting large stones that had been left around the fields when he witnessed certain events. He observed a French-built tank that had been disabled and abandoned and was able to identify it as a Hotchkiss H39. Although built by the French, the Germans captured and deployed them after defeating the French Army in 1940.[44] He also observed a tank that had been destroyed at the base of a clearing known as Rouge-Croix and identified it as a *Panzer* IV. As for the American tank that had been destroyed at the northern edge of the village, he identified it as an M10 Tank Destroyer. According to Pierre, this armored vehicle was struck on the right side just under the turret. A German antitank gun was also abandoned on the slope near the mill, but he has never been able to identify its model.[45]

As the 180th Infantry Regiment fought its way into the village, 2nd Battalion troops emerged from the wooded path near the site of the damaged tank destroyer at the foot of Hill 385. The group of soldiers moved directly past a wooden shed near the roadside that housed a natural spring and a watering trough; several of the troops paused to write words and statements on the horizontal support beams. The inscription on the east side of the beam reads, "ARMY 7th US 1944 USA TEXAS" and the inscription on the west side reads, "USA ARMY OCTOBR." Jean-Marie recently purchased and restored the shed in a successful effort to preserve the original support beams. As they reached the road several yards beyond the shed, the 2nd Battalion soldiers turned right and advanced into the village of Frémifontaine.

Following the path of the 2nd Battalion, we rode along with Jean-Marie up the narrow road into the center of town and stopped near the Frémifontaine church. As we walked up the street and approached the historic structure, church bells began to ring. Although the bell-tower roof had been replaced after sustaining severe damage from both German and American tank and artillery fire in October 1944, the bells are original to the structure.[46] The sounds heard as we approached the church were produced by the same bells the 180th Regiment troops heard in 1944. They are also the same bells that Private Chuck Shindler and his squad heard as they walked into a German ambush while patrolling the southern section of Frémifontaine on October 6. Shindler wrote in his journal:

> As we were crawling up the path the shells were hitting on both sides of us and tracer bullets were making a criss-cross pattern on the path in front of us. By the time I got to the top of the hill I was really exhausted lugging that BAR [Browning automatic rifle] and ammunition. When we started digging in, we took count of the noses left in the squad and found that we had lost five men of which one was killed, three other members of the platoon in the other two squads were also wounded in our attempt to get out of the trap. Now that I remember it, when we were entering the town, the church bell was tolling and I think that was some sort of a signal to the German soldiers laying in ambush for us.[47]

One of the company commanders reported on October 1 that a German tank to the left of his position continued to shell the church, as well as the nearby bridge.[48] The church had been a central point of interest during the multiday battle. The Germans had eventually blown up the bell-tower roof because of concerns American observers were using it to call in artillery strikes. The roof was subsequently replaced with a slightly different design and shape than the original. Prior to its destruction, the roof was round and domed in design. However, the church walls and the bell-tower structure remain in their original state. Extensive bullet and shrapnel damage remains clearly visible across the church and tower exterior walls. As found in most French villages, the local church is located on the high ground in the center of town. I stood in the road a few yards from the structure and quietly processed the history that had occurred on the site. The sound of the bells was the same tone heard by my father and his unit. The visions were becoming more vivid and increasingly rich as we progressed on our journey into my father's secret history. At times it felt as though I was moving between two realities in some form of time portal.

The small houses and homes surrounding the church, and all of the original structures throughout the village itself, were damaged to varying degrees during the battle that raged throughout October 1944. Some homeowners experienced direct structural damage to their property from artillery and small-arms fire, while others experienced complete loss of property and personal belongings. According to resident Madame Girault, in addition to the destruction inflicted upon the buildings and the homes, the Germans took jewelry, silverware, and other items of value they had pillaged throughout the years of occupation prior to the arrival of American forces in Frémifontaine. At some point in time after the war, Madame Girault was able to identify and reclaim her silverware from a village in the Alsace region of France. The only item missing was a dessert knife.[49] During the first few weeks of October, the Americans requisitioned furniture from villagers, in particular the dining-room furniture from the house of Marguerite Demangeon. They used it to equip their command post at the Bougigoutte farm. However, Marguerite acknowledged that the Americans returned all the furniture to their rightful owners near the end of October as they moved on and advanced toward Germany.[50]

Progressing with the journey, we entered a small house directly across the street from the Frémifontaine church and met with the owners, Monsieur Pierre Eymann and Madame Michele Eymann. Pierre shared with us a story that had been told by villagers on numerous occasions over the decades. In early October, two American soldiers took shelter inside a back bedroom of the house with a window facing the backyard. An American bazooka team was in place to the rear of the house 30 yards further up the hill. A German tank targeted the bazooka team—two local eyewitness accounts have confirmed this to Jean-Marie—but the shell missed the team and came in through the back window of the house, destroying the bedroom as well as the wall that separated it from the living room, killing the two American soldiers.

The Germans also utilized bazooka teams throughout the village, and within very close range of buildings and houses. Radio communication from a battalion commander to regimental headquarters indicated, "German bazookas are within range of the buildings. They are shooting them down one or two at a time. They are right in there close."[51] The 191st Tank Battalion assigned to the 180th Infantry Regiment lost several tanks to bazooka fire in and around Frémifontaine.[52]

The fighting from house to house became as personal and as traumatic for some of the villagers as it was for the soldiers. Madame Boheme-Anxionnat, who lived with her family at 19 Rue des Tilleuls during the fighting in Frémifontaine, recalled that a German soldier was killed in the kitchen of her family house without letting go of the grenade he was holding. She was struck by the youth of the soldier, who she estimated to be 17 or 18 years old, as he lay dead on the floor of her home.[53]

Madame Serriere-Laumont lived in Frémifontaine in the family home at 1 Rue de la Carriere. During the fighting in the lower half of the village, a German soldier had taken shelter in her family house and used his rifle to fire into the window of the nearby Boheme house, subsequently killing an American soldier who was in the process of shaving inside the kitchen window. His comrades fired in anger on the German sniper and killed him with a pistol shot from the area near the garage.[54]

A young woman who identified herself only by her initials, Mademoiselle C. D., watched as a German soldier, who had taken up a position behind the wall of a small garden near her house, was killed instantly during the fighting. She also described how a wounded American soldier was brought into the house by his comrades through the back window and was laid out on the bed. The soldier received first aid there in the house and was subsequently evacuated by medics. It was later necessary to scrub the mattress at the town fountain in an attempt to remove the bloodstains. At one point during the fighting, an American artillery shell entered C. D.'s family barn through the main door and created a breach through the back wall as it exploded. After the battle had finished and the fighting ceased, the breach was used to install an additional barn door.[55]

Georges Fortier, FFI member and Frémifontaine resident, described in a written testimonial several of his experiences during the fighting. Georges had planned to visit the orchard to pick some ripe apples during the afternoon of an early October day. The fighting had moved away from the village but continued to rage in the immediate outskirts and the surrounding forests. Around noon, Georges's friend and neighbor, identified only as M. J., came to him and asked for his assistance in replacing some roof tiles on his house—tiles that had been damaged and broken during some harassing artillery fire the prior night. Georges wanted to use the time to harvest the apples. But, after some hesitation, he agreed to assist M. J. with the roof repairs. At approximately 3:00 in the afternoon, while the two men were busy working on the roof, several artillery shells fell in the area. One fell behind the house, near the Anders's house, and then another fell further up in La Raplye orchards. At that point, Georges and M. J. abandoned their work and came down from the roof to take shelter. The next morning, Georges returned to the orchard to pick apples, as he had intended to do the prior afternoon. Upon arrival, he had the unpleasant surprise of finding that the second artillery shell they heard explode the day before had fallen on the same apple tree he had intended to climb. All that remained was the trunk and a couple of blackened branches. M. J.'s request for assistance had undoubtedly saved his life.[56]

John Reeves, of the 180th Regiment's Headquarters Company, wrote of his observation in the village of Frémifontaine:

> We were shelled some every day and sometimes the shelling was intense. One thing I remember about the shelling was how one man that lived in the village would climb on top of his house and replace the damaged tiles following a shelling. More than one time while he was on top of the house new shelling would begin and he would come down off the house like a squirrel. How he was not ever wounded or killed I do not know.[57]

Monsieur Robert Martin recalls witnessing an American tank destroyed along Departmental Route 70 at the north end of the village. A shell from a German antitank gun, set up in the Brules, struck the American armored vehicle, which Monsieur Martin described as an M4 Sherman. At the time, the fate of the crew was unknown to Robert. Prior to the attack on Frémifontaine, the Germans had established a command post in the Martin family farm, and he recalls the officers had laid out their maps on the kitchen table. A German field radio was placed in the barn and camouflaged for concealment. Only the radio antennas could be seen outside of the barn, which gave away the presence of the otherwise well-hidden device. The Germans quickly left the area when the initial American artillery shells began to fall shortly before the start of the 180th Regiment's offensive on Frémifontaine. Robert recalled his father, John Martin, and other occupants of the house continued to make FFI identification armbands in the bedroom despite the German presence in the area.[58]

The local villager, M. J., stated that during the fighting taking place in the woods, the Americans had set up an artillery battery along the Roseaux Stream on the north side of the Departmental Route 70 (D-70), which is the equivalent to a rural road. He described the vehicles as M7 Priests and stated that each had a 105-mm gun mounted on a tank chassis. When the battery was pulling out of the area, one of the artillery pieces was abandoned after becoming stuck in the mud. Monsieur Gravier later recovered the vehicle and used the engine to power his sawmill until1970.[59]

The M7 Priest was self-propelled artillery that weighed 50,000 pounds, could travel 26 mph on the road or 15 mph cross-country and was used as the primary artillery support for armored units during the war. The vehicle typically carried a crew of seven men: a commander, a driver, a gunner and four ammunition bearers. The Priest received its name from the British who believed the .50-caliber machine-gun ring resembled the pulpits in European churches.[60]

Our morning had passed quickly, and the sun had reached a point high in the sky. After a quick lunch at a small restaurant in the nearby town of Bruyères, less than two miles from Grandvillers, we returned to Frémifontaine. Our approach to the village this time was from the south, the path taken by the 180th Regiment's 3rd Battalion, which emerged from the woods and crossed the field from west to east toward the southern portion of the village. During the advance, one of the 191st Tank Battalion Shermans attached to the 3rd Battalion struck a landmine as it crossed the field in the direction of town and two other tanks became bogged down in the mud as they tried to pass it.[61] Jean-Marie shared local reports that the tanks were disabled but continued firing at the enemy that was well entrenched along the ridge above Frémifontaine. Consistent with their pattern, the Germans sent in several bazooka teams in an attempt to take out the damaged and disabled Shermans, but the tanks' machine gunners repeatedly silenced the teams before they could fire on the armored vehicles. The tanks remained stuck in the muddy field throughout the day and into the night. Lieutenant Cobbs from the tank battalion believed that the T2 tank recovery vehicles required to pull them out would also become stuck in the mud if he attempted to pull them out before daylight on the 2nd. The 3rd Battalion's commanding officer reported the Regimental S-3 officer, "It is slow going up here. We have only one tank and two Tank Destroyers left."[62] The Germans were positioned on the high ground across the road that separated the field and the ridge. They were spread across nearly 550 yards on the high ground and were dug in via foxholes.[63] Relentless pressure from advancing 2nd Battalion troops kept the enemy on its heels despite having the advantage of an elevated position. German troops were initially unable to retreat because the Americans were approaching from several sides.

Between the German line and the field lay a narrow road and a large barn on the field side of the road. Near the back of the barn, the entire apple harvest was being temporarily stored in burlap bags. The Germans had a machine gun set up behind the barn and concealed behind the bags of apples. One of the two Sherman tanks in the field noticed the position and in response fired a shell. It hit the intended target and destroyed the machine gun as well as all of the apples. The barn and its shell-damaged exterior walls remain today and serve as confirmation of the local story.[64]

Tank and artillery fire were often used to silence machine-gun nests in an attempt to preserve infantry lives. Gilbert Demangeon witnessed such an event and recalled that the American shell fired against a German machine gun set up in the corner of the shed near the Demongeon house did not immediately kill all of the Germans manning the gun. In fact, one of them, who had been seriously wounded in the stomach, was brought to shelter in the basement of the Boulay family house. He died early the next morning after having suffered deliriously throughout the night.[65]

Frémifontaine residents Lucien Guidat and Albert Thiriet had become accustomed to taking shelter in the basement of Monsieur Guidat's house. However, in between alerts, they watched, through the dining-room window, the events taking place in the lower section of Frémifontaine. On October 5, their presence in the window had been noticed by an American tank crew that was set up in the hollow near the house of Janine Begel. The two men had barely reached the cellar when a tank shell pulverized the window of the dining room as well as the buffet located inside. The top of the buffet was blown into the stairway leading down to the basement. Guidat and Thiriet assumed the tank crew mistook them for German observers. At that point, the basement was abandoned and they ran to the Fortier house to hide in the cellar and hope for safety.[66]

Monday October 2, 1944, was cold and foggy.[67] During the early morning hours, elements of the 3rd Battalion fought their way through the miserable weather to the high ground along the southern edge of Frémifontaine. Immediately, the Germans responded with three companies of infantry in a violent counterattack.[68] At 6:50 a.m., 3rd Battalion captured several veteran German soldiers, prompting the 3rd Battalion's commanding officer to request via radio, "Send MPs for 6–8 PWs. These babies seem to be the old type Germans—plenty tough."[69]

The fighting between American and German forces throughout the first few days of October involved small arms firefights, tank and mortar shelling. The intensity of conflict steadily increased with the gaining and losing of ground as the 180th advanced into the village and the surrounding forests. During the late afternoon hours of October 5, at approximately 4:00, 2nd Battalion relieved the 3rd Battalion and the four companies—E, F, G, and H—returned to the front lines and subsequently remained in close contact with the enemy throughout the evening and night.[70] At 8:50 p.m., after darkness had set in, F Company reported hearing a large number of vehicles in front of them, which aligned with the information shared by German prisoners indicating that they were ordered to initiate an attack at dark, but were already surrounded by Americans and couldn't move.[71] By 3:50 in the morning, all three 2nd Battalion companies reported hearing enemy vehicle movement in the darkness out in front of their positions. This was the beginning of what would become my father's most terrifying encounters in the dark forest of Frémifontaine, and the explanation for his lifelong silence and persistent nightmares.

CHAPTER 14

In the Dark Forest—The End

In order to understand my father's demeanor and his behavior, I needed to immerse myself in the history of this violent battle. Through meticulous research involving 180th Regiment military documents, review of letters and testimonials from local residents, and personal discussions with French villagers, I assembled a historically accurate description of the events that he experienced in early October 1944 as a 22-year-old soldier assigned to an H Company heavy-machine-gun squad. That research prepared me to wander across the actual ground where the combined experiences of the 180th and my father fused together. Frémifontaine was the final battle he experienced as a member of H Company. If there were answers to my ongoing questions related to his silent, introspective, and distant personality, they were to be found in this historic place nestled in the foothills of the Vosges Mountains.

Prior to this expedition, I hadn't been able to decisively determine the exact location on the battlefield where he had been fighting, although all of 2nd Battalion was concentrated in a small area of dense forest east of town throughout the multiday battle. According to the H Company morning reports, the company had been in brief regimental reserve in Nonseville and then, on October 5, was ordered to move up to Frémifontaine and relieve 3rd Battalion on the front lines. H Company marched across the countryside and positioned itself among the rifle companies. During the still dark early morning hours of October 6, 2nd Battalion noticed signs the Germans were fortifying their positions in the woods ahead of them. E Company heard vehicles moving around across the river and F Company reported enemy vehicle movement directly in front of its position.[1] C Company of the 191st Tank Battalion, attached to the 180th Infantry Regiment, received orders to prepare for an imminent German counterattack as evidenced by movement of enemy tanks. The American tanks repositioned themselves at a crossroads west of Frémifontaine.[2]

At sunrise on October 6, all three of the rifle companies, as well as the heavy weapons company of 2nd Battalion, attacked as the German assault began. E Company attacked in an easterly direction, F Company fought from its position, and G Company attacked to the southeast.[3] G Company jumped off at 7:30 a.m. under heavy German artillery fire.[4] At 9:35 a.m., Captain Murphy, Commanding Officer of M Company, reported to regimental headquarters, "About 25 Germans came in where we had an observation post behind F Company. We ran those off and they started into the woods toward Hill 385 and then everything broke loose over there."[5]

Shortly after the initial 2nd Battalion attack, at approximately 9:30 a.m., a large German force attacked along the entire 180th Regiment line, with a significant concentration on F Company's position. The Germans were supported by a large number of tanks and, at 1:50 p.m., these worked their way around and behind F Company.[6] Within a couple of hours, the Germans had infiltrated around both flanks of Company F. They drove a wedge between E and G Companies and infiltrated around G Company's right flank.[7] "The fighting that ensued was desperate. The enemy force included two battalions of the 111 Panzer Grenadiers [*sic*], together with five batteries of self-propelled artillery and ten tanks, backed by well-placed mortar fire, striking both swiftly and with great force."[8] In addition to the heavy armor and organized enemy groups, small groups of Germans were able to filter through the 2nd Battalion's forward positions under the cover of fog, dense forest, and miserable weather conditions that limited visibility.[9]

During the German counterattack, 2nd Battalion took the brunt of the assault, experienced the heaviest fighting, and sustained the most casualties. A farmhouse in a field to the southeast of Frémifontaine served as the F Company command post (CP) as the battle began.[10] American tanks from the 191st Tank Battalion were present in the vicinity of the farmhouse during the intense German counterattack near the Xeuty Farm. However, on the morning of October 6, the tanks were forced to withdraw along with F Company and its H Company attachments when the Germans infiltrated around and behind them from the northeast.[11] The weather and the terrain contributed to the difficulties of maneuvering American tanks in this area, which reduced the effectiveness of the armor and in turn affected the balance of power. German forces were well entrenched in the region following many weeks of preparation. Machine guns, mortars, bazookas and armor were dug in and concealed, providing a significant advantage over the approaching US soldiers during the initial days of the battle. American infantry was without the desired level of tank support in response to the heavy vehicles frequently becoming bogged down by mud and unstable ground as they attempted to cross open fields saturated by rain and navigate narrow unfamiliar paths in an effort to avoid heavily mined roads. The American tank battalion commander later wrote, "Continued rainfall had rendered the surrounding territory unfit for cross country maneuver. In addition, much of the action took place in densely wooded areas, where the employment of tanks was extremely dangerous. The roads, particularly through the woods, were little better than good trails."[12] When German tanks arrived, they were accurately directed across the local terrain by veteran troops familiar with the area and the conditions.

Local French resistance members witnessed the events after having spent the night of October 5/6 with the Americans at the Xeuty Farm. Realizing the lack of supplies, such as warm clothing and blankets, the leader of a group consisting of approximately thirty men from the Frémifontaine #42 resistance group made the decision to send a detachment to the village in an effort to obtain supplies, as well as a few bottles of wine. The selected group included Robert Martin, Marcel Demangeon, and Armand Pierrat. They departed in the morning and followed a path that allowed them to observe strong concentrations of German infantry hidden in the hollowed path leading from the village, to the Xeuty Farm, and to the intersection of La Rouge-Croix, the site of the current 45th Infantry memorial. They also observed that the

Americans held the intersection of Vache Lallemand (Hill #421) and the surrounding area. Several American tanks had been hidden in the low woods with their main guns aimed in the direction of Rouge-Croix and Chaudpoil. The three resistance fighters were intrigued by the presence of a white rope-like marker strung from tree to tree inside the woods parallel to the edge of the forest. The marker was used to show the line at which a soldier would be at risk of being seen and subsequently attract enemy fire. The unleashing of the German counterattack a few hours later prevented the men from rejoining the Americans at the Xeuty Farm.[13]

Jean-Marie's father-in-law was attached to F Company when it was positioned around the Xeuty farmhouse. The company commander, Captain Richard Buchanan, was using the farmhouse as the company CP when it began taking fire from multiple directions on the morning of October 6. According to eyewitness accounts shared with Jean-Marie over the years, German infantry and tanks appeared from around the bend in the road to the west of the farmhouse, just before the Germans began attacking through the dense woods on the east side of the structure. The American CP quickly evacuated as the German tanks fired on the farmhouse.

George Fisher's historical account of the 180th Regiment supports Jean-Marie's information:

> In the Company F sector at about 11:30 am the main attack struck around the Company Command post located in a house at the edge of the woods east of Frémifontaine. The German tanks moved around both sides of the farmhouse, firing as they advanced. They then began penetrating up through the woods towards the house.[14]

At 2:14 p.m., 2nd Battalion companies reported that several enemy tanks and infantry were breaking through their lines and radioed the situation to regimental headquarters. Six enemy tanks and scores of German infantrymen had overrun the mortar positions behind F Company and the situation became critical. In a radio report to regimental command, a 2nd Battalion officer stated, "This thing is getting serious … six tanks are in behind F Company now … the Krauts have broken through them … condition red."[15] The Americans took up positions just inside the edge of the woods to the east of the farmhouse. They were facing in the direction of the Germans, who were dug in 100 yards ahead in the dense pine forest. By 3:45 p.m., both E and G Companies were completely surrounded and cut off. There were more than six German tanks on their left flank and additional tanks between E and F Companies.[16] By 3:55 p.m., F Company was completely surrounded by German tanks and 200 enemy infantry.[17] The attack intensified as evening approached and the only road between 2nd Battalion and its headquarters in Frémifontaine was effectively cut off.[18]

Sergeant Troy Hottinger was an infantry soldier with H Company, the heavy weapons unit for 2nd Battalion. He was assigned to F Company on the morning of the German attack at the farmhouse. Captain Buchanan ordered his F Company men to pull back and readjust their lines, extending to several hundred yards in an attempt to protect their flanks. As the company withdrew, Sergeant Hottinger fired on the enemy from an exposed position. Hottinger radioed for artillery support as tanks bore down on him. "They are on me, bring fire down on me." American field-artillery shells landed in Sergeant Hottinger's immediate location, as he requested and some fell within 15 yards of him. "Despite the heavy shelling, one German tank rolled up sufficiently close to fire its cannon directly at the brave sergeant, and when the smoke cleared away from the explosion, he was dead."[19] Both F and E Companies quickly dug in along a line they had formed in the forest to the east of the farmhouse. The fighting was so heavy in this location that American machine gunners were holding up the bodies of their fallen comrades for protection against German bullets.[20] Fighting near Sergeant Hottinger during this battle was Staff Sergeant George Tipton of F Company. With his submachine gun, he fought against German tank, artillery, bazooka, and rifle fire at close range. German attack teams attempted to infiltrate around his position, throwing hand grenades at him as they approached. Although he was able to hold his position through seven hours of this intense fighting, the large numbers of attacking Germans eventually overtook his position and killed him.[21]

H Company's 1st Section of 1st Platoon was actively supporting G Company, while the 2nd Section of 1st Platoon was actively supporting F Company. H Company reported all of 2nd Battalion's companies along with their attachments were completely surrounded by enemy forces and that F Company was attempting to fight its way back through enemy lines, while E and G Companies were attempting to fight their way back to the H Company 81-mm mortar positions that were supporting the entire battalion.[22]

Major General W. "Birdie" Eagles, the 45th Division Commander, ordered unlimited artillery support of 2nd Battalion, despite a shortage of ammunition and daily quotas. "An Army Munitions Officer reminded General Eagles that his artillery had used a month's quota of ammunition during the morning of the 6th. General Eagles replied, 'To hell with the quota; my boys are dying up there and they are going to have artillery, if we use a year's quota.'"[23] The artillery and mortar shells fell furiously from the sky as multiple batteries fired toward the area.

A soldier with M Company, the heavy weapons company of the 180th's 3rd Battalion, and the equivalent to my father's company with the 2nd Battalion, was functioning as a forward observer with the 171st Field Artillery Battalion. In a letter written after the war, he described what it felt like to be on the front lines with the infantry when artillery shells were falling in significant number:

> I needed all the fire power I could get as quickly as possible, I called for "Fire for Effect" by radio communication. It is hard to fathom the fire power of all these battalions of artillery firing all at once; you literally unleash several tons of TNT and steel within 15 or 20 minutes. The shells came down furiously from the clear sky. Most awesome was the lightning like bursts of energy emanating from large caliber shells bursting in the air, on the ground and on the trees with bright orange explosions draped with irregular black smoke rings rising into the clear sky. This was followed immediately by flashing shock waves with a ground shaking, deafening crack of thunder that seemed to puff my cheeks as the blast pushed past me and vibrated the air with ear-popping furor. A better description might be explained as receiving over 400 bolts of lightning within 100 yards of your position. The screaming shells with their indelible whistling, whirring sound had become familiar to mortar and artillery forward observers close to the point of impact. I felt tiny and helpless before such awesome power. The sounds came in like fast freight trains over your head from all directions and quadrants, culminating in pinpoint accuracy right in front of your forward position. Imagine a football field grandstand and you are at the front and center of it with all this fire power falling in front of you. You literally destroy everything in the path of these barrages. The carnage of tree bark being ripped from the trees, leaving

> skeletons of upright splintered wood, it left you in a state of mourning for the beautiful trees, that once stood so magnificently a few moments ago.[24]

A German prisoner reported that two battalions were involved in the attack on the 2nd Battalion side of the river and that an estimated 600 enemy troops were involved overall.[25] Jean-Marie recounted statements made by several members of the French resistance group #42 in Frémifontaine who indicated the resistance was placed under the command of *Adjudant* Max Delaite from October 3 through the end of fighting in the village. They had done their best to assist the American soldiers, who had begun to gain a presence and a foothold in the surrounding forests. With three of their number trapped in the village after going there to obtain supplies on the morning of October 6, Max Delaite, Georges Fortier, Marcel Jeandel, Jean Lemasson, and Jean Miette were encircled at Xeuty Farm along with the 2nd Battalion troops. Late in the afternoon, recognizing the severity of the situation, American officers engaged in the battle advised the five resistance fighters to return to the village while they were able, in order to avoid capture with weapons in their hands. After a quick discussion, the group decided to hide their weapons, separate, and return to the village.

Georges and Marcel were surprised by a machine-gun crew, which opened fire on them. Marcel fired a long burst in the direction of machine-gun nest at a distance of approximately 45 yards. The late-day shadows assisted in concealing their presence in front of the German position. Miraculously, neither man was injured. Georges and Marcel were able to break free of the German encirclement and return to the village and their own homes.[26] While following a different route, Max and Jean were captured by the Germans on a hill near the Frémifontaine mill. As for Jean Miette, he was surprised by a German patrol and subsequently taken prisoner. All three were held at the Moulin de Frémifontaine (government office), before being taken under a large escort to Saint-Dié and were eventually deported. It was later learned Jean Miette had been shot and killed during an escape attempt from the Blechhammer concentration camp in Poland on January 26, 1945; Jean Lemasson disappeared under unknown circumstances at Buchenwald on March 13, 1945; Max Delaite was liberated from Dachau on April 29,

1945, by soldiers of the 157th Regiment, 45th Infantry Division.[27] It is ironic that Delaite was fighting with elements of the 45th Division when he was captured in France, and was eventually liberated six months later in Germany by other units of the division.

Georges Fortier recalled that, on the morning of October 6, the Americans were in defensive positions on Xeuty Farm and in the forest at the edge of the field. Several patrols were organized earlier on October 4 and 5, guided by local resistance members who had been armed with M1 rifles by the Americans. These patrols ventured into the woods at night via jeeps, which Fortier found to be somewhat strange. Georges believed the practice was unsuccessful in determining the locations or intentions of the infiltrating Germans because of the noise made by the vehicles. Knowing the location of enemy positions was critically important in surviving the bullets and mortars coming from all directions. Georges shared that, at the strongest part of the German counterattack, the Americans went so far as to build ramparts using the dead bodies of their comrades to protect themselves from German bullets, a description shared with me by Jean-Marie as well. An American machine gunner, with half his hand torn off, sought out first aid and, after receiving sulfa and a bandage, returned to operate his machine gun. Facing the gravity of the situation and the uncertainty of the outcome, the Americans were no longer concerning themselves with the assistance of the resistance fighters, thus giving them the option to return to the village.

Georges Fortier later described further to Jean-Marie his experience of escaping from the Xeuty Farm on October 6. After successfully avoiding the German machine gun, Georges and Marcel hid in a dense section of pine trees and waited there without movement until night had fallen. The two men very quickly realized the precariousness of their situation. Hearing the voices of German soldiers all around them, they anguished in the darkness without knowing what to do next as the voices seemed to surround them. Suddenly, a very large artillery piece in the Destord–Padoux area began to open fire at regular intervals. Georges and Marcel heard the firing of the gun very clearly, the shell overhead, and its explosion just past them in the river valley of the Mortagne. Georges noticed, with each artillery explosion, a brief, subtle glow illuminated the surrounding terrain just enough that the two men were able to determine how far to step in the dark between firings in order to work their way toward the village and away from the German lines. They moved in hopscotch fashion through the dark with each brief flash. It was later determined the Americans had used an M1 "Long Tom" artillery piece that fired 155-mm diameter shells to destroy the German command post. This powerful weapon was designed to destroy enemy trench positions and fortifications. It could fire a shell weighing approximately one hundred pounds as far as 14 miles. One of these unexploded shells was discovered in 2001 while workers were performing road paving near Frémifontaine and was subsequently taken into the custody of the bomb-squad section of the civil protection.[28]

Monsieur Delaite, brigadier of the police at Épinal, ex-sergeant of the 8th Regiment, and leader of the 30th FFI during the war, was born August 8, 1919, in Frémifontaine, and lived his entire life as a resident of the small village. In a written attestation dated September 18, 1946, he certified he was a member of the French resistance on a patrol with units of the 180th Infantry Regiment at Xeuty territory of Frémifontaine. He was fighting alongside his comrade, Sergeant Jean Lemasson, during the liberation of Frémifontaine in the first days of October 1944. Additional members of his group at that time included Jean Miette, Georges Fortier, and Marcel Jeandel. After the German attack, they received the order to fall back. But in the fighting, he, Marcel, and Miette were captured by the Germans. They were taken to the Jacquot Mill in Frémifontaine and were subsequently held there for three days. The tight German surveillance made it impossible for them to escape. The mill had to be evacuated after several days and, at 4:00 in the afternoon on October 8, they were taken to the Martraire sawmill at the dwelling of Monsieur Paul Barad in an area called Mossoux. After spending the night at the Barad house, the Germans took them to the police station at Saint-Dié, where they underwent interrogation by the Gestapo.[29]

F Company had been completely surrounded during this battle; the Germans took 80 prisoners, including the H Company machine-gun squads attached to F Company. This large number contributed to Jean-Marie's belief that virtually all of F Company had been captured—only a few had managed to escape and link up with E and G Companies. The fact that my father had not been a prisoner of war suggests he had not been assigned to F Company during this intense battle, and more likely was supporting G or E Companies. G Company was also surrounded during this phase of the German attack. However, Captain Benjamin Blackmer, G Company commander, was able to get his men out only through intense close-contact fighting through the dense forest and swamps. If my father and his heavy-machine-gun squad were assigned to support G Company, he would have been fighting for his life.

At approximately the same time F Company was ordered to withdraw in the afternoon of October 6, Captain Blackmer and G Company were ordered to withdraw some 900 yards to their original positions from which they had jumped off that morning. The Germans had built up a very strong line behind G Company, including a heavy-machine-gun position, and effectively blocked the company's withdrawal. Captain Blackmer crawled and ran up to the machine-gun nest and fired his M1 rifle, killing three members of the crew. He crawled to within thirty feet of another German machine-gun nest and destroyed it by throwing a hand grenade at the fire team. When Blackmer and G Company reached their original jump-off point, they found the Germans had surrounded them again and were using the original foxholes dug by the company. Blackmer and his men attacked the foxholes and, after fierce and stubborn fighting, killed 40 Germans.[30] G Company was eventually able to fight its way to E Company positions to the north and the two companies joined their lines. Despite this reinforcement, German forces continued to place great pressure on the Americans. "Both Companies E & G were surrounded by the hordes of Germans that had infiltrated through. At 5:45 p.m. the Germans drove a wedge into the center of Company E's positions with a fierce attack, which forced Company E to move toward the lines of Company G."[31] The companies continued to fight and make their way through the darkening forest in an attempt to withdraw to the west and make contact with the 179th Regiment on the right and the 180th's 3rd Battalion on the left.[32] Captain Blackmer received the order to withdraw at 7:00 in the evening. However, the Germans blocked all escape routes. "Besides having cut off the road to the left of Companies E & G, the Germans had, by that time, set-up on both flanks of the companies and were deep into the woods behind them."[33] Captain Blackmer later received the Distinguished Service Cross for his "extraordinary heroism" associated with his actions during the horrific fighting on October 6. His actions played a significant role in preventing the capture and/or demise of his company,[34] including, potentially, my father.

At some point during the intense fighting, Captain Buchanan of F Company was noted to be missing. Many months after the battle, it was learned he had been liberated from a German prisoner of war camp, alive and well.[35] It is assumed he was captured along with the majority of F Company in the dark forest outside of Frémifontaine.

As the fighting intensified during the afternoon of October 6, the Americans set up a battery at the double curve near the Pourcher family house. Two armored vehicles fired almost continually until the middle of the night to stave off the German counterattack. These vehicles left their positions the following dawn; the only remaining items were two piles of shell casings more than a yard high. According to witnesses, each armored vehicle was armed with a machine gun and a 37-mm cannon. One battery of 81-mm mortars was set up in the yard of the Rochet house and it also sent fire in the direction of the German counterattack.[36]

Throughout the night and into the dark early morning hours of October 7, all elements of 2nd Battalion, including Headquarters Company, were engaged with the Germans in hand-to-hand combat as the battalion continued to improve upon its defensive positions. Jean-Marie stated that, following the intense battle, bodies were so numerous that they were piled up along the side of the road like firewood (both American and German).

Sergeant Joseph Margotta, who I had interviewed at his home in Sleepy Hollow, New York, several years before, when I was unaware of my father's involvement in this battle, was a member of H Company's 1st Platoon. During our discussion, he shared with me that the Germans captured him, along with the entire company to which he was attached at the time, during a daylight attack near a small French village during the first week of October. His description of the scene was horrific

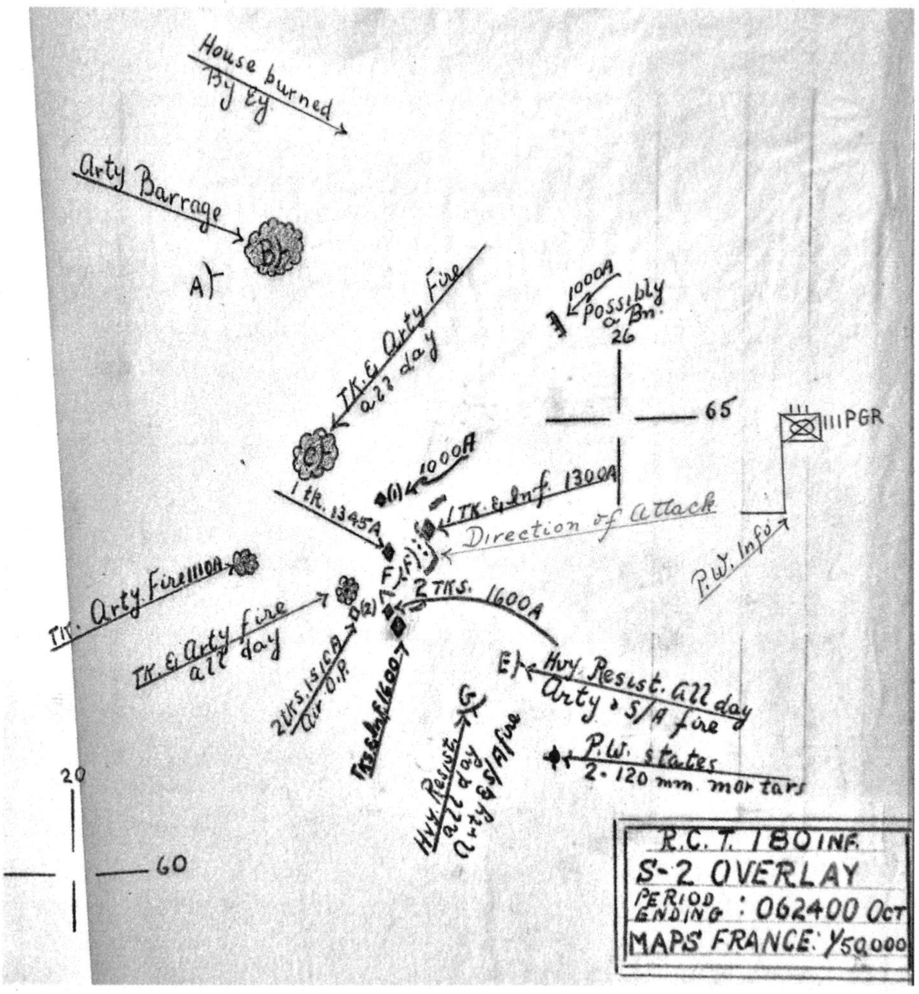

Sketch depicting the fighting on the morning of October 6, 1944. Enemy tanks moved in from all directions and surrounded 2nd Battalion. F Company is shown in the center of the map, E and G Companies to its south and slightly forward. The map shows where enemy tanks and infantry split F and E Companies and encircled all three units. Map overlay located in the 45th Infantry Report of Operations, Headquarters, 180th Infantry Regiment, S-2 Journal, October 1944. (Courtesy of the 45th Infantry Division Museum archives. Photo taken by Michael Reyka on location in Oklahoma City, Oklahoma)

and involved hand-to-hand fighting in dense, foggy, and dark woods. Although he did not recall the name of the village, there is little doubt

Joseph Margotta of H Company was assigned to F Company during this fighting in Frémifontaine. It corresponds with his stated date of capture and his assertion the entire company was captured with him. After many decades, he remained angry with the captain that commanded his unit, stating, "We kept telling him that we shouldn't be there." The captain he referred to was most likely Captain Buchanan. Sergeant Margotta told me the Germans surrounded them after a fierce battle and subsequently captured the company by working their way around both flanks and surrounding the entire unit with infantry and tanks. He recalled, "It was pretty horrible. My number 2 man got blown apart by a grenade."[37] The H Company morning reports reflect intense fighting on these dates that included squads from the heavy weapons company:

> October 6:
>
> Biggest enemy artillery barrage since Anzio. Began at 10:00 AM and is still going on intermittently at about 5 minute intervals.[38]
>
> October 7:
>
> All companies with attachments completely surrounded by enemy. F Company had to come back through enemy lines. E & G were ordered to fight way back to the 81mm mortar positions which were in general support of the Battalion. 3rd Bn moved up from reserve and thrown in at E & G Company sector. Battalion reorganized in Fremifontaine [*sic*] and E & G Companies back on the line with attachments.[39]

The H Company morning report mentions E and G Companies reorganizing and returning to the lines with their H Company attachments, but there is no reference to F Company after reports that all companies had been surrounded. In addition, the same report indicates that nine H Company enlisted men were reported missing in action (MIA) on October 6. This is a large single-day number of MIA for a heavy weapons company. The number was likely larger than what was reported, given that Sergeant Margotta is not included in the initial list of names. The Headquarters Company of 2nd Battalion's morning report recorded similar events. Heavy mortar, tank, and artillery shelling began at 9:00 in the morning, resulting in seven direct hits on the 2nd Battalion CP. All three rifle companies were completely surrounded and cut off, along with three communications wire men attached to G Company. The report states, "The Battalion caught hell today … the situation looks bad."[40]

News of the initial German counterattack on October 6, followed by the withdrawal of the Americans from several positions held earlier, quickly spread throughout the village. A German patrol, having been spotted on the morning of the 7th near the Calvaire (the intersection where the large stone cross is located), served to confirm the fears of the villagers. To see the German occupiers come back in force was very unsettling. When villagers witnessed this turn of events, they quickly discarded all of the supplies, arms, ammunition and other items they had picked up, in fear of retribution from the Germans. The items were buried in yards or thrown down shallow wells in order to hide them.[41]

The German counterattack continued all night on October 6 and throughout the day and night of October 7. It wasn't until several days later that the Americans took to the offensive. H Company was in defensive positions in Frémifontaine on the 8th. The company morning reports summarize the unit's activity for the previous 24 hours. The report for October 7 indicates that 1st Section of 1st Platoon was supporting G Company and that 2nd Section of 1st Platoon was assigned to an assault-team platoon that moved out at 4:45 a.m. In addition, the October 8 report indicates that 1st Section remained with G Company and that 2nd Section of 1st Platoon was assigned to F Company.[42] H Company had two platoons of Browning water-cooled heavy machine guns. The morning report confirms 1st Platoon was split between rifle companies during this intense battle. Previous research suggests my father had been a member of 1st Platoon and records indicate he was present during this fighting in and around Frémifontaine.

Madame Lucienne Girault recalled events that occurred at the Frémifontaine mill during the intense fighting. The occupants of the mill were evacuated on October 10 and moved in the direction of Saint-Dié by way of Mortagne and Les Rouges Eaux. She assumed that many were prisoners.[43] Madame Denise Durant was living in upper Frémifontaine on a tiny farmette, owned by Pierre Heymann. Her husband was being held prisoner in Germany at the time. She recalled that the Americans had placed a battery of several mortars along the road situated up against the mound across from the house owned by Roland Demangeon. The mortars were directed toward the Germans positioned in the woods opposite the farm. She noted that, several days prior, the Germans had also placed mortars in the same location but pointed in the opposite direction—toward the Americans. She also recalled seeing a small cannon, manned by two Americans, in a hollow, and dug in at the top of a trench behind the house. Three additional soldiers were staying in the house nearby. The Germans apparently spotted the gun because an enemy tank emerged from the woods and fired a shell in the direction of the cannon. The shell missed its mark, went through a window, and exploded within the house, destroying everything inside. Madame Durant later watched as their comrades took the bodies of three terribly mutilated Americans, wrapped in sheets and covered in bloody blankets, out of the house.[44]

A girl in the village recalled that very young German soldiers were using the trenches along the orchards toward Chaudpoil to fall back into when shelling or firefights occurred. She could clearly hear what she believed to be their teeth chattering in fear. For several days, trailers that were hooked up to jeeps and 4×4 Dodge trucks were bringing the bodies of dead American soldiers out of the woods. The bodies were covered with blankets and tied onto the trailers. Heads, arms and legs were sometimes hanging out and you could see traces of blood flowing. The sight of a dead body with half its head missing had an emotionally traumatic effect on a young girl named Mademoiselle Fortier.[45]

My daughter, a young woman similar in age to the French girl who witnessed these horrors, listened to the graphic stories in deep contemplation. As Tara listened to the English translation of these personal stories, her face quietly showed concern, disbelief, and subtle despair in response to the sights and experiences that became painful lasting memories for the youth of this small village. Now, on October 10, we were here in this same spot, many years after my father had experienced this horrifying encounter.

As we walked into the dark pine forest at the site of the brutal fighting where E, F, G, and H Companies had been surrounded, Jean-Marie suggested the entire forest had been cleared and replanted at some point following the fighting that occurred during October 1944. However, numerous foxholes and artillery shell craters remain as evidence to the violence. Other than occasional loggers and Jean-Marie's personal excavations, no one visits these remote wooded areas. There has therefore been no compelling reason to designate the time or energy to fill in the foxholes. It was dense, old growth forest at the time of the battle and, although the current tree trunks are not quite as large in diameter as the original tall pine trees, the forest remains dark and concerning. The rain and fog of 1944, however, were missing during our visit, which at least improved the ability to navigate.

I stood in the dim light and imagined what it would have been like to be here in these woods during the fighting, including the sound of rifle fire, artillery, grenades, and the sight of German tanks approaching. I stepped down into one of the remaining 2nd Battalion foxholes that had been dug nearly seventy years before. Based upon the map overlay and the general location of the foxhole, it most certainly belonged to F Company. I crouched down in the direction of the enemy attack, looked around the forest at other nearby foxholes and recalled the description of one soldier who commented after the battle, "The tree bursts from German mortar and artillery fire were terrific. Many of the bravest men of our Second Battalion fell in the deep dark woods southeast of Frémifontaine."[46] I felt the damp air on my face and imagined the smell of gunpowder. I envisioned the soldiers and their faces in the foggy darkness, the colors of their uniforms, the weapons and the debris scattered around the forest. I could visualize everything. This was the location of the battle—I was standing on the same ground during the same October week many decades after the intense fighting had occurred. This must have been the most frightening experience in my father's life to that point—and most likely beyond. The emotional impact of this insight encompassed my thoughts and I simultaneously felt both despair and comfort in response to being in this place and experiencing his history. It was an odd and perplexing mixture of emotions. Yet, I still didn't know exactly what happened to him

I knew my father had been in these woods and that he spent time in these foxholes. I know for a fact he had been assigned to H Company of 2nd Battalion and I know from his medical records that he had been surrounded by enemy forces multiple times during the fighting in this region. He somehow evaded capture by the Germans, which means he and his machine gun squad were probably not attached to F Company. G Company was able to avoid capture and eventually made it out of the German trap by fighting its way back through its own lines. So, it is likely he was attached to either G or E Companies during October 6 and 7.

Despite extensive efforts, I had been unsuccessful in locating any information or official records that conclusively identified which rifle company my father had been attached to during this extended fierce battle. The original unit rosters had been long lost, allegedly discarded due to lack of storage space and the belief they offered no value to future researchers. I therefore had been unable to determine whether he was a member of 1st Platoon or 2nd Platoon or to which section he had been assigned. In an effort to address the unanswered question related to his exact position on the battlefield, I decided to approach the mystery through assessment of the information known to me, and the application of objective deductive reasoning to determine the exact rifle company to which he was assigned. I knew the exact positions of E, F, and G Companies during the battle based upon military maps and official radio transcripts.

Heavy weapons companies such as H Company had a specific structure during World War II. Each company included two .30-caliber heavy machine-gun platoons. Each platoon included two sections and each section included two squads, each of which contained one machine gun. In total, H Company had eight heavy-machine-gun teams when operating at its full strength (full roster of men and equipment). Sergeant Arthur Heeringa, the soldier sitting next to my father on the back of the tank destroyer in Bourg, was a member of H Company's 1st Platoon—this has been confirmed through a 1st Platoon photograph taken in the spring of 1945.

Since squads had a tendency to stay close together as they traveled and fought, I can speculate my father was a member of H Company's 1st Platoon. Joseph Margotta had been a member of H Company's 1st Platoon and responsible for two machine-gun squads when he was

1st Platoon, H Company, spring 1945. (Courtesy of the 45th Infantry Division Museum)

captured along with the majority of a rifle company during the fighting in Frémifontaine—this has been confirmed through his personal statements. Numerous resources indicate that F Company had been surrounded and decimated during this battle, while E and G Companies fought their way out of the perilous situation after sustaining heavy casualties. The official H Company morning reports for this period indicate 2nd Section of 1st Platoon was assigned to F Company during the fighting on October 6 and 7 at Frémifontaine. Therefore, I can reasonably speculate that Sergeant Margotta had been a member of the 2nd Section of 1st Platoon and assigned to F Company, since he and the majority of F Company were captured. The H Company morning reports also indicate that 1st Section of 1st Platoon had been assigned to G Company on the dates the fighting occurred in these woods. Since my father and Sergeant

Heeringa were members of 1st Platoon, they were likely affiliated with 1st Section and assigned to G Company during this fighting. In addition to the morning report, the fact that they had not been captured by the enemy during this battle supports my theory regarding assignment to 1st Section. The map overlay for October 6, drawn by the S-2 (intelligence and security) officer, shows not only the approach of the enemy tanks and infantry during the attack, but also the exact positions of E, F, and G Companies during the fighting on October 6 and 7. If my father had been manning a heavy machine gun in support of G Company on these dates, his specific location on the battlefield is known—slightly more than a mile southeast of F Company and among a grouping of foxholes within a radius of approximately 100 yards. I decided to press on and test the limits of my deductive reasoning in an effort to find the answers I felt were now within my reach.

Each section of a heavy-machine-gun platoon includes two Browning water-cooled machine-gun squads when operating at full capacity. Since official H Company records confirm 1st Section of 1st Platoon had been assigned to G Company, there had been at least one heavy-machine-gun nest, or foxhole, in G Company's immediate vicinity on October 6 and 7. The terrain occupied by 2nd Battalion on the outskirts of Frémifontaine between October 6 and 8 spanned approximately a mile and a half between the flanks of its defensive line. Through decades of archeological exploration across this ground, Jean-Marie has collected countless artifacts from numerous foxholes and has been able to identify those used by machine guns because of the large number of .30-caliber cartridge casings found in the holes (only machine guns could have produced hundreds of spent cartridge casings piled up in one small foxhole). In several of those foxholes, he also found empty ammunition boxes, lids from boxes, sections of cloth machine-gun ammunition belts, and several partially fired belts. The specific foxholes he identified were few in number and spaced far apart across the 2nd Battalion's battlefield, also suggesting they were used by machine-gun squads and not riflemen.

I explained to Jean-Marie that my father had likely fought with G Company during the battle southeast of the Xeuty farmhouse. I shared my reasoning and referenced the original S-2 map overlay for October 6 in an effort to gain additional insight regarding his presence during the battle. Jean-Marie's familiarity with the battlefield around Frémifontaine, and his personal knowledge of specific archeological sites, brought an immediate response. Jean-Marie believed he knew the location of my father's foxhole. As I suspected, it was slightly more than a mile from where I stood in the F Company foxholes. Second Battalion had been spread out on a slightly arched line that ran southeast from the farmhouse across several hills overlooking the Mortagne valley, with F Company at the northwest end, E Company in the middle and G Company at the southeast end covering the right flank of the line. The 179th Regiment was located on G Company's right flank to the southwest.

Jean-Marie's assertion that he knew the location of my father's foxhole was linked to an event that occurred 20 years before our visit to France. At that time, he located and excavated a specific foxhole in G Company's sector. The site was positioned on the crest of a hill facing east in the direction of the Mortagne valley and the location of German troops. During the excavation, Jean-Marie found several hundred spent .30-caliber cartridges on the parapet and in the bottom of this particular foxhole, before he stopped counting and collecting the artifacts. In addition, he found ammunition cans and their lids. This was the only foxhole in the G Company sector of October 6 that contained machine-gun-related items. The 1st Section of 1st Platoon had a maximum of two machine-gun squads, but likely deployed only one during this battle because of casualties and reduced resources associated with the relentless fighting throughout the prior weeks. Based upon a logical assessment of the facts, Jean-Marie was convinced he knew the exact location of my father's foxhole and his final combat experience while assigned to H Company. This small section of forest in the foothills of the Vosges Mountains was the pinnacle of the events that had produced my father's nightmares, and likely contributed to the quiet, introspective personality, emotional distance and demeanor I experienced throughout my time with him.

★★★

When 2nd Battalion initially liberated Frémifontaine on October 2, the attack drove a wedge between some of the German regiments and pushed them back to several small hills to the west along the Mortagne River. While enemy forces continued to defend Hill 385, additional German infantry and armor prepared for a counterattack. After receiving reinforcements on October 5, ten Mark IV tanks and four enemy infantry battalions assembled in the Mortagne valley, three-quarters of a mile east of Frémifontaine. The Germans planned to retake several strategic hills behind my father's position and, in the process, isolate and destroy the 180th Regiment.[47] Slightly before 4:00 a.m. on the 6th, E, F, and G Companies heard a great deal of enemy vehicles moving around in front of their positions. Expecting an imminent attack, G Company initiated a preemptive assault in a southeasterly direction. Shortly thereafter, the company began receiving fire from several German machine guns on their right flank.[48] At 9:00 a.m., the German counterattack began in strength and approached G Company from both flanks. My father and his machine gun were caught in between two attacking forces.

During the initial German counterattack on the 6th, G Company had advanced several hundred yards before being completely cut off after enemy tanks and artillery moved up the road leading to their location. My father was likely carrying the Browning heavy machine gun or the tripod at this point. The company was ordered to fight its way back to the battalion's 81-mm mortar positions behind the lines. Relentless enemy artillery and mortar shelling continued to fall on G Company's position throughout the day and the night and into the following day. The company was surrounded and using large quantities of ammunition with no means of resupply. It remained in the fight as 3rd Battalion was thrown in to assist G and E Companies in repelling the fierce German attack. G Company continued to receive intense artillery, machine gun, and small-arms fire as the enemy attacked, and counterattacked, from the east and southeast throughout the day and night. For several relentless days, my father and his squad members endured this horrific scenario. He no doubt questioned whether or not he would survive.

Although 20 years had passed since Jean-Marie originally found the artifacts in this particular foxhole, he returned to the secluded, forested site. When looking out over the foxhole, the reason for selecting the location to set up a machine gun was self-evident. The remains of the foxhole are located at the crest of a hill that slopes down in three directions, with the flat ground of a narrow plateau behind. The rampart faces the Mortagne valley, which was clear of vegetation in 1944, offering an unobstructed view to the east and the German troops positioned along the river. A machine-gun squad would have been able to see any threat as it approached this elevated position. However, the fog, rain, and darkness likely reduced the effect of this strategic advantage. The remains of numerous foxholes exist immediately behind the machine-gun location, and extend back more than 50 yards across the plateau, indicating the machine gun was positioned at the forward edge of the company's lines. During this return visit to the site, additional spent .30-caliber casings and the rusted remains of a machine-gun ammunition can were excavated from the same foxhole.

Several compelling factors indicate my father's heavy machine gun was located at the site. First, the foxhole was placed at the crest of a hill at the forward point of G Company's infantry position and faced east/southeast toward a large force of dug-in enemy troops and vehicles. Second, the hundreds of spent casings found by Jean-Marie 20 years before, and the ones subsequently found during this visit, strongly suggested it was the location of a Browning water-cooled heavy machine gun and not an air-cooled light machine gun. The air-cooled version would have overheated during such intense, extended fighting. There is no doubt in my mind this foxhole served as G Company's heavy machine gun, supplied by H Company, during the fighting on October 6. Since Jean-Marie's extensive investigations had identified only one machine-gun foxhole in G Company's sector of October 6, and since 1st Section of 1st Platoon had been assigned to G Company during this particular battle, I had no doubt my father fought in this specific foxhole. As extraordinary and improbable as it seemed, we had found my father's exact location during this horrific battle. By combining his exact location on the morning of October 6 along with the G Company communication transcripts contained in the original S-2 and S-3 (operations and mission planning) officer reports, I was able to identify and understand his unique experiences and expose the memories responsible for awakening him from sleep throughout his life.

★★★

With this new information, a detailed reconstruction of the events is possible. At 8:47 on the morning of October 5, 2nd Battalion received its battlefield orders and was to relieve the 3rd Battalion on the front lines. Typically, two companies remained on the front lines and one company was kept in reserve at all times, rotating to assure adequate strength on the battlefield. Colonel Dulaney, the 180th Regiment's commanding officer, informed Colonel Cruikshank, 2nd Battalion's commanding officer:

> Your mission is to continue to the South, staying on the West side of the Railroad (RR) and proceed to the initial objective at about 253605. You will put one company on the high ground overlooking Brouvelieures and the wide-open valley down there ... The reason we limit it to one company for you is that the other two can protect your left flank and left rear.[49]

Colonel Cruikshank ultimately selected G Company to lead the mission, given that it was dug in on a hill slightly north of the 61 grid line between the 24 and 25 lines, and E and F Companies were positioned to its left flank and rear by mid-afternoon on October 5. G Company's high ground position faced east toward the Mortagne valley and southeast toward Brouvelieures directly into the enemy's defensive position. Having been relieved, 3rd Battalion moved back and positioned itself to the south and rear of G Company. Shortly before 6:00 p.m., the 3rd Battalion commanding officer reported, "There is definitely a German out there with an American machine gun, field jacket and helmet." Some of the Germans spoke English and yelled, "We are Americans, don't shoot." But, when 180th Regiment troops responded with, "Come out if you are Americans," they would continue firing their weapons. Soon after, G Company reported receiving enemy machine-gun fire on their right flank.[50] Although artillery was called

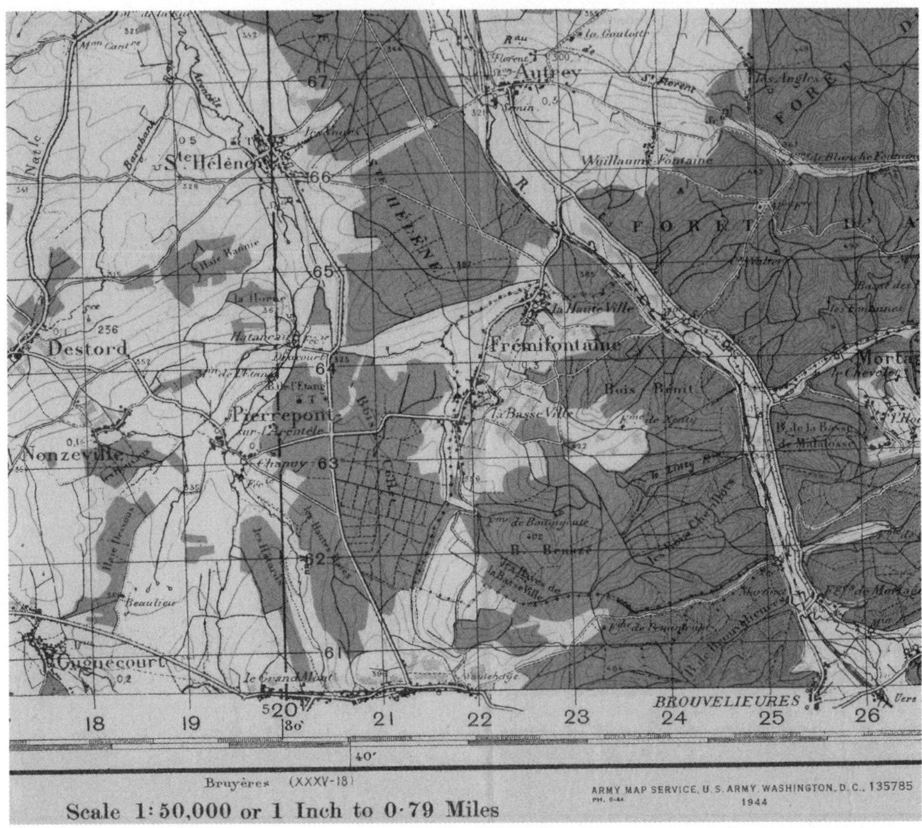

Map of the Frémifontaine region showing grid lines that correspond to unit position references within the text. (Department of Defense. Department of the Army. Office of the Chief of Engineers. U.S. Army Topographic Command)

in to silence the machine guns, this scenario was a foreshadowing of what was to come.

Complying with their mission orders, G Company troops initiated an attack at 7:30 a.m. and advanced in a southerly direction down the hillside toward Brouvelieures from their dug-in position on the high ground, with my father's machine gun covering their initial advance from the crest of the hill as the riflemen moved past him. As the company advanced down the wooded hillside and toward the swamps at the bottom, he and his squad undoubtedly disassembled the machine gun and moved with the company to assure supportive firepower along the way. After they'd advanced several hundred yards, the Germans initiated a fierce counterattack on all sections of 2nd Battalion. The initial assault on G Company came from their right. Captain Blackmer, G Company's commanding officer, notified Colonel Cruikshank, "We got a little firefight over to the right. We moved only a little ways. The Germans have a few machine guns down there."[51] E Company followed close behind and at the same time F Company began to realize it was becoming surrounded. The attack on G Company intensified to the right and to the rear of its position, involving heavy mortar barrages and machine-gun fire directed as enemy infantry advanced from the southeast.

The overall assault was intense and overwhelming. A German prisoner confessed he witnessed 20 wounded American soldiers taken prisoner and moved to a location behind the enemy lines during the early moments of the attack. Captain Blackmer had been fighting in a different section of the company's position when the attack began, but ran through the heavy mortar and machine-gun fire to the spot of the intense enemy assault. He quickly organized his men and successfully stopped the advance. During the initial firefight, Blackmer killed four Germans. Within moments, the enemy initiated an attack on G Company's forward platoons. My father and his crew were likely ordered to quickly set up the machine gun in the direction of the attack, since it is primarily a defensive weapon. Blackmer moved to the forward units, organized some of his men, and fought alongside the riflemen, effectively fighting off several additional enemy attacks.[52] Shortly after 11:00 a.m., Colonel Cruikshank told G Company via radio to temporarily hold at their current location as the situation along the entire 2nd Battalion line rapidly escalated. At 11:54 a.m., 2nd Battalion HQ reported to the Regimental S-3:

> Company F reports tanks working in on them. They really hit this place with mortars and direct fire from tanks. We're moving the Tank Destroyers up to check point #4. That doesn't leave us anything back in town. We got a big gap between Companies E and F … Company E is in a fight all around them. Mortars have been shooting from out in front of them about 400 yards. Company G is at 250610 and they say there are more Germans in back of them than there are

> in front of them. Company G is going to try to scout that road out and work down the right to contact the 179th Infantry. Company E has a platoon trying to fill the gap between E and G. We're fighting in three separate groups.[53]

Second Battalion S-2 and S-3 officers received multiple reports of enemy tanks breaking through company defensive lines, firing their cannons as they approach E, F, and G Company positions. Enemy artillery and tank fire had knocked out all of the communication wire lines between the forward companies and battalion headquarters. Field radios and small patrols moving between units were the only available options to communicate at that point in time. In response to the massive attack from all directions, G Company received orders to fight its way back to the positions it occupied the previous night, before jumping off earlier in the morning.

Captain Benjamin A. Blackmer, G Company Commander, 180th Infantry Regiment, photographed in front of a barn near Frémifontaine, France. (Photo courtesy of Jean-Marie Siret)

As Captain Blackmer and his men moved back toward the high ground, they met heavy enemy resistance, including a German heavy machine gun blocking their path. Blackmer attacked the machine guns blocking G Company's path, leading to his heroics in silencing two enemy machine gun crews with his rifle and grenades at dangerously close range.

> With Blackmer in the lead, his men had a fierce fight with the Germans, who fought like a band of thoroughly indoctrinated Nazis, and refused to surrender. The Germans resisted to the last man, and when the fighting was over at the foxholes, forty of them lay dead.[54]

My father and his heavy-machine-gun squad moved constantly,

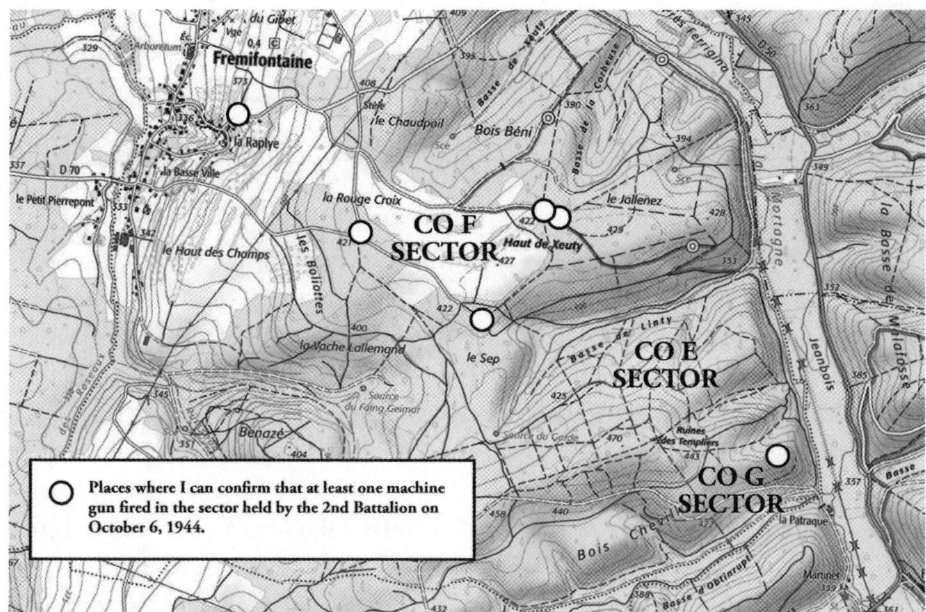

Locations of E, F and G Companies on the morning of October 6, 1944. The locations of confirmed machine gun positions are marked by circles. (Map and markings provided by Jean-Marie Siret)

setting up momentarily to fire the weapon, and then repositioning over and over again as G Company advanced through the forest, engaging in frequent firefights with enemy troops in their attempts to emerge from the trap.

Shortly before 3:00 in the afternoon, 2nd Battalion officers had decided that a new strategy was necessary as the number of German tanks, flak wagons, and infantry continued to build behind E, F, and G Companies. The situation had become critical as the three companies were fighting in complete circles. By 3:45 p.m., plans were developed to bring the three companies, all of which were surrounded by enemy forces, back to form a defensive line near the edge of town. The regimental executive officer reported to Colonel Dulaney:

> I just talked to Colonel Cruikshank and he says that Companies E and G are completely cut off. There's also more than six tanks out there. There are six on the left flank and there are tanks between Companies E and F. Colonel

> Cruikshank seems to think they can't hold much longer the way they are. He wants to pull Companies E and G back on a line with Company F. They will have to fight their way back.

Dulaney had a different plan. "I think it is better to use 3rd Battalion rather than bring those people back … the 3rd Battalion could make a push up from, and through, F Company."[55]

By 4:15 p.m., 3rd Battalion initiated a counterattack with plans to advance a company to both flanks of F Company's position. Several minutes later, B Company from the 179th Infantry Regiment initiated a counterattack toward the northeast in an effort to contact E and G Companies. However, the 179th was in a similar situation, with Germans all around, and regimental command was skeptical they would be able to break through. Meanwhile, E and G Companies were fighting for their survival. Captain Blackmer was organizing an all-around defense, and was trying to tie-in with E Company on the left. After a conference with Captain Satterfield of E Company, Blackmer reorganized his company's positions, so as to repel German attacks from any direction. My father and his heavy machine gun would have undoubtedly been involved in this action, using the Browning water-cooled machine gun as a powerful defensive weapon against the attacking enemy troops. It was arranged that, should either company be required to withdraw, it would close in with the other and the two would fight their way out together. "Both Companies E and G were surrounded by hordes of Germans that had infiltrated through. At 5:45 p.m., the Germans drove a wedge into the center of Company E's position, with a fierce attack that forced Company E to move toward the lines of Company G."[56] Being surrounded by attacking enemy forces meant 2nd Battalion soldiers were burning through ammunition as they attempted to repel the Germans. It also meant supply lines were completely cut and no more ammunition was accessible. G Company was fighting for its life and quickly running out of firepower to defend itself.

Shortly after 8:00 p.m., the regimental executive officer received a report that E Company had been split in half during the relentless German attack and that one half of the company was trapped on the south side of the swamp with G Company and the other half was located in the forest north of the swamp. The company had found itself in an "every man for himself" situation. A 16-man patrol had somehow worked its way back to headquarters from that location. The eight men from G Company and eight from E Company said they were completely cut off, were short on ammunition, and more enemy troops were coming in on them. Darkness had set in when G Company reported taking eight German prisoners, who stated they had arrived the prior night with the mission of driving the 180th Regiment out of the forest and into town for better observation and concentration of artillery fire. At 9:00 p.m., Colonel Dulaney revised his strategy and the S-3 officer notified the 179th:

> The situation on our Companies E and G is bad. They got Germans behind them … there's Germans all around them. So, Colonel Dulaney has elected to bring Companies E and G back and establish a line along the 24 grid … that is if we can get word to those companies to come back. At that point, or someplace close by, we'd like to make contact with your people [the 179th].

The same S-3 then contacted the 3rd Battalion and said, "This situation with Companies E and G is critical. We're out of communication with them. Get some of those people and find out something."[57] The Germans had cut off the only road leading to E and G Companies. They had also set up on both flanks of the companies and were deep into the woods behind them:

> Captain Blackmer oriented his men as to the disposition of the German forces. Then, under the cover of darkness, he led his company through the thick woods and swamps. From time to time, they encountered German strong points, and had fierce firefights in the darkness. Traveling by compass, Blackmer led his men through the German held woods.[58]

Finally, a small patrol in the 179th's area made field-radio contact with E, G, and H Companies at around 10:30 p.m. The companies were together and positioned 300 yards short of where they were earlier in the morning, still completely surrounded by enemy forces and described as being in "pretty poor shape." They were instructed via radio message to continue fighting their way back and to eventually organize a defensive line. Several minutes after midnight, four men from either E, G, or H

Company walked into the 179th Infantry's I Company position. They had followed a power line for about 1,000 yards before reaching I Company. The men said their companies were receiving fire from all directions and that they needed ammunition and any supplies they could locate. One of the men was Sergeant Frances Able from G Company. I Company was alerted to expect more men from G and E Companies approaching their left flank, as the companies had been given orders to fight their way back to the 24 line between the 61 and 62 grid lines.

At 3:15 a.m., Captain Blackmer and some of his G Company men made physical contact with the 179th Regiment's Anti-Tank Company in the dark woods south of Frémifontaine. He contacted regimental command via either radio or communication line, gave his position, and said, "I am going to move East to try to contact K Company. Where are they?" Having less than fifty of his men with him, they set out in the darkness to the coordinates provided. Despite their courageous efforts, contacting K Company proved impossible because the woods were heavy with enemy troops and machine guns. In response, regimental command directed Blackmer and what remained of G and E Companies back to town. This order meant the remaining men of G Company would need to fight directly through the powerful enemy forces scattered throughout the dark forest and swamp. With supplies of ammunition low or exhausted, the men undoubtedly knew they would be fighting hand-to-hand in the darkness.

Guided only by Blackmer's compass, the remaining soldiers redirected their path, intensely scanning each tree and rock as they slowly advanced toward Frémifontaine throughout the night. Artillery, mortar, and tank fire continued to explode in all directions as they fought to survive through the German rifles and machine guns hidden within the forest. Then, as dawn approached at 5:46 on October 7, Colonel Cruikshank notified the regimental S-3 officer that the G and E Company commanders had returned with some of their men and were with him at the command post. He said, "They brought back approximately 45 men each. I got 12 more men from F Company, which makes a total of 29. They have little or no ammunition. They brought none of their weapons back with them except the Heavy Machine Guns."[59] Rifles without ammunition are useless to soldiers in combat. M1 Garand rifles are heavy and would

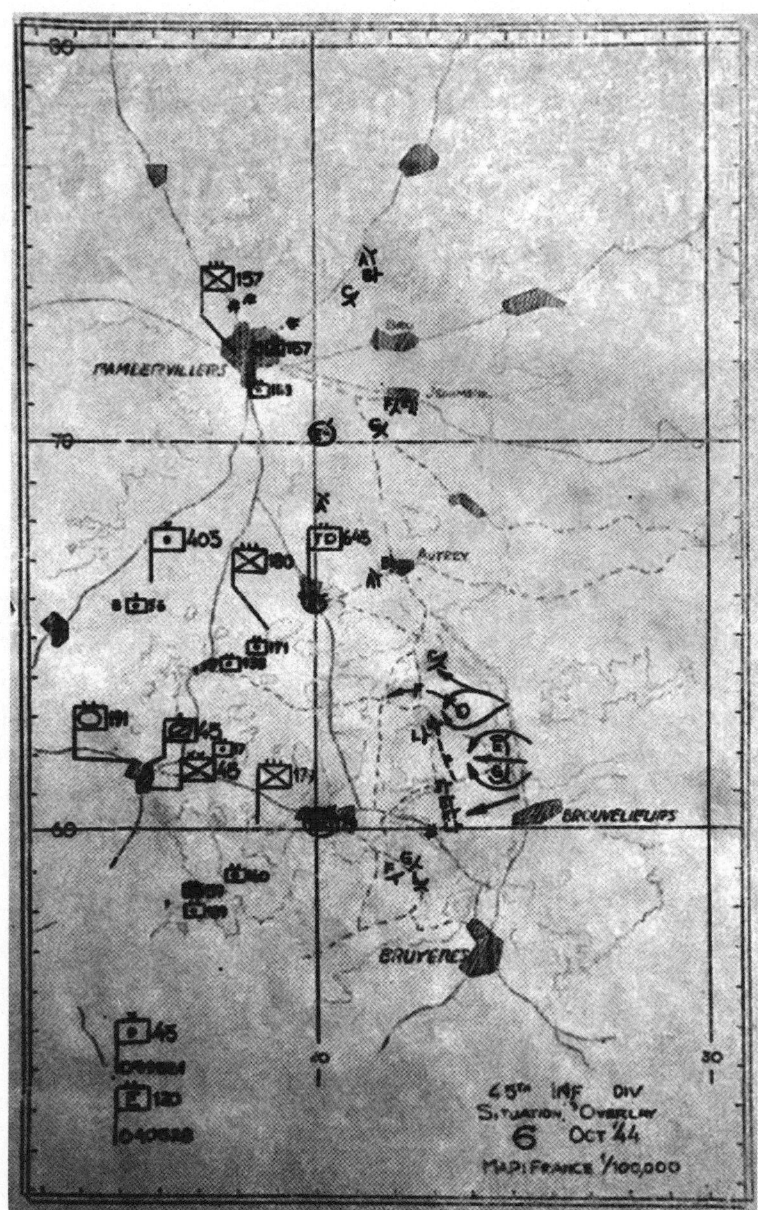

Sketched map overlay showing the 180th Infantry Regiment positions at the end of the day on October 6, 1944. Arrows indicate the direction of the German attack. Map overlay located in the 45th Infantry Division G-3 Period Report, October 1944. (Courtesy of the 45th Infantry Division Museum archives. Photo by Michael Reyka on location in Oklahoma City, Oklahoma)

have been cumbersome if unusable while navigating the dark forest and swamps. I can only speculate that continuing to carry them under such conditions would have been as pointless as clinging tightly to a flashlight without batteries. No doubt my father was out of ammunition as well, yet he must have carried the heavy, useless machine gun through the dark woods and swamps. Their primary weapons at that point would have been survival knives. The heavy machine guns assigned to G and E Companies were likely brought back because of the limited number available to the regiment and perhaps in response to the recent memory of a German soldier in disguise using an American machine gun against 2nd Battalion troops.

My father was without any doubt one of the remaining men who returned with Captain Blackmer for two significant reasons. First, he survived the battle and avoided capture and, second, Captain Blackmer would have assured that the only heavy-machine-gun squad available to G Company remained in close proximity to him so he could deploy it at a moment's notice. Somehow, my father made it out of this perilous situation, along with a fragment of his unit—only 45 men. More than half of the men he had been fighting with throughout the day and night were gone—either dead, captured, or missing. The fighting overnight was in close proximity with knives, fists, or whatever else the men could find to use as weapons. Despite the horrifying night, the remnants of E, G, and H Companies were immediately directed back to the front line and placed on K Company's right flank facing east toward the German troops. The 180th Regiment was still at significant risk of annihilation as enemy artillery and mortar barrages continued throughout the day. At that time, G Company was located several hundred yards west of the hilltop position it had occupied the previous morning.

Nevertheless, in the predawn hours of October 7, G and E Companies had joined a strong defensive line east of Frémifontaine, with I, K, and L Companies of the 179th Infantry Regiment positioned on their right flank facing southeast. Throughout the morning, a few additional men were reunited with their units. But the overall company strength of 2nd Battalion had improved very little. By noon, G Company had reached a strength of 50 men, E Company 44 men, and F Company 42 men in response to reassignment from other jobs or individual soldiers

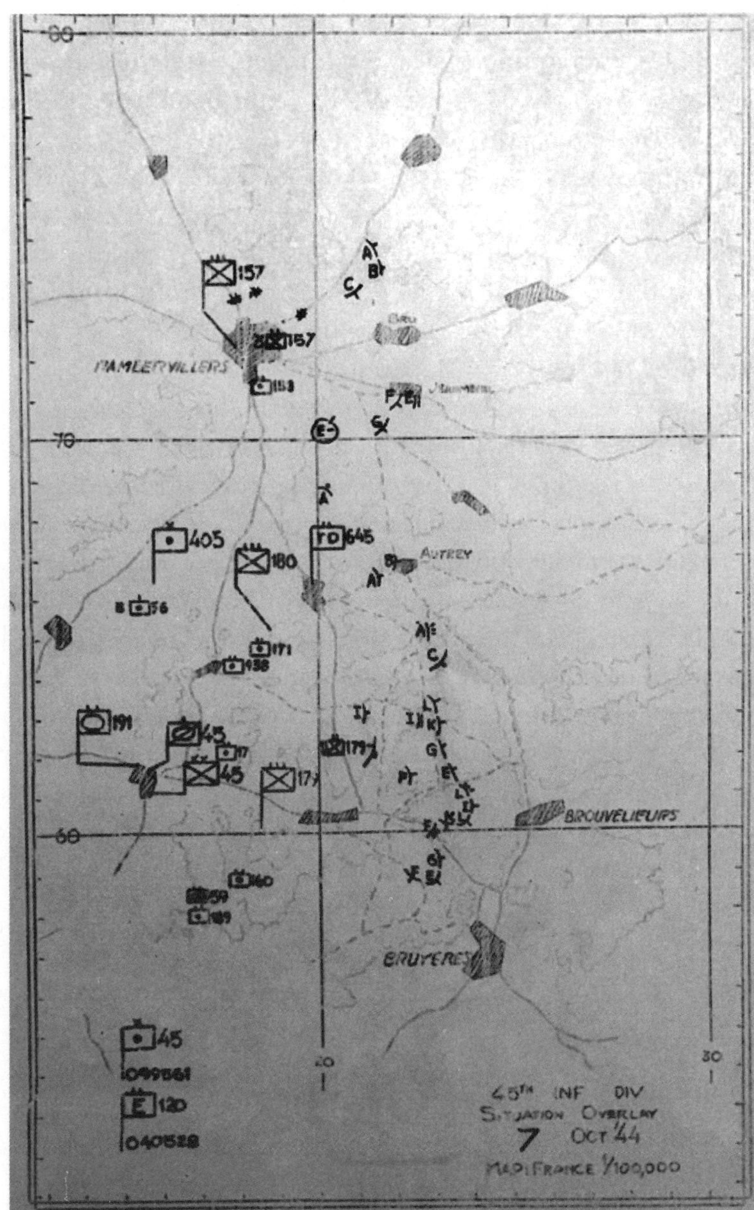

180th Infantry Regiment positions end of October 7, 1944. E, F and G Companies are back on the line after losing more than 50 percent of their men and most of their weapons. Map overlay located in the 45th Infantry Division G-3 Period Report, October 1944, map #7. (Map overlay courtesy of the 45th Infantry Division Museum archives. Photograph by Michael Reyka on location in Oklahoma City, Oklahoma)

finding their way back through the enemy infested forest and swamp. For comparison, full strength of a rifle company during a non-combat situation can be as high as 180 men and six officers. Second Battalion had received a beating and small scattered pockets of men were still fighting for their lives through the forest to the east and south of the village. From its new position on October 7, E Company reported hearing American small arms firing out in front of them to the east and believed a platoon was still out there, intact and trying to fight its way back to safety. Some speculated it was the E Company soldiers that had been split and stranded north of the swamp.

Throughout the remainder of the day and into the night, German artillery, tank, and mortar fire continued to fall on what remained of E, F, and G Companies as they held their defensive line. It is certain my father and his heavy machine gun were active on this defensive line throughout the day—cold, exhausted, hungry, dehydrated, and scared as hell.

There is a compelling argument that my 22-year-old father fought in the G Company machine-gun foxhole Jean-Marie identified. The original unit rosters may have validated this theory, given they included individual names and corresponding platoon assignments, but they no longer exist. Regardless, the argument remains strong without them. The H Company morning reports for this period confirm that 1st Section of 1st Platoon was assigned to G Company from October 6 to October 10, the day my father was medically evacuated from the battlefield. The H Company morning report on this date recorded:

> Reyka, Steve C. Pfc
> Relieved of assignment & duty & transferred to Det. of Pat. 7th Army (LOD).
> Dispensory slip 120th Medical Battalion, 10th of October, 1944,
> (59th Evacuation Hospital).
> Authorization: Cir #82, NATO USA. Cs.

He and the rest of his heavy weapons company performed bravely during this intense fight, as did every able-bodied man present. "Excellent support was rendered the line companies by both Company H and Second Battalion Headquarters Company during the 6th."[60]

The intensity of this battle was beyond my comprehension. I didn't know what to think with regard to my father's presence and engagement in this conflict. I was baffled, confused, and saddened. I stood on the same ground nearly seven decades after the fighting had occurred, and many years after my father's death, with a strange sense of fulfilment and closure. The reason for his post-traumatic stress disorder, which manifested itself through silence, emotional distance, and nightmares, had finally been exposed. I had stepped into his most challenging, stressful, and frightening life experience. The medical note written by the attending physician at the 35th Station Hospital, where he was treated for an acute respiratory infection, indicates tension, anxiety, restlessness, and exhaustion were present when he was admitted on October 18, 1944. I don't know how he physically survived these battles, or how he managed to repress such emotional trauma throughout the course of his life. I felt strangely close and connected to him at that moment, more than at any other point in my life. I realized I was the only person who knew the truth about my father. In the years that followed the war, he said nothing to his family regarding these events. His parents and siblings only knew he had had a "bad experience" during the war. My mother and my siblings certainly knew nothing of the factors responsible for his periodic nightmares and his emotional distance. Feelings of both sadness and relief rushed through my thoughts as well as my body. I felt a deep sadness for him in relation to the silent pain he endured, yet I felt a strange sense of relief for both of us. The secret that created a subtle unspoken distance between us and that occasionally caused me to silently question our relationship had emerged from the darkness and was out in the open.

With all of this weighing on my mind, our small group left the forest and proceeded again to the location of the 45th Division monument, where Jean-Marie had planned the small ceremony later that evening in honor of our visit. As we drove into Frémifontaine and toward the monument, Jean-Marie pointed out the other side of the German counterattack that occurred on the 6th and 7th. This segment of the assault came from the high ground to the west into the center of the village. The enemy's advance progressed to the large stone-cross monument in the middle of the intersection and the nearby house that served as the 180th Regiment's 2nd Battalion CP, which was subsequently evacuated during the intense counterattack.[61]

At the onset of the fighting in Frémifontaine, the Germans were dug in as the Americans initiated their attack from the west. That process reversed itself several times across the same ground throughout the escalating fighting during the first weeks of October. Because of this, both sides used each other's foxholes for shelter.[62] Jean-Marie had found several foxholes that contained both German and American equipment and artifacts. One such foxhole was likely used by an American Browning automatic rifleman as evidenced by the location along the side of a wooded path and artifacts found in the hole. These and other artifacts were found in foxholes throughout a particular area that had been defended by E and G Companies on the 15th of the month. Over the decades, Jean-Marie had personally found more than eighty grenades, dozens of M1 Garand clips and countless numbers of empty .30-caliber cartridges in this small area surrounding the 2nd Battalion foxholes. He located several specific sites where he found hundreds of 30.06 cartridges in a condensed area, suggesting the likelihood of machine-gun installations.

Larger debris and military vehicles were scattered across the battlefield immediately following the fighting. Monsieur M. J. recalled seeing a damaged American tank that had been towed into the village of Frémifontaine and parked along the side of the road near the intersection where the large stone cross is located. He believed the tank had hit a landmine because one of the tracks was damaged and other parts were missing. One subsequent morning, M. J. noticed the tank had been removed, having been taken during the night by a repair crew attached to the division.[63]

We drove past a house that had served as the American first-aid station in Frémifontaine; it was the only medical station in Frémifontaine, referred to as Collection Station C.[64] Later in the evening, at the ceremony, I met a villager who was a child living in Frémifontaine during the battle; he and his younger brother were hiding in the basement of their house in response to the artillery shelling. His brother touched a hot wood stove and severely burned his hand, requiring medical attention. With nowhere else to go, they went to the American first-aid station. My father was most certainly taken to this location when he was evacuated from the front lines near Frémifontaine. The house is located at the intersection of the stone cross, directly across from 2nd Battalion's CP. I walked to the yard and stood in front of the house, imagining the sights and sounds of October 1944, and visualized my father walking up the front path to receive medical treatment in this unassuming structure. He must have felt relieved, and perhaps finally safe, as he focused on the front door.

My father was removed from the front lines on the morning of October 10 with a medical diagnosis of pneumonia, fever, and chest pain.[65] His medical condition was most likely recognized, addressed, and treated at this particular time because the intensity of the fighting had subsided and the opportunity to assess the troops for illness and injury had presented itself. In addition, the fever, difficulty in breathing, chest pain, and sheer exhaustion had reached the point of compromise. According to the 180th Infantry's organizational history, "Operations during the period of 9–10 October were limited to extensive patrol activity to the regiment's front and flanks. The patrols engaged the enemy in numerous firefights and also reported the location of enemy roadblocks and positions. Considerable enemy tank and artillery fire of mixed caliber was received on the regiment's forward position."[66] As a heavy machine gunner, my father would not have participated in patrols. Rather, he would have been stationary at a fixed machine-gun emplacement in a defensive position. As such, he would have been a priority target of the enemy,[67] and he was certainly well aware of that after so many months on the front lines. The weather and the intense fighting had taken a tremendous toll on the 180th Regiment's troops. Infantry soldiers fought hand-to-hand under extremely harsh weather conditions both day and night. Lack of sleep, lack of hot food, inadequate hydration, and exposure to the elements reduced their resistance to disease. According to the 180th Regiment Organizational History Record:

> October was a busy month for the Medical Detachment. The number of evacuees reached an all [time] high total of 1,036. Constant severe fighting against tenacious resistance through heavily wooded areas, inclement weather, lack of rest, continuance of reclassification of enlisted men, all played an important part in reaching this high total.[68]
>
> Exhaustion cases leaped skywards with a total of 125, of which 52 were sent for reclassification. In spite of the rain, mud, cold and lack of waterproof shoes, only 18 men were evacuated with trench foot.[69]

John Reeves, a communications lineman for the 180th Regiment, described the effect the fighting around Frémifontaine had on the soldiers' mental health during early October 1944. He and a fellow soldier were repairing a line after dark near the spot where they had witnessed several men burn to death after their vehicle was hit by a German shell earlier that same day. When the repair was finished and he asked his comrade if he was ready to leave, the soldier didn't respond. Reeves recalled, "He did not answer and I noticed that he was crying. We went to the aid station and they said he had battle fatigue and he was sent to the hospital for a few days and was able to return to duty, but only as a switchboard operator. All of our switchboard operators were one-time linemen."[70] Several days later, near Hill #385, Reeves encountered a similar response from another soldier. He recalled:

> We were pinned down under machine gun fire. During this firing a medic brought a soldier from a little further up the hill to where we were. He was completely out of his mind. Another case of battle fatigue. Lt. Tykeman talked to him and quieted him until the machine gun opened up again. This sent him over the edge again. I didn't know him or what became of him.[71]

Disease and exhaustion contributed to the physical health of troops. Pneumonia killed even young and relatively healthy people during the 1940s. It was considered a serious medical condition at any age. Pneumonia causes the tiny air sacs in the lungs to fill with fluid and become inflamed, reducing the amount of oxygen that is able to reach the blood and subsequently cells throughout the body. If the infection spreads, it can lead to sepsis and death. During the 1930s and 1940s, pneumonia was a leading public-health concern throughout society. In 1937, it was the "leading infectious cause of death" in the United States.[72] For soldiers living outdoors in cold, damp, deplorable conditions with inadequate nutrition, pneumonia was an exceptionally life-threatening condition.

The rapid and constant advance of the 180th Regiment from southern France to the Vosges Mountains had significantly drained the soldiers, both physically and emotionally. When the advance slowed near Frémifontaine, as the Germans turned to fight, the regimental commanders attempted to address the exhaustion:

> The long bitter fighting and the inability to supply front-line troops with clean clothing and hot food, plus the cold damp weather, made it imperative to set

> up a rest camp where units could be withdrawn from the lines and rested for a period. On 6 October [*sic*], the 180th Rest Camp was opened at Aydoilles. Hot showers, movies, a day room, complete with radio, library, and phonograph, were provided.[73]

Unfortunately, my father and the remainder of 2nd Battalion were engaged in fierce hand-to-hand combat and fighting for their lives on the day the rest camp opened.

I experienced a multitude of thoughts and emotions about my father as I sorted through everything I had learned during this journey. At the Xeuty farm several hours earlier, I had paused in silent refection while standing in an F Company foxhole as my eyes gradually adjusted to the lack of light among the dense pines. I wondered what factors drove these men. What motivated them to keep fighting and driving forward despite the fear that must have consumed their thoughts? The individual accounts of tenacity, courage, and selfless bravery associated with the men of the 45th Division are seemingly innumerable. As detailed in the introduction, General Jacob Devers said of these men, "The officers and men of the 45th Infantry Division have reached heights of bravery and self-sacrifice which all Americans may well set before themselves as future standards of conduct. Seldom has a group of men been called upon to endure such hardships, and never has man responded more gallantly than did the infantrymen of the 45th."[74] This reputation can be seen in the 180th's actions in and around Frémifontaine during the autumn of 1944. Was it the division's slogan, *Semper Anticus*, "Always Forward," that inspired, empowered, and drove them—a legacy to be honored? Or was it instead the spirit, passion, and character of these men that supported the slogan? Perhaps it also involved the commitment among soldiers to support and defend each other in battle.

The fighting during the liberation of Frémifontaine and the surrounding area was extremely costly for all those involved. For the 180th Regiment troops, French fighters, Frémifontaine villagers, and Germans as well, the intensity continued as the autumn weeks evolved into bitter-cold winter months. My father's involvement ceased on October 10, but the remainder of his unit continued to experience death and destruction that challenged the limits of the human body and mind.

An officer with the French resistance, fighting alongside the 180th Regiment in Frémifontaine, commented that it wasn't until October 14 that a powerful attack of American infantry, supported by tanks, put an end to the German resistance in and around the village. During this fighting, the combined forces suffered heavy losses, including an American tank destroyer disabled by a German antitank shell just a few yards from the spot where the French group was positioned during its assault on Hill 385. The officer commented that of the five members of its crew, three perished, burned alive while trapped in the armored vehicle.[75]

The close fighting and the stiff German resistance remained strong and costly, even after the liberation of Frémifontaine, as the 2nd Battalion continued to push the enemy further back toward the German border.

The body of a German soldier and a knocked-out tank barely distract these 45th Division infantrymen as they don a new type of winter combat jacket on October 31, 1944, after crossing the Mortagne river east of Frémifontaine (U.S. Signal Corps, 111-SC 195862/NARA)

Third Battalion launched an attack on the morning of October 20 and was successful in breaking through the enemy's front line of foxholes and trenches. "Very close contact was maintained with numerous grenade duels and small arms engagements. Slowly the advance continued for approximately 300 yards, where the enemy's wire entanglements halted the advance."[76]

Georges Fortier noted that, later in the month, near October 20, the Germans created breaches in the embankments of the canals near the sawmill situated above the valley, thereby successfully flooding the fields and the road surface all along the D-50 route. During the crossing in force of the Mortagne by the 180th Regiment's 1st Battalion on the 23rd, the unit suffered heavy losses under German machine-gun fire from carefully placed positions across the river. Fortier looked over the site shortly after the crossing and remembered seeing many bodies of dead American soldiers floating in the water. He also noted that the sawmill, which is today known as La Sciegotte, had been used as a German infirmary during the fighting.[77] His accounts are supported by the 45th Division Headquarters journal:

> Company A launched an attack at … [2:45 p.m.] … with the mission of securing the bridge across the Mortagne River and the high ground one kilometer to the northeast. The attack met very heavy machine gun fire from the east bank of the river, which caused heavy casualties and compelled the attacking elements to withdrawal to positions on the west side of the river.[78]

The numerous German attempts to block and delay the American advance continued to harass the 180th Regiment throughout the Vosges Mountains region. "Progress was slow through the dense woods and against enemy [forces] entrenched in well camouflaged positions."[79] Yet, the 45th Division Thunderbirds pressed forward in a relentless manner. Along the way, the soldiers left memories and lasting impressions with the French villagers.

Madame Perot-Demangeon was nine years old in October 1944. In 2007, she shared with Jean-Marie her memory of an American soldier named John, whose last name she has forgotten. Some of the American soldiers billeted in the village following the liberation struck up conversations and friendships with the villagers. This was the case with John, who befriended Madame Perot-Demangeon's older sister, Therese. Later, John sent Therese notes and photographs—on the back of one photograph he wrote the dedication, "To my sweetheart, Therese. Beaucoup of love, John." He also sent the family several unique bank notes with dedications written on them, one of which was a 50 Franc note, better known to coin collectors as a "liberation note."[80]

I remember my father as a gentle, quiet, and generous man. I can envision him as another young American soldier giving chocolate bars to French children and politely conversing with villagers who approached him in appreciation for his presence in their community.

CHAPTER 15

Coping

My journey retracing my father's steps across France, from the tank photo in Bourg to the village of Frémifontaine, uncovered his personal story involving the battles to liberate French villages and created a detailed image of his engagement in the brutal fighting in and around Frémifontaine. He witnessed death and destruction all around him and was no doubt convinced he would be wounded, killed, or captured in the dark forest near Xeuty Farm or in the forest west of Frémifontaine. I'm convinced this experience changed him forever.

Emotions play a role in the individual's appraisal of the situation or event, which in turn establishes the degree of stress. Appraisal is more than mere perception—it is a personal evaluation of what is happening.[1] The way in which a person appraises a situation or an encounter is largely responsible for the assessment of threat, the coping response selected, and the type of response demonstrated. While stress is a complex process involving interaction and appraisal, the phenomenon of stress and coping begins with a stressor and a response. This complex process is often described in the context of structural engineering. For example, environmental conditions such as gravity, wind, rain, ice, snow, and the weight of vehicles place stress on a bridge, which produces structural strain. In a similar manner, environmental conditions such as interpersonal conflict, social and economic pressures, fear, and threats to personal safety act as stressors because they place stress on the individual and produce psychological strain.[2] From this perspective, stress is a physical and psychological response experienced when the demands on one's environment outweigh one's available resources. While some stress is a normal aspect of life and beneficial in regard to motivation and action, such as a soldier trying to survive a specific battle, stress that becomes intense, repeated, or sustained can lead to an inability to cope and a negative situation referred to as distress.[3] Like many frontline soldiers during World War II, my father and his comrades were engaged in relentless and sustained brutal battles, often at close range and sometimes involving hand-to-hand fights to the death. The 45th Division Thunderbirds spent more consecutive days on the front lines than any other US Army unit during the war. Their threat was real, not merely a perception influenced by emotion, and the traditional coping mechanisms available were limited to their training and the biological "fight or flight" response. As an infantry soldier in battle, flight is not an option unless ordered to do so as a strategic battle plan. So, they fought, relentlessly—day after day, month after month—facing death and destruction with every passing moment. Modern psychology suggests that, when coping processes are no longer effective, fear and anxiety become pathological and the condition expands to the level of trauma, often involving paralyzing fear, panic, depression, and hopelessness.

Everyday encounters between individuals influence, shape, mold, and create the individuals themselves. In a sense, people are unique in large part due to their patterns of behavior with others through various situations over time. The concept can be described as "not men and their moments. Rather, moments and their men."[4]

Appraisal occurs constantly during human interaction. In fact, it operates at both conscious and unconscious levels and can be defined as primary or secondary appraisal. Primary appraisal involves an initial assessment and evaluation of whether or not the situation or event poses a threat to once's safety and security. If the individual appraises that the situation does indeed pose a threat to personal safety, a condition of stress will result. Secondary appraisal is a cognitive-evaluative process that determines what can be done in response to the stressful situation or event—the coping options. The process of coping involves the manner in which individuals manage stressful situations and events in their lives. The coping process involves questions such as: Do I need to do something? What should I do? Can I do it? When should I do it? What are the risks? Appraisal and coping are collaborative processes that work together in responding to stress. The more confidence a person has in his or her ability to face danger and overcome obstacles, the more probable it is the person will experience challenge as opposed to threat when experiencing stress.[5] I don't know anything about my father's level of personal confidence or self-esteem prior to the war. In fact, I don't know of any stories related to his youth, other than what I have learned through this research. Regardless, it is difficult to imagine that anyone, at any level of self-confidence, could emerge from these experiences across France without emotional scars. The difference between them appears to be related to the coping mechanisms selected following the events.

When a person is confronted with a life-or-death situation, the body responds with heightened awareness, caused by chemical reactions throughout the body. This natural process prepares the person for the well-known fight or flight response. But, when this natural survival mechanism is engaged for a sustained period of time, as with infantry soldiers during prolonged combat, the strain on the body and the mind often leads to side effects that have a disruptive influence on the ability to function. Trembling, anxiety, dizziness, confusion, and hyperventilation are merely a few of the common manifestations that result from the physical, emotional, and mental demands of prolonged combat. During the war, the general term associated with the immediate aftereffects is "battle stress" or "battle fatigue." According to resources at the National WWII Museum, the symptoms or side effects of battle fatigue subside over time for most veterans after they leave the battlefield and return home.[6] For others, the powerful memories and deep emotional wounds have long-lasting effects and can progress to post-traumatic stress disorder (PTSD). Perhaps the cruelest of these symptoms attack veterans at their most vulnerable times through nightmares where flashbacks cause them to relive the traumatic events as if for the first time. My father's nightmares were a window into his past trauma. As a family, we didn't understand this because he didn't talk about his affiliation with the 45th Infantry Division or his brutal hand-to-hand combat with German soldiers. He buried the memories in an intentional effort to erase the events that carried with them so much pain, fear, and stress. I have since learned that avoidance is one of the most-common symptoms of PTSD.

Monsieur Prieur, the retired superintendent of the American Cemetery in Épinal, wrote to me following our visit and attempted to offer some explanation as to why my father remained silent about his wartime experiences:

> … please do not worry about the fact that your Dad didn't talk about his war experience. By my own experience, and by what I have learned over the years, I can assure you that it is nearly always the case [that experiences are not shared]. Why? I don't really know, but it may be because the most important thing is to be back in one piece, the rest doesn't matter so much. And, the veteran often feels that others might not believe his stories; they're so awful. The real Hero doesn't need to tell! Perhaps there is a good reason why your Dad didn't say much.

I suspect my father fished because he felt safe in that activity as well as the opportunity to engage with the calming and centering effect of nature. He had not been safe during the relentless fighting across the French countryside during World War II. Certainly, he was immersed in nature throughout his experiences as an infantry soldier, but not engaged from a healthy psychological perspective. He was in conflict with nature, trying to stay dry, warm, and safe in a foreign environment. The dark forest was filled with danger and threat to life, not relaxing and peaceful sounds. If owls and crickets were present, he would have perceived them as enemy troops disguising their voices or stepping on twigs as they approached. Monsieur Prieur also wrote in his letter to me that "war always brings a lot of misery, tragedy, wounds, death, disasters, separations of family … but also, unexpected love and wonders." Perhaps for my father the soothing sights and sounds of nature were overpowered by the elements of war.

My father's fishing habits and adventures began with the companionship of his poker buddies following World War II. In reality, the social outings involved comradery and solidarity among a group of Army veterans. It was a special group of men who shared similar but silent combat experiences and memories. They didn't need to openly discuss the details associated with their combat memories. It was sufficient to spend time together knowing the group understood in ways others could not comprehend.

At some point in time, the fishing trips transformed into poker games, perhaps in response to marriages, children, work responsibilities, or financial costs associated with large-scale excursions to Canada. The activity had changed, but the group maintained its cohesiveness and silent bond.

By the time I was a senior in high school, my father was fishing alone along the river near our home. During the early autumn months, he came home from work, calmly and silently ate dinner, and then carried his fishing pole to the truck and drove to the location that had become his favorite salmon-fishing spot. On Saturdays, he fished during the early morning. Fishing was his safe zone—shelter from aspects of his environment beyond his control and a stable, predictable structure that provided emotional balance and a place for him to manage his emotions and his memories. A place where he didn't need to be on guard. Fishing with his Army buddies offered shelter from painful combat memories associated with stress, heightened emotions, and entrapment. Fishing alone provided a place to balance similar stressors later in his civilian life related to feeling trapped in his job, and unfulfilled and bored with his routines and the life he had created.

That which I had interpreted as introspectiveness throughout my youth had changed to emotional isolation and profound loneliness as I approached high-school graduation. The Canadian fishing trips with his group of Army comrades had stopped many decades earlier. Their poker games tapered off and stopped completely somewhere during my high-school years and he rarely mentioned the group after that, other than occasional references to their individual names. The fishing trips to Crossville stopped during my senior year. Ed Kmet had retired and the Crossville Rubber Company processes had changed, no longer requiring face-to-face business meetings. My father had lost his primary support systems. A few days after high-school graduation, he asked if I had any plans for the future. He waited for my response while continuing to read the newspaper as he sat in his usual place on the living-room sofa. I had nothing specific on my agenda. College had not crossed my mind—I knew our family couldn't afford the tuition and I would not risk inflicting embarrassment or unintentional humiliation by asking him for the money required to pay for college. His question surprised me—he rarely asked me or my siblings about individual aspects of our lives. In part I wondered why he decided to ask at that particular time, and in part I was pleased he was actually asking me. I felt slight resentment as well as joy in response to his simple question. When I said, "No, I don't have any plans, other than finding a job," he said, "You can come and work with me." Again, I experienced simultaneous conflicting thoughts. First, I thought, "You hate your job, why would I do that?" and then I thought, "It's a full-time job. I can get an apartment and go out on my own."

The next week we began a daily rideshare routine. Just me and my father for 20 minutes in the morning and 20 minutes in the evening. Forty minutes of mostly awkward silence. The few conversations we shared often lacked depth and substance. A month later, he began picking me up in front of my apartment and dropping me off in the same spot at 5:30 every evening. The location had changed but the routine and the communication pattern in the truck remained consistent. I believe he wanted to have meaningful conversation, he just didn't know how to. A year later, I recognized this employment opportunity was not a path that would lead to a bright future so I sought and accepted a job as an orderly in the recovery room of a large Cleveland teaching hospital. This was the start of my lengthy and productive career in healthcare and the catalyst for my relentless pursuit of formal academic education. It was also the point in time at which I began to slowly lose contact with my father. We talked briefly on the phone after that and I occasionally stopped at the house to say hello, but the visits were brief in large part because the awkward silence had become uncomfortable. His quiet nature was not associated with anger or resentment toward visitors, and he wasn't mean, hostile, curmudgeonly, or unwelcoming. He was simply quiet and reserved, as if faithfully and diligently protecting something deeply personal he wouldn't risk sharing.

My father's preferred coping mechanisms associated with hiding away emotional pain and seeking silent solidarity with those who understood eventually failed him when his Army buddies were no longer present and active in his life, when the fishing trips to Tennessee and the peaceful hours fishing with Ed on City Lake ended, and when there was no one remaining with whom to silently connect after my four siblings and I had all left the nest. The silent trips to and from work that year were possibly his final attempt to keep the fragile social framework from crumbling. But he didn't know what to say because his defense mechanisms were well-entrenched by then, and I didn't know where to start meaningful conversations because I didn't understand the factors contributing to the pattern of awkward communication.

He always seemed to be emotionally guarded. He retired the next year and my parents sold our childhood home before moving to Florida. I made only one visit to their rented condominium near Fort Lauderdale before his diagnosis of metastatic cancer. My busy schedule attending school on a full-time basis Monday through Friday and working every weekend at the hospital prevented me from visiting him once he was home and spending all his time in a living-room hospice bed. At least, that was my plausible public excuse. In part, I didn't know how to bring closure because too many unanswered questions remained and I had been unsuccessful in my naive attempts to break through the silence. So, I avoided the conflict—just as he did throughout his life.

Reflection

> Like a giant hand clutching an eraser, troops of the VI Corps US Army have rubbed out the centuries-old "T" on the big word "can't" as it applies to the military conquest of the Vosges Mountains.[1]

Several years have passed since completing this very personal journey and I continue to reflect on the factors that compelled me to make the trip. The thoughts often return unexpectedly—prompted by some seemingly random and unrelated statement, conversation, visual trigger, or simply during a moment of silence. The memories associated with the journey are extremely clear and I can play them back as if I were watching a movie re-run.

Throughout our journey across France, the weather conditions were perfect—mild temperatures, mostly sunny, and no rain. The mornings were cool and misty, the days were warm and clear, the nights cold and crisp. The weather on the day we located the field where the 27th Evacuation Hospital was briefly based was absolutely beautiful—a dramatic difference from the conditions in October 1944.

Through the completion of this amazing journey, I gained a deeper appreciation for the men of the 180th Infantry Regiment and for my father. I understand him as a human being, with the same strengths, weaknesses, fears, apprehensions, scars, wounds, limitations, mistakes, and questions as each of us. I understand him as a strong and good-looking naive young man that, while searching for his identity as a proud young soldier, experienced the dramatic realities of war and the brutality of which mankind is capable. I understand his silence as the result of painful emotional scars, deep-seated fear, and emotional trauma that he buried within his psyche. Today, the medical profession refers to this process and condition as post-traumatic stress disorder. He witnessed profound and sustained violence and destruction, and he likely inflicted the same as a heavy machine gunner. I understand him as a fragile and vulnerable person who became a survivor. His silence was a reflection of his pain, and the absence of transparency and emotional conversations were the result of defense mechanisms to contain the powerful emotions associated with his memories. I understand him from a much broader and more-realistic perspective. I still look up to him, but with admiration and empathy for his struggles, pain, courage, and humanity, not the larger-than-life mystical figure that always seemed elusive during my youth and confusing to me as an adult. At the same time, I feel sad for him and his lifetime of silent personal struggle. I have become closer to him for all of these reasons.

Even after leaving the front lines, my father was not out of harm's way, and his life remained threatened. The scar on the side of his neck, resulting from a traumatic laceration in 1945, was quite large. If it had been slightly lower, it would have likely cut the carotid artery, and he would have bled to death at the scene of the attack. The bone along the lower edge of his jaw apparently served to stop the wound from becoming too deep and protected the major blood vessels in his neck. The only time he mentioned the scar was in response to my questioning him as a nine-year-old child sitting cross-legged on the living room floor in front of the television.

"Where did you get that scar?"

"In the war."

"What happened?"

"A guy went crazy."

"What did you do?"

He then turned the page and continued reading his newspaper, while avoiding eye contact with his young son. Whoever the attacker was, he could have easily taken my father's life from him at that moment. He told me, "They had to shoot him." Despite my research, I still don't know who "they" were.

The only medical reference to a neck wound and subsequent scar is contained in his medical-discharge examination summary completed in January 1946 after returning to the United States. The record indicates he received the laceration in the line of duty when hit with a broken bottle during a riot in March 1945. He was in Paris, assigned to a military police (MP) unit at the time and was treated at the 7th Convalescent Hospital to repair the wound. Paris was a popular area for leave—over one hundred thousand officers and enlisted men visited each week during this time of the war. If he was serving as an MP called to break up a riot somewhere in Paris, and was attacked by a broken-bottle-wielding soldier, it is possible my father had to shoot in self-defense. If so, it would merely have added to the emotional scars he carried with him after returning home from Europe.

My father passed away in the autumn of 1984 and took with him these profound secrets. I hope he is at peace and that his pain, fears, regrets, wounds, and scars have resolved. I hope they have evaporated like the morning mist and fog of the forest when I first stood in front of the 45th Division monument in Frémifontaine on the morning of October 10 nearly 70 years after my father left the field of battle in this village.

I have very few regrets in my life. One is that my father did not have the opportunity to meet my daughter. She is his first-born grandchild and she was born less than a year after he died. To be accompanied by her meant two generations were connecting with him. Tara shared these reflections following our journey:

> Although I never met my grandfather, I know that he was a truly wonderful man. I also know how proud he is of his son and the man he has become. I will forever cherish this journey across the French countryside.
>
> To begin our journey by standing in the exact spot in Bourg, France, that the tank photo was taken so many years ago connected me to my grandfather in a way I could never have imagined. It was then that I knew this would be one of the most impactful experiences of my life.
>
> Eager to learn, we met an elderly woman outside her home as she broke into tears of appreciation for my grandfather's efforts in WWII. She invited us into her home as she cast a vision for the past. The significance of my grandfather's time in France hit me like a tidal wave of emotion when I heard this testimony.

> It showed how important my grandfather and the other troops had been in helping so many people.
>
> A quick visit to a field in Xertigny turned into so much more when we located the exact location of the Evacuation Hospital and met an elderly woman that remembers delivering food to the soldiers in that Hospital so vividly from her childhood. This experience more than anything painted a picture of the perilous road my grandfather traveled. Hearing this story from a woman that could have potentially served my grandfather food was the closest thing to hearing it from my grandfather directly. Standing in that field, for a moment, it was as if we were there with him.
>
> The powerful culmination of our journey began with the arrival into the village of Fremifontaine [*sic*]—arriving on the same October date my grandfather left the field of battle from this village many decades earlier. With much anticipation, we drove up the narrow and picturesque winding streets to the 45th Infantry Division monument that Jean-Marie had worked so hard to create. I will forever remember the moment my father walked up to the monument perched on its small hill—as he crouched down, the clouds instantly parted and beautiful rays of sun cast down on him. In that moment, I knew that my grandfather was with us on this journey and we could consider our mission accomplished.

So, what was the point of this journey? In part, finding answers to a lifetime of unanswered questions specific to the emotional distance of an important person in my life—my father. Although I recall sensing something elusive in his personality throughout all stages of my childhood, I could never describe nor understand the subtle behavior. Therefore, the appropriate questions never formed in my thoughts or in my words, even if the opportunity to ask them had presented itself. There was nothing within my environment—family, siblings, friends, house, neighborhood, school, hobbies—that explained the subtle distance and sadness. So, I quietly continued to wonder. His death in the autumn of 1984 was difficult for me. Parents are irreplaceable and they leave a permanent imprint upon our lives. My silent challenge in saying goodbye was compounded by a lifetime of not knowing, and subconsciously believing I would never know. Several decades later, my relentless personal journey finally exposed the dramatic reasons for his emotional distance and introspective personality. I could never have speculated that the strong, handsome, kind, quiet family man I knew had experienced such intense personal trauma.

This journey also facilitated emotional closure specific to an important aspect of my life that has remained through adulthood—I can stop wondering. Perhaps most importantly, when I encounter future moments in life that generate concern, worry, fear, despair, and even panic—when there seems to be no way out—I will think of my dad in the dark forests near Frémifontaine. I will take a long, deep breath, gently shake my head and softly say out loud, "*Semper Anticus!*" And, I will keep going. If he had given up, he would not have survived the German attack on October 6 and 7 and I subsequently would not exist. He had two choices—fight or give up. He certainly didn't apply a great deal of calm analysis to the decision. He was undoubtedly in survival mode and terrified his life was about to end in the dark forests of France far from his family and friends. It seems my journey was also a uniquely personal lesson at a specific time in my life. As a child, the lesson would have been missed. As an adult, the lesson is clear and profoundly meaningful. I've experienced events in my life that were perceived as devastating while actively involved in those moments. Broken relationships, unexpected job loss, and emotional conflict seemed overwhelming and hopeless at the time. But, despite the anxiety, fear, and tension, they were merely brief moments associated with the challenges and struggles of daily life compared to what my fathered endured in the forests of eastern France. As I closed my thoughts on this journey, I imagined that the man with no formal education, and who once told me he regretted dropping out of high school, had inadvertently facilitated a profound moment of learning long after his death.

I have often learned through the mistakes of others. I learned what not to do by observing their failures and this applied to my parents as well. I had successfully broken free from the roadblocks that trapped my father in his work and his job. I had avoided the barriers that prevented him from finishing high school and his regret associated with not pursuing and obtaining a formal education. However, I hadn't discovered or processed the factors responsible for his emotional distance and silence, so avoiding this path proved to be more difficult than the first two objectives. I briefly saw him cry only once. It was at the funeral service for his mother, my grandmother. The Russian Orthodox priest was chanting and after mentioning her name several times within the chant, I saw my father lower his head, turn, and walk toward the back of the room. As I turned toward him, my mother reached out her arm and said, "He's okay. He's just upset and needs some air." He left the funeral home and stepped out onto the sidewalk just as several of his poker buddies walked from the parking lot up to the entrance. My mother later said the timing of their arrival was fortunate. As a young adult, I had inadvertently adopted some of his behaviors simply through observation. He didn't openly share emotion, so I didn't share my emotions. I hadn't realized the connection until gaining insight through this journey across France. He apparently had a legitimate reason for at least some degree of the protective nature observed in his personality; I didn't.

This journey opened the door to a secret emotional vault and revealed aspects of the man that I could never have imagined during my youth. He spent so much time and energy protecting himself and hiding his trauma. His silence and lack of shared emotion were not behaviors to be patterned and copied. Rather, they were protective shrouds designed to hide away pain and suffering from the brutality of war and the emotional scars of battle. Research shows that this pattern of persistent behavior over an extended period of time can lead to devastating outcomes involving an emotional explosion of violence or slow erosion and destruction of the body from within. This journey revealed his painful secrets, but also corrected the earlier self-imposed lessons I had learned by watching him throughout my life. In hindsight, the challenging aspects of his life that served as self-destructive forces helped me to understand three important lessons, all of which have had a positive effect. Do meaningful work that is enjoyable and financially beneficial, continuously learn and expand upon knowledge, and bring transparency and authenticity to the important relationships in one's life. Emotional armor did not serve him well over the course of time.

My father's lessons included teaching me to fish, something I do frequently May through September for enjoyment and relaxation. I don't brag about my catches, nor do I boast about my sportsman-related skills. Fishing isn't a competition, nor is it an elaborate process. I just fish, an activity that will continue throughout my life and that will include many meaningful hours teaching my grandchildren to do the same.

The remains of a 30-caliber machine-gun ammo can and six 30-caliber spent cartridges retrieved from the G Company foxhole overlooking the valley used by my father during the fighting on October 6 and 7, 1944. (Michael Reyka)

A shadow box of Steve Reyka's medals and awards above the remains of a German pop-up mine, a vintage Thunderbird patch, and artifacts from my father's foxhole as well as his dog tags and uniform cap. (Michael Reyka)

Michael Reyka and Jean-Marie Siret shaking hands in front of the 45th Division Monument in Frémifontaine, France.

Several years after returning home from France, I received a small parcel from Jean-Marie along with a separate small, white, padded envelope. The cardboard parcel was about the size of a breakfast cereal box wrapped in brown paper and taped securely at both ends. I opened the container and removed the severely rusted remains of a metal machine-gun ammunition can. The padded envelope contained six empty .30-caliber brass cartridge casings taped to a thin piece of cardstock. A message from Jean-Marie confirmed he had returned to the remote site on the plateau overlooking the Mortagne and retrieved the artifacts from my father's foxhole more than 70 years after they had been left there. Jean-Marie had written in a note slid into the envelope that he thought the relics would be meaningful to me. He was correct. They are currently displayed on an oak platform under a glass dome in my home with my Dad's framed boot-camp photo on the wall above them.

Biography of Jean-Marie Siret

Jean-Marie Siret, born in 1941, is married to Yvette Fortier, and lives in the small village of Frémifontaine (Vosges, east of France).

Yvette's father, Georges Fortier, was a member of the French resistance forces, formally known as the *Forces françaises de l'intérieur* (FFI, French Forces of the Interior) during World War II. Georges fought alongside the American soldiers of the 180th Infantry Regiment in this region during the early autumn months of 1944. He and five of his French comrades, along with F Company of the 180th Regiment, were surrounded by German forces at the Xeuty farm. Only Georges and one of his comrades succeeded in escaping.

Georges passed away in 2006. After Georges shared these personal wartime experiences, Jean-Marie decided to recognize and pay tribute to all the men who fought for the liberation of Frémifontaine and the surrounding region. Jean-Marie initiated the design and erection of a monument dedicated to the 45th Infantry Division soldiers, as well as a commemorative plaque dedicated to the FFI squad of Frémifontaine. His tireless efforts serve to preserve the memory of the sacrifices made by the FFI and American soldiers of the 45th Infantry Division. He is a lifelong member of the 180th Infantry Association.

Endnotes

Prologue

1 Siret, email to author, confirmation of location where jeep hit a mine, 2011.

2 Siret, written testimonial describing "the place of the jeep," 2010.

3 L. Remond, transcript of words read during the ceremony on October 10, 2010. Via Jean-Marie Siret, translation by L. Gregorio. Frémifontaine, France, October 10, 2010.

4 R. Phulpin, statement made to author during the town-hall reception following the ceremony, information confirmed by Jean-Marie Siret in email dated April 25, 2011. Frémifontaine, France, October 2010.

Chapter 1

1 Chuck Schindler, Personal diary, January–March 1944, 45th Infantry Division Museum Archives, Oklahoma City, Oklahoma.

2 Flint Whitlock, *The Rock of Anzio: From Sicily to Dachau: A history of the U.S. 45th Infantry Division* (Westview Press, 1998), 258.

3 Christopher Hibbert, *Anzio: The Bid for Rome* (New York: Ballantine Books), 113–20.

4 Whitlock, *The Rock of Anzio*, 248.

5 Ibid.

6 Order of Battle of the US Army WWll ETO 45th Infantry Division, n.d.

7 L. Frazier, "S-2 Army Officer Duties," *Careertrend*, 28 December, 2018. Accessed January 8, 2022, https://careertrend.com/list-6692783-s2-army-officer-duties.html.

8 N. H. Fuss, "Back to the Basics: the Battalion S2." *Military Intelligence Professional Bulletin*, 23(2), April–June 1997, 19.

9 M. Reyka, *A Son's Journey: Uncovering my father's life as a Thunderbird* (Gettysburg, Pennsylvania: Thomas Publications, 2009).

10 J. Vincent, "Memories of War and Sacrifice," Tom Mathews interview by Libby Smith, *45th Division*. Accessed January 8, 2017, https://www45thdivision.org.
11 W. T. Zoepf, *Seven Days in January with the 6th SS Mountain Division in Operation Nordwind* (Bedford, Pennsylvania: Aberjona Press, 2001), 118.
12 J. Devers, Letter of appreciation to the commanding general of the 45th Division, September 28, 1945. In G. A. Fisher, *The Story of the 180th Infantry Regiment* (San Angelo, Texas: Newsfoto Publishing, 1947).
13 B. Austin, interview with author, 45th Division Reunion 2008, Oklahoma City, Oklahoma, 2008.
14 C. Bell, interview with author, 45th Division Reunion 2008, Oklahoma City, Oklahoma, 2008.
15 C. Charles, telephone interview with author, November 30, 2006.
16 J. Margotta, interview with author, Sleepy Hollow, New York, December 2006.

Chapter 2

1 S. Zaloga, *Operation Dragoon—France's other D-Day* (Oxford: Osprey Publishing, 2009).
2 A. Tucker-Jones, *Operation Dragoon: the Liberation of Southern France, 1944* (Barnsley: Pen & Sword Military), 113.
3 Zaloga, *Operation Dragoon—France's other D-Day*, 45.
4 The US Army Campaigns of World War II, Southern France, brochure, p. 15. Accessed November 19, 2017, http://www.army.mil/cmh-pg/brochures/sfrance/sfrance.htm.
5 George A. Fisher, *The Story of the 180th Infantry Regiment* (San Angelo, Texas: Newsfoto Publishing, 1947).
6 Zaloga, *Operation Dragoon—France's other D-Day*, 87.
7 Fisher, *The Story of the 180th Infantry Regiment.*
8 Headquarters 180th Infantry Regiment, S-2 Journal, 0052, 2003 & 2140 hours, September 1, 1944.
9 L. V. Bishop, *The Fighting Forty-Fifth* (Baton Rouge, Louisiana: Army and Navy Publishing, 1946), 101.
10 Ibid., 103.
11 Regiment, Headquarters S-2 Journal, 1944 September, September 8, 0822 hrs.
12 Ibid., September 8, 0914 hrs.

Chapter 3

1 L. V. Bishop, *The Fighting Forty-Fifth* (Baton Rouge, Louisiana: Army and Navy Publishing, 1946), 103.
2 Jean-Marie Siret, conversation with author, October 2010.
3 Regiment, Headquarters S-2 Journal, 1944 September, September 7, 0315 hrs.

4 Regiment, Headquarters S-2 Journal, 1944 September, September 7, 0425 hrs.
5 Regiment, Headquarters Transmittal of Organizational History, 1944 September.
6 Bishop, *The Fighting Forty-Fifth*, 103.
7 Ibid., 103–4.
8 Regiment, Headquarters Transmittal of Organizational History, 1944 September.
9 Regiment, Headquarters S-2 Journal, 1944 September, September 7, 1341 hrs.
10 Ibid., September 7, 1902 hrs.
11 G. A. Fisher, *The Story of the 180th Infantry Regiment* (San Angelo, Texas: Newsfoto Publishing, 1947).
12 Ibid., Chapter 8, September 8.
13 Regiment, Headquarters S-2 Journal, 1944 September, September 8, 1145 hrs.
14 Ibid., September 8, 1506 hrs.
15 Ibid., September 8, 2050 hrs.
16 Regiment, Headquarters Transmittal of Organizational History, 1944 September, 4–5.
17 Fisher, *The Story of the 180th Infantry Regiment*, Chapter 8, September 9.
18 Regiment, Headquarters S-2 Journal, 1944 September, September 9, 1015 hrs.

Chapter 4

1 Regiment, Report of Operations, 1944 September, 6.
2 Regiment, Headquarters S-2 Journal, 1944 September, September 11, 1125 hrs.
3 Ibid., September 11, 1201 hrs.
4 Ibid., September 11, 1759 hrs.
5 B. Echohawk, *Drawing Fire* (Lawrence, Kansas: University Press of Kansas, 2018), 145.
6 Regiment, Headquarters S-2 Journal, 1944 September.
7 Ibid., September 11, 1125 hrs.
8 Ibid., September 11, 1653 hrs, 1759 hrs, 1940 hrs.
9 Massif des Vosges [Vosges Mountains]. Accessed March 23, 2025, http://www.vosges-mountains.com.

Chapter 5

1 G. A. Fisher, *The Story of the 180th Infantry Regiment* (San Angelo, Texas: Newsfoto Publishing, 1947), Chapter 8, September 11.
2 Regiment, Headquarters S-2 Journal, 1944 September, September 11, 1823 hrs.
3 Ibid.
4 Fisher, *The Story of the 180th Infantry Regiment.*
5 Regiment, Headquarters Transmittal of Organizational History, 1944 September, 6.
6 Regiment, Headquarters S-2 Journal, 1944 September, September 11, 1352 hrs.
7 Ibid., September 11, 1433 hrs.

8 Ibid., September 12, 0755 hrs.
9 Ibid., September 12, 0845 hrs.
10 Ibid., September 12, 0953 hrs.
11 Ibid., September 13, 0923 hrs.
12 Ibid., September 13, 0930 hrs.
13 Regiment, Headquarters Field Order, 1944 September 12.
14 Regiment, Headquarters S-2 Journal, 1944 September, September 13, 2035 hrs.
15 Ibid., September 12.
16 Ibid., September 12, 1940 hrs.
17 Ibid., September 13, 2400 hrs.
18 Information provided by Ghislaine Vuillier, mayor of Bonnal, via email to Jean-Marie Siret, March 31, 2025.

Chapter 6

1 R. Grosjean, interview with author, Villersexel and Fougerolles, France, October 2010.
2 "Cushman 1944 Model 53 Airborne Motor Scooter," *International Military Antiques*, n.d. Accessed August 2017, https://www.ima-usa.com.
3 "White Motor Company half-track military vehicle," *National WWII Museum*, n.d. Accessed August 2017, https://www.nationalww2museum.org/visit/museum-campus/us-freedom-pavilion/vehicles-war/white-m3-half-track.
4 M3 Half-track military vehicle, *Tank Encyclopedia*, n.d. Accessed August 2017, https://tanks.encyclopedia.com.
5 Ibid.
6 Regiment, Headquarters S-2 Journal, 1944 September, September 13, 2400 hrs.
7 Ibid., September 14, 1233 hrs.
8 Ibid., September 12, 2400 hrs.
9 Ibid., September 14, 2035 hrs.
10 Ibid., September 14, 2400 hrs.
11 Ibid., September 16, 0245 hrs.
12 Ibid., September 16, 2245 hrs.
13 M. F. Demangeon, written testimonial describing German soldier with fatal abdominal wound, via Jean-Marie Siret, translation by L. Gregorio, Frémifontaine, France, October 2010.
14 Regiment, Headquarters S-2 Journal, 1944 September, September 18, 2025 hrs.

Chapter 7

1 R. Prieur, interview with author, retired Superintendent American Cemetery at Épinal, Épinal, France, October 2010.

2 Regiment, Headquarters Second Battalion Journal, 1944 September, September 12, 2400 hrs.
3 Prieur, October 2010.

Chapter 8

1 A. Boissonet, email to author, town council member, information regarding location of 27th Evacuation Hospital.
2 Hospital, Annual Report—Supplement #2 Nurses Diary, 1944, 34.
3 Ibid.
4 Ibid.
5 Hospital, Annual Report—Supplement #2 Nurses Diary, 1944.
6 Hospital, Annual Report—Supplement #1 Medical History Data, 1944.
7 Hospital, Annual Report—Supplement #2 Nurses Diary, 1944, 34.
8 Hospital, Annual Report—Supplement #2 Nurses Diary, 1944.
9 Ibid.
10 Hospital, Annual Report—Supplement #1 Medical History Data, 1944.
11 Ibid., 12.
12 Ibid.
13 Hospital, Annual Report—Supplement #2 Nurses Diary, 1944, 34.
14 Ibid.
15 J. Pierre, interview with author, Xertigny Farm family member, regarding 27th Evacuation Hospital location, October 2010.
16 Pierre, October 2010.

Chapter 9

1 Jean-Marie Siret, conversation with author, October 2010.
2 G. A. Fisher, *The Story of the 180th Infantry Regiment* (San Angelo, Texas: Newsfoto Publishing, 1947), Chapter 8.
3 L. V. Bishop, *The Fighting Forty-Fifth* (Baton Rouge, Louisiana: Army and Navy Publishing, 1946), 105.
4 Regiment, Report of Operations, 1944 September, 9.
5 Fisher, *The Story of the 180th Infantry Regiment*, Chapter 8.
6 Regiment, Headquarters S-2 Journal, 1944 September, September 21, 1634 hrs.
7 Ibid., September 22, 1356 hrs.
8 Ibid., September 22, 1945 hrs. White 3 to Regiment.
9 Regiment, Report of Operations, 1944 September, 9.
10 Regiment, Report of Operations, 1944 September, 9–10.
11 Siret, conversation with author, October 2010.
12 Fisher, *The Story of the 180th Infantry Regiment*, Chapter 8.

13 Regiment, Headquarters S-2 Journal, 1944 September, September 22, 0836 hrs.
14 Ibid., September 22, 1248 hrs.
15 Siret, conversation with author, October 2010.
16 Regiment, Headquarters S-2 Journal, 1944 September, September 22, 1841 hrs.
17 Ibid., September 23, 1121 hrs.
18 "For the First Time in History an Army Crossed the Vosges," *Beachhead News*, December 10, 1944, Army, 1–3.
19 Siret, conversation with author, October 2010.
20 "For the First Time in History an Army Crossed the Vosges."
21 Fisher, *The Story of the 180th Infantry Regiment*, Chapter 8.
22 Regiment, Headquarters S-2 Journal, 1944 September, September 22, 2150 hrs.
23 Ibid., September 22, 2020 hrs.
24 "For the First Time in History an Army Crossed the Vosges."
25 Jean-Marie Siret, email to author, confirmation of Bailey Bridge across Moselle River, March 14, 2011.
26 Regiment, Headquarters S-2 Journal, 1944 September, September 22, 2150 hrs.
27 Ibid., September 23, 0001 hrs.
28 Siret, email to author, March 14, 2011.
29 Fisher, *The Story of the 180th Infantry Regiment*, Chapter 8.
30 Ibid.
31 Siret, email to author, March 14, 2011.
32 Regiment, Report of Operations, 1944 September, 10.
33 Fisher, *The Story of the 180th Infantry Regiment*, Chapter 8.
34 Ibid.
35 Regiment, Headquarters S-2 Journal, 1944 September, September 24, 0730 hrs.
36 Fisher, *The Story of the 180th Infantry Regiment*, Chapter 8.
37 Regiment, Headquarters S-2 Journal, 1944 September, September 24, 1233 hrs.
38 Bishop, *The Fighting Forty-Fifth*, 108.
39 Fisher, *The Story of the 180th Infantry Regiment*, Chapter 8.
40 Bishop, *The Fighting Forty-Fifth*, 106–7.
41 Regiment, Headquarters S-2 Journal, 1944 September, September 24, 2300 hrs.
42 Ibid., September 25, 1345 hrs.
43 Ibid., September 24, 1320 hrs.
44 Ibid., September 24, 1104 hrs.
45 Bishop, *The Fighting Forty-Fifth*, 108.
46 Ibid., 111.
47 Regiment, Report of Operations, 1944 September, 12.

Chapter 10

1 G. A. Fisher, *The Story of the 180th Infantry Regiment* (San Angelo, Texas: Newsfoto Publishing, 1947), Chapter 8.

2 Regiment, Headquarters S-2 Journal, 1944 September, September 26, 1446 hrs.
3 Ibid., September 26, 1540 hrs.
4 Ibid., September 26, 1610 hrs.
5 Regiment, Headquarters Field Order No. 46 September 27, 1944 September 27.
6 Regiment, Headquarters S-2 Journal, 1944 September, September 27, 1019 hrs.
7 P. Triboulot, interview with author (L. Gregorio, translator), Girecourt resident—facial trauma during childhood from land mine, October 2010.
8 Jean-Marie Siret, conversation with author, October 2010.
9 Triboulot, October 2010.
10 Ibid.
11 Ibid.
12 L. V. Bishop, *The Fighting Forty-Fifth* (Baton Rouge, Louisiana: Army and Navy Publishing, 1946), 109.

Chapter 11

1 Jean-Marie Siret, conversation with author, October 2010.
2 L. V. Bishop, *The Fighting Forty-Fifth* (Baton Rouge, Louisiana: Army and Navy Publishing, 1946), Chapter 8.
3 Siret, conversation with author, October 2010.
4 Regiment, Headquarters S-2 Journal, 1944 September, September 26, 1515 hrs.
5 Ibid., September 26, 1610 and 1723 hrs.
6 Ibid., September 27, 1415 and 1445 hrs.
7 G. A. Fisher, *The Story of the 180th Infantry Regiment* (San Angelo, Texas: Newsfoto Publishing, 1947), Chapter 8; Memorial of John W. Puckett. Accessed April 25, 2025, https://www.fold3.com/memorial/657824645/john-w-puckett.
8 Ibid.
9 Ibid.
10 Ibid.
11 Ibid.
12 Regiment, Report of Operations, 1944 September, 12.
13 Fisher, *The Story of the 180th Infantry Regiment*, Chapter 8.
14 Regiment, Headquarters Field Order No. 46 Sept. 27, 1944 September 27.
15 Regiment, Headquarters S-2 Journal, 1944 September, September 27, 1945 hrs.
16 Fisher, *The Story of the 180th Infantry Regiment*, Chapter 8.

Chapter 12

1 Regiment, Headquarters S-2 Journal, 1944 September, September 28, 0135 and 2020 hrs.
2 Ibid., September 28, 1225 hrs.

3 Ibid., September 28, 0700 hrs.
4 Ibid., September 28, 0835, 1007, and 1114 hrs.
5 Ibid., September 28, 1900 hrs.
6 Ibid., September 28, 1940 hrs.
7 Jean-Marie Siret, conversation with author, October 2010.
8 Regiment, Headquarters Transmittal of Organizational History, 1944 September.
9 Regiment, Headquarters Field Order #47 September 28, 1944, September 28.
10 Regiment, Report of Operations, 1944 September.
11 Regiment, Headquarters S-2 Journal, 1944 October, October 1, 0850 hrs.
12 Regiment, Report of Operations, 1944 October.
13 Ibid.
14 Siret, conversation with author, October 2010.
15 Regiment, Report of Operations, 1944 September, 16.
16 Regiment, Headquarters S-2 Journal, 1944 September, September 28, 1115 hrs.
17 Regiment, Second Battalion H Company Morning Reports, 1944 October, October 2.
18 Ibid., October 3–4.
19 Ibid., October 5.
20 George, FFI Action Order calling for disruption to German operations prior to October, written Action Order via Jean-Marie Siret, translation by L. Gregorio, Frémifontaine, France, October 2010.
21 J. Moulin, Written testimonial of Allied escapees hiding in the forest, via Jean-Marie Siret (translation by L. Gregorio), Frémifontaine, France, October 2010.
22 Regiment, Headquarters Transmittal of Organizational History, 1944 September.
23 A. Kershaw, *The Liberator* (New York, New York: Penguin Random House, 2012).
24 Ibid.
25 Ibid.
26 Ibid.
27 Ibid.

Chapter 13

1 Jean-Marie Siret, written testimonial examples of villager passive resistance to Germans, via Jean-Marie Siret (translation by L. Gregorio), Frémifontaine, France, October 2010.
2 A. Begel, villager frustration with German soldier in his home, via Jean-Marie Siret, translation by L. Gregorio, Frémifontaine, France, October 2010.
3 J. Moulin, Written testimonial of Allied escapees hiding in the forest, via Jean-Marie Siret (translation by L. Gregorio), Frémifontaine, France, October 2010.
4 Regiment, Headquarters Transmittal of Organizational History, 1944 October, 2.
5 Ibid., 4.

6 G. A. Fisher, *The Story of the 180th Infantry Regiment* (San Angelo, Texas: Newsfoto Publishing, 1947), Chapter 8.
7 Ibid.
8 Regiment, Headquarters Transmittal of Organizational History, 1944 October, 2.
9 L. V. Bishop, *The Fighting Forty-Fifth* (Baton Rouge, Louisiana: Army and Navy Publishing, 1946), 110.
10 L. Delaite, written testimonial related to the Allied use and return of local furniture, via Jean-Marie Siret (translation by L. Gregorio), Frémifontaine, France, October 2010.
11 M. Demangeon, written testimonial regarding artillery and tank shell activity in the village, via Jean-Marie Siret (translation by L. Gregorio), October 2010.
12 Regiment, Headquarters S-3 Report, 1944 October, October 1, 2036 hrs, entry #9 & #55.
13 Regiment, Headquarters S-2 Journal, 1944 September, September 30, 1721 hrs, entry #53.
14 Ibid., September 30, 1905 hrs, entry #56.
15 Ibid., September 30, 1923 hrs, entry #57.
16 Bishop, *The Fighting Forty-Fifth*, 111.
17 Regiment, Headquarters S-2 Journal, 1944 October, October 1, 1.
18 Regiment, Headquarters Transmittal of Organizational History, 1944 October, 16.
19 Pernot, written testimonial of the first artillery shells falling on October 1, 1944, via Jean-Marie Siret (translation by L. Gregorio), Frémifontaine, France, October 2010.
20 L. Balland, written testimonial of a German soldier killed and his rifle preserved, via Jean-Marie Siret (translation by L. Gregorio), Frémifontaine, France, October 2010.
21 J. Alix, written testimonial of shell hitting their home, via Jean-Marie-Siret (translation by L. Gregorio), Frémifontaine, France, October 2010.
22 L. Begel, written testimonial of violent nightime fighting behind her house, via Jean-Marie Siret (translation by L. Gregorio), Frémifontaine, France, October 2010.
23 Ibid.
24 A. Delaite, written testimonial of the protection offered by kitchen water stones, via Jean-Marie Siret (translation by L. Gregorio), Frémifontaine, France, October 2010.
25 G. Fortier, written testimonial of the death of his friend, Hubert, via Jean-Marie Siret (translation by L. Gregorio), Frémifontaine, France, October 2010.
26 Jean-Marie Siret, written testimonial—anonymous author—the test of the buried barrels, via Jean-Marie Siret (translation by L. Gregorio), Fremifontaone, France, October 2010.
27 Regiment, Headquarters S-2 Journal, 1944 October, October 1, 2007 hrs.
28 Ibid., October 1, 1725 hrs.
29 Ibid., October 2, 0650 hrs.
30 Ibid., October 2, 0930 hrs.
31 Ibid., October 2, 2129 hrs.
32 Ibid., October 2, 1000 hrs.
33 Ibid., October 4, 1407 hrs.

34 Fisher, *The Story of the 180th Infantry Regiment*, Chapter 8.
35 Regiment, Headquarters S-2 Journal, 1944 October, October 4, 1740 hrs.
36 Regiment, Headquarters Transmittal of Organizational History, 1944 October, 5.
37 R. D. Martin, written testimonial of FFI losses while fighting on Hill 385, via Jean-Marie Siret (translation by L. Gregorio), Frémifontaine, France, October 2010.
38 Regiment, Headquarters S-2 Journal, 1944 October, October 5, 2100 hrs, entry #28.
39 Jean-Marie Siret, conversation with author, October 2010.
40 C. Balland, written testimonial of the arrival of German tanks in Frémifontaine, via Jean-Marie Siret (translation by L. Gregorio), Frémifontaine, France, October 2010.
41 Siret, conversation with author, October 2010.
42 J. Reeves, letter from 180th HQ Lineman John Reeves to Jean-Marie Siret, February 17, 2000, via Jean-Marie Siret, Frémifontaine, France, October 2010.
43 J. Morgan, letter from Company A Commander 645th Tank Destroyer Battallion to Jean-Marie Siret, via Jean-Marie Siret, Frémifontaine, France, October 2010.
44 Hotchkiss H39 Fast Reconnaissance Light Tank, Military Factory. Accessed April 25, 2025, https://www.militaryfactory.com/armor/detail.php?armor_id=383.
45 P. Grenot, written testimonial of damaged armored vehicles around Fremifontine, via Jean-Marie Siret (translation by L. Gregorio), Frémifontaine, France, October 2010.
46 Siret, conversation with author, October 2010.
47 C. Schindler, personal diary, October 1944, 45th Infantry Division Museum Archives, Oklahoma City, Oklahoma.
48 Regiment, Headquarters S-2 Journal, 1944 October, October 1, 1449 hrs, entry #13.
49 L. Girault, written testimonial related to events at the Frémifontaine mill in early October 1944, via Jean-Marie Siret (translation by L. Gregorio), Frémifontaine, France, October 2010.
50 L. Delaite, October 2010.
51 Regiment, Headquarters S-2 Journal, 1944 October, October 1, 2007 hrs, entry #23.
52 Battalion, 1944 October.
53 Boheme-Anxionnat, written testimonial of young soldier killed in her childhood home, via Jean-Marie Siret (translation by L. Gregorio), Frémifontaine, France, October 2010.
54 Serriere-Laumont, written testimonial of soldier killed while shaving in local house, via Jean-Marie Siret (translation by L. Gregorio), Frémifontaine, France, October 2010.
55 M. C. D., written testimonial of wounded soldier in her home and scrubbing the bloody mattress, via Jean-Marie Siret (translation by L. Gregorio), Frémifontaine, France, October 2010.
56 G. Fortier, written testimonial of assisting M. J. in repairing roof tiles on his home, via Jean-Marie Siret (translation by L. Gregorio), Frémifontaine, France, October 2010.

57 Reeves, October 2010.
58 R. Martin, written testimonial of events in early October 1944 as the 180th arrived, via Jean-Marie Siret (translation by L. Gregorio), Frémifontaine, France, October 2010.
59 M. M. J., written testimonial about the M7 Priest armored vehicles in Frémifontaine, via Jean-Marie Siret (translation by L. Gregorio), Frémifontaine, France, October 2010.
60 J. Brabenac, "Great Guns: M7 'Priest' Backs WWII Armor," *US Army*, September 29, 2011. Accessed January 8, 2020, https://www.army.mil/article/66398/great_guns_MY_Priest.
61 Battalion, 1944 October.
62 Regiment, Headquarters S-3 Report, 1944 October, October 1, 0850 hrs, entry #10 & #55.
63 Siret, conversation with author, October 2010.
64 Ibid.
65 G. Demangeon, written testimonial describing German soldier with fatal abdominal wound, via Jean-Marie Siret (translation by L. Gregorio), Frémifontaine, France, October 2010.
66 L. Guidat, written testimonial of artillery hitting their home and fleeing to the basement, via Jean-Marie Siret (translation by L. Gregorio), Frémifontaine, France, October 2010.
67 Bishop, *The Fighting Forty-Fifth*, 112.
68 Fisher, *The Story of the 180th Infantry Regiment*, Chapter 8.
69 Regiment, Headquarters S-2 Journal, 1944 October, October 2, 0650 hrs, entry #4.
70 Ibid., October 5, 2.
71 Ibid., October 5, 2050 hrs, entry #27.

Chapter 14

1 Regiment, Headquarters S-2 Journal, 1944 October, October 6, 0350 hrs, entry #4.
2 Battalion, 1944 October, 3.
3 Regiment, Headquarters Transmittal of Organizational History, 1944 October, 5.
4 Regiment, Headquarters S-2 Journal, 1944 October, October 6, 0700 hrs, entry #7.
5 Ibid., October 6, 0935 hrs, entry #12.
6 Ibid., October 6, 1350 hrs, entry #36.
7 G. A. Fisher, *The Story of the 180th Infantry Regiment* (San Angelo, Texas: Newsfoto Publishing, 1947), Chapter 8.
8 L. V. Bishop, *The Fighting Forty-Fifth* (Baton Rouge, Louisiana: Army and Navy Publishing, 1946), 113.
9 Ibid., 114.
10 Jean-Marie Siret, conversation with author, October 2010.
11 Battalion, 1944 October, 3.
12 Ibid., 1.

13 R. Bedel, written testimonial describing FFI and Allied positions on the night of October 5, 1944, via Jean-Marie Siret (translation by L. Gregorio), Frémifontaine, France, October 2010.
14 Fisher, *The Story of the 180th Infantry Regiment* Chapter 8.
15 Regiment, Headquarters S-2 Journal, 1944 October, October 6, 1414 and 1420 hrs, entry #44 and 45.
16 Ibid., October 6, 1554 hrs, entry #53.
17 Ibid., October 6, 1555 hrs, entry #54.
18 Siret, conversation with author, October 2010.
19 Fisher, *The Story of the 180th Infantry Regiment*, Chapter 8.
20 Siret, conversation with author, October 2010.
21 Fisher, *The Story of the 180th Infantry Regiment*, Chapter 8.
22 Regiment, Second Battalion H Company Morning Reports, 1944 October, October 7.
23 Fisher, *The Story of the 180th Infantry Regiment*, Chapter 8.
24 A. Barron, Letter from Albert Barron, 2nd Lt. M Co. 180th, to Jean-Marie Siret postwar describing fire for effect, via Jean-Marie Siret, Frémifontaine, France, October 2010.
25 Regiment, Headquarters S-2 Journal, 1944 October, October 6, 2110 hrs, entry #68.
26 G. Fortier, written testimonial describing how his group escaped the German trap on October 6, 1944, during the night, via Jean-Marie Siret (translation by L. Gregorio), Frémifontaine, France, October 2010.
27 Jean-Marie Siret, written testimonial—anonymous author—of FFI group #42 activity on October 5 and 6, 1944, via Jean-Marie Siret (translation by L. Gregorio), Frémifontaine, France, October 2010.
28 Siret, conversation with author, October 2010.
29 M. Delaite, 2010.
30 Fisher, *The Story of the 180th Infantry Regiment*, Chapter 8.
31 Ibid.
32 Regiment, Headquarters Transmittal of Organizational History, 1944 October, 5.
33 Fisher, *The Story of the 180th Infantry Regiment*, Chapter 8.
34 "Hall of Valor Benjamin Blackmer," *Military Times*, n.d. Accessed January 8, 2022, https://valor.militarytimes.com/recipient/recipient-6434/.
35 Fisher, *The Story of the 180th Infantry Regiment*, Chapter 8.
36 R. Moulin, written testimonial describing American armored vehicle positions on October 6, 1944, via Jean-Marie Siret (translation by L. Gregorio), Frémifontaine, France, October 2010.
37 J. Margotta, interview with author, Sleepy Hollow, New York, December 2006.
38 180th Regiment H Company Morning Report, October 6, 1944.
39 180th Regiment H Company Morning Report, October 7, 1944.
40 Regiment, Second Battalion Headquarters Company Morning Reports, 1944 October.

41 Jean-Marie Siret, testimonial regarding the German reoccupation of Frémifontaine on October 6 and 7, 1944, Frémifontaine, France, October 2010.
42 Regiment, Second Battalion H Company Morning Reports, 1944 October, October 8.
43 L. Girault, written testimonial related to events at the Frémifontaine mill in early October 1944, via Jean-Marie Siret (translation by L. Gregorio), Frémifontaine, France, October 2010.
44 D. Durant, written testimonial of events observed during the battle, via Jean-Marie Siret (translation by L. Gregorio), Frémifontaine, France, October 2010.
45 Fortier-Balland, written testimonial of casualties observed during the fighting, via Jean-Marie Siret (translation by L. Gregorio), Frémifontaine, France, October 2010.
46 Fisher, *The Story of the 180th Infantry Regiment*, Chapter 8.
47 J. S. Clark, *Riviera to the Rhine* (Washington, D.C.: Center of Military History, 1993).
48 Regiment, Headquarters S-2 Journal, 1944 October, October 6, 0350, 0700, and 0823 hrs.
49 Regiment, Headquarters S-3 Report, 1944 October, October 5, 0847 hrs.
50 Ibid., October 5, 1700, 1756, and 1835 hrs.
51 Ibid., October 6, 0823 hrs.
52 Fisher, *The Story of the 180th Infantry Regiment*, Chapter 8.
53 Regiment, Headquarters S-3 Report, 1944 October, October 6, 1154 hrs.
54 Fisher, *The Story of the 180th Infantry Regiment*, Chapter 8.
55 Regiment, Headquarters S-3 Report, 1944 October, October 6, 1554 hrs.
56 Fisher, *The Story of the 180th Infantry Regiment*, Chapter 8.
57 Regiment, Headquarters S-3 Report, 1944 October, October 6, 1816, 1838, 1842, 1905, and 1915 hrs.
58 Fisher, *The Story of the 180th Infantry Regiment*, Chapter 8.
59 Regiment, Headquarters S-3 Report, 1944 October, October 6, 2240, 2247, 2300, and 2400 hrs. and October 7, 0012, 0315, and 0546 hrs.
60 Fisher, *The Story of the 180th Infantry Regiment*, Chapter 8.
61 Siret, conversation with author, October 2010.
62 Fisher, *The Story of the 180th Infantry Regiment*, Chapter 8.
63 M. J. M., written testimonial describing damaged tanks in Frémifontaine, via Jean-Marie Siret (translation by L. Gregorio), Frémifontaine, France, October 2010.
64 Military records denote it was the only a post. Jean-Marie had verified the location through personal accounts and the testimonials of villagers.
65 Regiment, Second Battalion H Company Morning Reports, 1944 October, October 10.
66 Regiment, Headquarters Transmittal of Organizational History, 1944 October, 7.
67 Siret, conversation with author, October 2010.
68 Regiment, Headquarters Transmittal of Organizational History, 1944 October, 18.
69 Ibid.
70 J. Reeves, letter from 180th HQ Lineman John Reeves to Jean-Marie Siret, February 17, 2000, via Jean-Marie Siret, Frémifontaine, France, October 2010.

71 Reeves, October 2010.

72 S. Podolsky, "The Changing Fate of Pneumonia as a Public Health Concern in 20th-Century America and Beyond," *American Journal of Public Health*, 95(12), December 2005, 2144–54.

73 Regiment, Headquarters Transmittal of Organizational History, 1944 October, 17.

74 J. Devers, Letter of appreciation to the commanding general of the 45th Division, September 28, 1945. In Fisher, *The Story of the 180th Infantry Regiment.*

75 Bedel, October 2010.

76 Regiment, Headquarters Transmittal of Organizational History, 1944 October, 11.

77 G. Fortier, written testimonial decsribing events and losses on October 20, 1944, after the battle, via Jean-Marie Siret (translation by L. Gregiorio), Frémifontaine, France, October 2010.

78 Regiment, Headquarters Transmittal of Organizational History, 1944 October, 12.

79 Ibid.

80 M. Pernot-Demangeon, written testimonial of friendships and notes sent to villagers by soldier. Via Jean-Marie Siret, translation by L. Gregorio. Frémifontaine, France, October 2010.

Chapter 15

1 R. Lazarus, *Stress and Emotion: A new synthesis* (New York, New York: Springer Publishing, 1999).

2 S. S. Hobfall, "Disentangling the stress labyrinth: Interpreting the meaning of the term stress as it is studied in health context," in *Anxiety, Stress & Coping*, 11(3), n.d.: 181–213.

3 P. Kane, "Stress Causing Psychosomatic Illness Among Nurses," *Indian Journal of Occupational and Enviromental Medicine*, 13(1), 2009: 28–32.

4 E. Goffman, *Interaction Ritual: Essays on face-to-face behavior* (Chicago, Illinois: Aldine Press, 1967), 3.

5 Lazarus, *Stress and Emotion: A new synthesis.*

6 "WWII Post-Traumatic Stress," The National WWII Museum, New Orleans, June 27, 2020. Accessed April 25, 2025, https://www.nationalww2museum.org/war/articles/wwii-post-traumatic-stress.

Reflection

1 Army, "For the First Time in History an Army Crossed the Vosges," *Beachhead News*, December 10, 1944, 1–3.

Bibliography

Primary sources

Alix, J. Written testimonial of shell hitting their home. Via Jean-Marie-Siret, translation by L. Gregorio. Frémifontaine, France, October 2010.

Austin, B. Interview by Michael Reyka at the 45th Division Reunion 2008. Oklahoma City, Oklahoma, 2008.

Balland, C. Written testimonial of the arrival of German tanks in Frémifontaine. Via Jean-Marie Siret, translation by L. Gregorio. Frémifontaine, France, October 2010.

Balland, L. Written testimonial of a German soldier killed and his rifle preserved. Via Jean-Marie Siret, translation by L. Gregorio. Frémifontaine, France, October 2010.

Barron, A. Letter from Albert Barron, 2nd Lt. M Co. 180th, to Jean-Marie Siret postwar describing fire for effect. Via Jean-Marie Siret. Frémifontaine, France, October 2010.

Bedel, R. Written testimonial describing FFI and Allied positions on the night of October 5, 1944. Via Jean-Marie Siret, translation by L. Gregorio. Frémifontaine, France, October 2010.

Begel, A. Villager frustration with German soldier in his home. Via Jean-Marie Siret, translation by L. Gregorio. Frémifontaine, France, October 2010.

Begel, L. Written testimonial of violent nighttime fighting behind her house. Via Jean-Marie Siret, translation by L. Gregorio. Frémifontaine, France, October 2010.

Bell, C. Interview with author at the 45th Division Reunion 2008. Oklahoma City, Oklahoma, 2008.

Boheme-Anxionnat. Written testimonial of young soldier killed in her childhood home. Via Jean-Marie Siret, translation by L. Gregorio. Frémifontaine, France, October 2010.

Boissonet, A. Email to author. Information regarding location of 27th Evacuation Hospital provided by town council member.

C. D., M. Written testimonial of wounded soldier in her home and scrubbing the bloody mattress. Via Jean-Marie Siret, translation by L. Gregorio. Frémifontaine, France, October 2010.

Charles, C. Telephone interview with author, November 30, 2006.

Delaite, M. Written testimonial of the FFI fighting throughout the region prior to October. Max was a platoon leader within the FFI. Via Jean-Marie Siret, translation by L. Gregorio. Grandvillers, France, October 2010.

Delaite, A. Written testimonial of the protection offered by kitchen water stones. Via Jean-Marie Siret, translation by L. Gregorio. Frémifontaine, France, October 2010.

Delaite, L. Written testimonial of artillery shell hitting their house. Via Jean-Marie Siret, translation by L. Gregorio. Frémifontaine, France.

Delaite, L. Written testimonial related to the Allied use and return of local furniture. Via Jean-Marie Siret, translation by L. Gregorio. Frémifontaine, France, October 2010.

Demangeon, G. Written testimonial describing German soldier with fatal abdominal wound. Via Jean-Marie Siret, translation by L. Gregorio. Frémifontaine, France, October 2010.

Demangeon, M. Written testimonial artillery and tank shell activity in the village. Via Jean-Marie Siret, translation by L. Gregorio, October 2010.

Demangeon, M. F. FFI attempted assault on German ammo depot. Via Jean-Marie Siret, translation by L. Gregorio. Frémifontaine, France, October 2010.

Durant, D. Written testimonial of events observed during the battle. Via Jean-Marie Siret, translation by L. Gregorio. Frémifontaine, France, October 2010.

Fortier, G. Written testimonial decsribing events and losses on October 20, 1944, after the battle. Via Jean-Marie Siret, translation by L. Gregiorio. Frémifontaine, France, October 2010.

Fortier, G. Written testimonial describing how his group escaped the German trap on October 6, 1944, during the night. Via Jean-Marie Siret, translation by L. Gregorio. Frémifontaine, France, October 2010.

Fortier, G. Written testimonial of assisting M. J. in repairing roof tiles on his home. Via Jean-Marie Siret, translation by L. Gregorio. Frémifontaine, France, October 2010.

Fortier, G. Written testimonial of the death of his friend, Hubert. Via Jean-Marie Siret, translation by L. Gregorio. Frémifontaine, France, October 2010.

Fortier-Balland. Written testimonial of casualties observed during the fighting. Via Jean-Marie Siret, translation by L. Gregorio. Frémifontaine, France, October 2010.

George. FFI Action Order calling for disruption to German operations prior to October. Written Action Order via Jean-Marie Siret, translation by L. Gregorio. Frémifontaine, France, October 2010.

Girault, L. Written testimonial related to events at the Frémifontaine mill in early October 1944. Via Jean-Marie Siret, translation by L. Gregorio. Frémifontaine, France, October 2010.

Grenot, P. Written testimonial of damaged armored vehicles around Fremifontine. Via Jean-Marie Siret, translation by L. Gregorio. Frémifontaine, France, October 2010.

Grosjean, R. Interview with author. Villersexel and Fougerolles, France, October 2010.

Guidat, L. Written testimonial of artillery hitting their home and fleeing to the basement. Via Jean-Marie Siret, translation by L. Gregorio. Frémifontaine, France, October 2010.

M. J., M. Written testimonial about the M7 Priest armored vehicles in Frémifontaine. Via Jean-Marie Siret, translation by L. Gregorio. Frémifontaine, France, October 2010.

M. J., M. Written testimonial describing damaged tanks in Frémifontaine. Via Jean-Marie Siret, translation by L. Gregorio. Frémifontaine, France, October 2010.

Margotta, J. Interview with author. Sleepy Hollow, New York, December 2006.

Martin, R. Written testimonial of events in early October 1944 as the 180th arrived. Via Jean-Marie Siret, translation by L. Gregorio. Frémifontaine, France, October 2010.

Martin, R. D. Written testimonial of FFI losses while fighting on Hill 385. Via Jean-Marie Siret, translation by L. Gregorio. Frémifontaine, France, October 2010.

Morgan, J. Letter from Company A Commander 645th Tank Destroyer Battallion to Jean-Marie Siret. Via Jean-Marie Siret. Frémifontaine, France, October 2010.

Moulin, J. Written testimonial of Allied escapees hiding in the forest. Via Jean-Marie Siret, translation by L. Gregorio. Frémifontaine, France, October 2010.

Moulin, R. Written testimonial describing American armored vehicle positions on Oct 6, 1944. Via Jean-Marie Siret, translation by L. Gregorio. Frémifontaine, France, October 2010.

Pernot. Written testimonial of the first artillery shells falling on October 1, 1944. Via Jean-Marie Siret, translation by L. Gregorio. Frémifontaine, France, October 2010.

Pernot-Demangeon, M. Written testimonial of friendships and notes sent to villagers by soldier. Via Jean-Marie Siret, translation by L. Gregorio. Frémifontaine, France, October 2010.

Phulpin, R. Statement made to author during the town-hall reception following the ceremony, information confirmed by Jean-Marie Siret in email dated April 25, 2011. Frémifontaine, France, October 2010.

Pierre, J. Interview with author regarding 27th Evacuation Hospital location with Xertigny Farm family member, October 2010.

Prieur, R. Retired Superintendent American Cemetery at Épinal. Interview with author. Épinal, France, October 2010.

Reeves, J. Letter from 180th HQ Lineman John Reeves to Jean-Marie Siret dated February 17, 2000. Via Jean-Marie Siret. Frémifontaine, France, October 2010.

Remond, L. Transcript of words she read during the ceremony on October 10, 2010. Via Jean-Marie Siret, translation by L. Gregorio. Frémifontaine, France, October 10, 2010.

Schindler, C. Personal diary, October 1944. 45th Infantry Division Museum Archives. Oklahoma City, Oklahoma.

Serriere-Laumont. Written testimonial of soldier killed while shaving in local house. Via Jean-Marie Siret, translation by L. Gregorio. Frémifontaine, France, October 2010.

Siret, J.-M. Testimonial regarding the German reoccupation of Frémifontaine on October 6 and 7, 1944. Jean-Marie Siret's verbal statements. Frémifontaine, France, October 2010.

Siret, J.-M. Conversation with author. Second Battalion headquarters in Girecourt. Validated in HQ 180th Field Order No. 46 Sept. 27 1944. Girecourt, France, October 2010.

Siret, J.-M. Conversation with author. Frémifontaine, France, October 2010.

Siret, J.-M. Written testimonial—anonymous author—of FFI group #42 activity on October 5 and 6, 1944. Via Jean-Marie Siret, translation by L. Gregorio. Frémifontaine, France, October 2010.

Siret, J.-M. Written testimonial—anonymous author—the test of the buried barrels. Via Jean-Marie Siret, translation by L. Gregorio. Fremifontaone, France, October 2010.

Siret, J.-M. Written testimonial describing the place of the jeep. Via Jean-Marie Siret, translation by L. Gregorio. Frémifontaine, France, October 2010.

Siret, J.-M. Written testimonial examples of villager passive resistance to Germans. Via Jean-Marie Siret, translation by L. Gregorio. Frémifontaine, France, October 2010.

Siret, J.-M. Email to author, April 19, 2011. Confirmation of location where jeep hit a mine.

Siret, J.-M. Email to author, March 14, 2011. Confirmation of Bailey bridge across Moselle River.

Siret, J.-M. Email to author, March 14, 2011. German fortifications along the river in Épinal.

Triboulot, P. Interview with author (L. Gregorio, translator), October 2010. Girecourt resident—facial trauma during childhood from land mine.

Secondary sources

Army, 6. "For the First Time in History an Army Crossed the Vosges." *Beachhead News*, December 10, 1944: 1–3.

Battalion, 1. T. *Commander's Narrative—Activities of the 191st Tank Battalion*. US Army, October 1944.

Bishop, L. V. *The Fighting Forty-Fifth*. Baton Rouge, Louisiana: Army and Navy Publishing, 1946.

Bonn, K. *When the Odds Were Even: the Vosges Mountains Campaign*. New York, New York: Presidio Press, 2006.

Brabenec, J. "Great Guns: M7 'Priest' Backs WWII Armor." *US Army*, September 29, 2011. Retrieved January 8, 2020, https://www.army.mil/article/66398/great_guns_MY_Priest.

Clark, J. S. *Riviera to the Rhine*. Washington, D.C.: Center of Military History, 1993.

"Cushman 1944 Model 53 Airborne Motor Scooter." *International Military Antiques*. Retrieved August 2017, https://www.ima-usa.com.

Devers, J. Letter of appreciation to the commanding general of the 45th Division, September 28, 1945. In Fisher, G. A. *The Story of the 180th Infantry Regiment*. San Angelo, Texas: Newsfoto Publishing, 1947.

Echohawk, B. *Drawing Fire*. Lawrence, Kansas: University Press of Kansas, 2018.

Fisher, G. A. *The Story of the 180th Infantry Regiment*. San Angelo, Texas: Newsfoto Publishing, 1947.

Frazier, L. "S-2 Army Officer Duties." *Careertrend*, December 28, 2018. Retrieved January 8, 2022, https://careertrend.com/list-6692783-s2-army-officer-duties.html.

Fuss, N. H. "Back to the Basics: the Battalion S2." *Military Intelligence Professional Bulletin*, 23(2), April–June 1997, 19.

Goffman, E. *Interaction Ritual: Essays on face-to-face behavior.* Chicago, Illinois: Aldine Press, 1967.

"Hall of Valor Benjamin Blackmer." *Military Times*, n.d. Retrieved January 8, 2022, https://valor.militarytimes.com/recipient/recipient-6434/.

Hobfall, S. S. "Disentangling the stress labyrinth: Interpreting the meaning of the term stress as it is studied in health context." *Anxiety, Stress & Coping*, 11(3), n.d., 181–213.

Hospital, 2. E. *Annual Report—Supplement #1 Medical History Data*. US Army, 1944.

Hospital, 2. E. *Annual Report—Supplement #2 Nurses Diary*. US Army, 1944.

Kane, P. "Stress Causing Psychosomatic Illness Among Nurses." *Indian Journal of Occupational and Enviromental Medicine*, 13(1), 2009, 28–32.

Kershaw, A. *The Liberator*. New York, New York: Penguin Random House, 2012.

Lazarus, R. *Stress and Emotion: A new synthesis.* New York, New York: Springer Publishing, 1999.

"M3 Half-track military vehicle." *Tank Encyclopedia*, n.d. Retrieved August 2017, https://tanks.encyclopedia.com.

McLaughlin, M. "The British Bailey Bridge." *Warfare History Network*, May 2005. Retrieved 2017, https://warfarehistorynetwork.com/article/ordnance-the-british-bailey-bridge/.

Order of Battle of the US Army WWII ETO 45th Infantry Division. US Army Center of Military History, n.d. Retrieved 2017, https://history.army.mil.

Podolsky, S. "The Changing Fate of Pneumonia as a Public Health Concern in 20th-Century America and Beyond." *American Journal of Public Health*, 95(12), December 2005, 2144–154.

Regiment, 1. I. *Headquarters S-2 Journal*. US Army, 45th Infantry Division, October 1944.

Regiment, 1. I. *Headquarters S-3 Report*. US Army, 45th Infantry Division, October 1944.

Regiment, 1. I. *Headquarters Second Battalion Journal*. US Army, 45th Infantry Division, October 1944.

Regiment, 1. I. *Headquarters Transmittal of Organizational History*. US Army, 45th Infantry Regiment, October 1944.

Regiment, 1. I. *Report of Operations*. US Army, 45th Infantry Division, October 1944.

Regiment, 1. I. *Second Battalion H Company Morning Reports*. US Army, 45th Infantry Division, October 1944.

Regiment, 1. I. *Second Battalion Headquarters Company Morning Reports*. US Army, 45th Infantry Division, October 1944.

Regiment, 1. I. *Headquarters Field Order*. US Army, 45th Infantry Division, September 12, 1944.

Regiment, 1. I. *Headquarters Field Order No. 46 Sept. 27*. US Army, 45th Infantry Division, September 27, 1944.

Regiment, 1. I. *Headquarters Field Order No. 47 Sept. 28*. US Army, 45th Infantry Division, September 28, 1944

Regiment, 1. I. *Headquarters S-2 Journal*. US Army, 45th Infantry Regiment, September 1944.

Regiment, 1. I. *Headquarters Second Battalion Journal*. US Army, 45th Infantry Division, September 1944.

Regiment, 1. I. *Headquarters Transmittal of Organizational History*. US Army, 45th Infantry Division, September 1944.

Regiment, 1. I. *Report of Operations*. US Army, 45th Infantry Division, September 1944.

Reyka, M. *A Son's Journey: Uncovering my father's life as a Thunderbird*. Gettysburg, Pennsylvania: Thomas Publications, 2009.

Tucker-Jones, A. *Operation Dragoon: the Liberation of Southern France, 1944*. Barnsley: Pen & Sword Military, 2009.

US Army Campaigns of WWII, Southern France. Retrieved November 19, 2017, http://www.army.mil/cmh-pg/brochures/sfrance.htm.

Vincent, J. "Memories of War and Sacrifice"—Tom Mathews interview by Libby Smith. *45th Division*. Retrieved January 8, 2017, https://www45thdivision.org.

"White Motor Company half-track military vehicle." *National WWII Museum*, n.d. Retrieved August 2017, http://www.nationalww2museum.org.

Zaloga, S. *Operation Dragoon—France's other D-Day*. Oxford: Osprey Publishing, 2009.

Zoepf, W. T. *Seven Days in January with the 6th SS Mountain Division in Operation Nordwind*. Bedford, Pennsylvania: Aberjona Press, 2001.